Attack on the Self

Commentary

"Derek Miller has written an excellent, timely book about the prevention and treatment of behavioral disturbances in adolescents. As Miller states, the incidence of symptomatic attack by adolescents on the bodily self has increased, as evidenced in drug abuse, illegitimate pregnancy, suicide, violent deaths, accidents, and self-starvation.

"Always thoughtful, often provocative, Miller's approach to understanding the cause of disturbance and the goal of treatment is unwaveringly developmental. As a gifted teacher and author, he provides us with a fundamental and integrated point of view, a much-needed guide for our use now and for years to come. His work will be of interest not only to mental health professionals, but to all who are involved and concerned with adolescents."

—Silvio Onesti, M.D.

"I strongly recommend *Attack on the Self* to anyone who is professionally or otherwise concerned with the growth, development, and pathological possibilities of contemporary adolescents. Whether you are a psychotherapist, a teacher, a pediatrician, or a social service worker, there is sure to be considerable knowledge to be gained from reading this book."

—Ronald Blank, M.D.

"The feature of this book that gives it its power and zest is the forceful attack that is made on the pessimism that exists regarding the successful treatment of these children. The reader is educated to the view that adolescents who are waging war on their own lives can be really helped and successfully treated. There is real hope that a well-done comprehensive evaluation and a treatment plan based on it can put an end to the syndrome of multiple evaluations at the expense of adequate treatment.

"This is an informative, easily readable, and enjoyable book that should be read by all who work with . . . adolescents."

—David Smith, M.D.

Attack on the Self

ADOLESCENT BEHAVIORAL DISTURBANCES AND THEIR TREATMENT

Derek Miller, M.D.

with the assistance of Barry Carlton, M.D.

Jason Aronson Inc.

Northvale, New Jersey
London

THE MASTER WORK SERIES

First softcover edition 1994

Copyright © 1994, 1986 by Jason Aronson Inc.

Library of Congress Cataloging-in-Publication Data *pending*

ISBN: 1-56821-214-3

Manufactured in the United States of America. Jason Aronson Inc. offers books and cassettes. For information and catalog write to Jason Aronson Inc., 230 Livingston Street, Northvale, New Jersey 07647.

To my wife

Acknowledgments

Thanks are due to Ellen Karp, who typed numerous manuscript drafts; the medical students of Northwestern University, who read the manuscript and offered useful comments; and my colleagues and friends, who were most helpful. Mark Walker, M.D., was particularly helpful, as was Diane Friedman, R.N., and Margo Toscano, M.S.W. Special thanks are due to Barry Carlton, M.D., who has exchanged ideas with me over a decade of collaboration in our clinical work.

Derek Miller, M.D.

Contents

Introduction

This book is about the prevention and treatment of behavioral disturbances in adolescents. The specific symptoms that appear as a result of these disturbances vary among cultures and social groups and change across historical times. A study of the significant developmental issues and the biopsychosocial roots of behavior, in conjunction with sophisticated treatment, should help improve both the quality of care and the outcome of therapy.

In the last decades there has been a remarkable split in the attitudes of adolescents and adults toward their bodies. On the one hand, the incidence of symptomatic attacks on the bodily self has increased, as seen in drug abuse, illegitimate pregnancy, suicide, violent death, accidents, and self-starvation. On the other hand, more people than ever before are making efforts to keep fit. Ironically, exercise clubs exceed in number the special centers designed for those who abuse their bodies.

Development over the life course is influenced by a set of simultaneous but ever-changing biological, psychological, and sociocultural factors. The vast majority of individuals negotiate age-specific developmental tasks smoothly, although a sizable

1

number encounter significant psychological difficulties at some point during their lives. Many are then temporarily derailed from the normal developmental track.

A behavior, or conduct disorder is defined—albeit unsatisfactorily—as "a repetitive and persistent pattern of conduct in which either the basic rights of others or major age-appropriate societal norms and rules are violated" (DSM III 1980, p. 45). This symptomatic definition can apply at once to eating disorders, illegitimate conception, law breaking, drug abuse, and self-destructive and violent behavior. Generally, this definition is used especially for those who are violent but violence is nonspecific and does not qualify as a valid diagnostic entity (Lewis et al. 1984).

Preoccupation with symptoms is not new in medicine. For example, in the nineteenth and early twentieth centuries, "fevers" were considered to be a significant entity. Special isolation hospitals were created for, and people received special training in, their treatment. Likewise, just as the relief of fever symptoms meant that some sufferers recovered, so the relief of behavioral symptoms allows some people to return to their developmental track. There are many reasons why the relief of symptoms may seem to cure the disease. First, the severity of symptomatic behavior does not directly correspond to the severity of the underlying disturbance. Second, interrupting an individual's antisocial symptomatology may stop the persecutory response of those who have become angry, coercive, or rejecting because their attempt to help the boy or girl has failed. The adolescent then is able to view the world as being more supportive. Third, the cessation of symptomatic behavior also relieves the antidevelopmental pathological instinctual gratification that it produces. An example of this is the control and power over others that are implicit in eating disorders.

The reasons that emotional disturbances in adolescence are expressed through behavioral symptoms are largely developmental. Adolescents act to avoid intolerable psychic tension, and when such action is not socially acceptable, it is considered to be a behavior disorder. Interestingly, overconformity to socially acceptable behavior, which may be at least as developmentally destructive, is not so labeled by those societies that value passive obedience. Those who are hypersensitive to stress because of a genetic central nervous system vulnerability may show extreme self-absorption and isolation, along with inappropriate mood shifts, sometimes including delusions and hallucinations. Such people's verbalizations and private thoughts may also be bizarre:

> One 16-year-old boy, unable to relieve his tension behaviorally, wore quite inappropriate clothing, such as a cutoff T-shirt in cold weather. When an adult male suggested to him that he dress properly to go outside, he retorted, "Why should I, do I turn you on?"

Adolescents who can control their disturbed behavior at isolated times—although this may produce superficial improvement—do not necessarily return to an appropriate developmental track. It thus becomes important to differentiate those young people who respond favorably to behavioral control alone from those whose biopsychosocially induced vulnerability to stress and maturational deficits also require treatment.

There are special centers for those with symptoms such as drug and alcohol abuse, sexual problems, eating disorders, or delinquent behavior. Some of these centers offer a boutique approach to treatment; that is, they use only one specialized technique, such as behavior therapy, peer counseling, or cognitive therapy. Likewise, those therapists who use these approaches may not consider the disorder's biopsychosocial etiology or the patient's developmental state as being of therapeutic significance. For example, behavior modification has been enshrined as the treatment of choice for those suffering from self-starvation syndromes (Stunkard 1972), with little or no consideration given to the causes of the syndromes.

The American correctional system, particularly, may effectively ignore the therapeutic implication of etiology. Although elaborate psychological and social diagnostic studies are sometimes performed, generally they are not followed up by specific recommendations that the correctional staff can directly apply and the staff rarely considers biological etiology. In any case, the system is starved of resources.

A specific behavior often stems from social processes. Indeed, sometimes quite blatant instruction as to how to misbehave is unconsciously given to those who are vulnerable. For example, the phenomenon of early and middle adolescents' excessive use of purgatives followed an article in *Seventeen* magazine decrying their use by older adolescents. Typically, the more subtle conflicts in social systems are significant; that is, the difference between what is said and what is done affects the way that disturbed young people exhibit their difficulties. Contradictory explicit and implicit verbal and nonverbal communications from large and small social systems influence adolescent behavior. For example, adolescents may feel that society permits deviant behavior that is not externally controlled. Or the presence of youth gangs in some large cities may seem to some adolescents as implicitly condoning violent behavior. In turn, violent behavior in adolescents may also be encouraged by the absence of gun control. The United States' refusal to ban handguns may grant implicit, if not explicit, permission for lethal violence.

Sometimes policymakers adopt a social policy without understanding the causes of the behavior that they seek to control. Adolescent sexual activity leading to illegitimate pregnancy is an example, and in addition, apart from many societies' refusal to provide birth control information to vulnerable populations, educational techniques and intervention programs may ignore social-class differences in attitudes toward intercourse and contraception.

Drug abuse, as well, has been subject to massive societal indifference, and only lately have there been efforts at its control. Indeed, parents and teachers may not even notice symptoms of drug use, and many adolescents may view the effective decriminalization of marijuana as permission for its use. Just as with alcohol, parents who smoke marijuana implicitly are giving permission to their children to do the same, and the use both of drugs and alcohol may lead to antisocial behavior and violence.

Marijuana, however, generally makes young males, in particular, less violent as well as less vigorous in their attempts to gain sexual satisfaction. Those who have recently smoked marijuana will have intercourse if it is available and acceptable. But if a young man is "stoned," he is less likely to seek out sex. In contrast, alcohol increases the probability of both violent and sexual behavior, although alcohol does diminish sexual performance. If alcohol is used at adolescent parties the noise level is high, a fight may be a possibility, and there probably will be an active search for sexual partners. But if the drug of choice for the evening is marijuana, the atmosphere will be quieter, several may seem to be sleeping or just sitting and staring into space, and there will be little effort to seek out active sexual contact.

Although there is some disagreement over the best techniques for controlling disturbed behavior, the evidence suggests that helping adolescents develop positive emotional attachments to an individual, group, or social system that has consistent socially acceptable expectations is often effective (Miller 1967). In addition, the more opportunities that are available to meet developmental needs, the easier it is to control destructive behavior. Such opportunities educate the adolescent both creatively and cognitively, enhance a sense of personal worth, and offer physical outlets in which work and play can substitute for less acceptable behavior. Both control and the satisfaction of developmental needs are necessary; the provision of one does not eliminate the necessity for the other. Having a job increases one's sense of worth, although it does not necessarily eliminate unacceptable sexual, drug-abusing, and violent behavior. Even in those societies with relatively little youth unemployment, such as Britain in the 1960s, such behavior remained a preoccupation of the community at large.

Societally inflicted punishment is often thought to be an effective means of control, though it actually deters only those with good reality testing. Most impulsive behavior is not controlled by fear of punishment: those involved commonly feel omnipotent, may believe that they will get away with their behavior, or deny its unacceptability.

The response of adult authority figures to adolescents' antisocial behavior may also not be immediately punitive or coercive. That is initially, the disturbed behavior may not be noticed, but when it is, adults may offer understanding and empathy. When this fails, however, the adults' response may then alter. The speed with which it changes seems to depend on the concerned adults' degree of helplessness. For example, parents often display a cycle of understanding, impatience, rage, and rejection resulting from their child's unacceptable behavior. Depending on the parents' response, the child's behavior may change in its quality and its frequency, but depending on how much the child "needs" the behavior, it may never cease. Adolescents will indeed learn that certain types of behavior will bring predictable responses, and sometimes when these responses are evoked, the behavior ceases. But shortly thereafter, the adolescent's internal tension rises, the behavior occurs again, and the cycle is repeated.

> A 17-year-old high school boy would come home "stoned" each evening. He would become increasingly irritable, and eventually his parents would notice and confront him. He would deny the allegation; they would persist; and eventually he would confess, all this was accompanied by understanding, rage, frustration, and rejection. The parents would threaten to throw him out of the house. He then would conform and improve his schoolwork. But within weeks the cycle would begin again.

Thus, the principal issue for parents and professionals is to decide when adolescent misbehavior is a transient part of growing up and when it represents a symptomatic attempt to resolve excessive tension.

Rebellious behavior, which is often associated with developmental turmoil, may not be developmentally destructive, even though it may arouse considerable anger and irritation in others. This may well be because problematic adolescent behavior tends to take place in areas of unresolved conflict for adults. Such behavior, usually negativistic and clearly oppositional for the sake of being separate, is like the negativism of two-year-olds. It is sometimes exhibitionistic and is rarely well hidden: the forbidden empty cans of beer are hidden behind the father's tool kit in the garage. If parents say "be home by midnight," the adolescent must argue for an hour later. Sometimes negativism may take place over issues that seem relatively insignificant to the noninvolved observer.

Like rebellion, regressive behavior may also be associated with a developmental striving for autonomy. Such behavior seems to arouse a much less negative adult response, but it is more likely to impede satisfactory emotional development, as the person exhibiting it may be insufficiently involved in the external world.

Destructive and regressive behavior that produces a developmental impasse is often blamed on the parents' personal or marital difficulties. But adolescents are not that easy to mold, and too much is expected of the nuclear family. For example, if adolescents are struggling for autonomy and do not have relationships with significant other adults outside the nuclear family, their emotional entanglements with peers and parents will be more intense. They may become overinvolved with peers and overly oppositional toward their parents, as they may feel that accepting any parental involvement will threaten their emotional independence.

The environmental response to adolescence is further distorted by this group's minority role. Adults' disapproval of issues of sex, violence, and drugs are typically projected onto adolescents, and like other minorities, they become the objects of prejudice. The problem is even greater for adolescents because their intense sexuality, high potential for creativity, and imaginative productivity may arouse intense, if unconscious, envy in adults. Adolescents may also "act out" the unconscious conflictual wishes of their parents in particular or of adults in general.

Apart from possibly inappropriate responses to specific disturbed behavior, adults' general reactions to adolescents are often startlingly negative. For example, the environments within which disturbed adolescents are housed are often hideously insensitive. The dormitories, classrooms, and living areas of both psychiatric hospitals and youth correctional centers often have to be seen to be believed:

In 1980, New York City kept adolescents over 16 who were on remand—not yet convicted but not able to make bail—on Rikers Island. There was a special wing for those youths who were emotionally disturbed. The youths were not supplied with underclothes; the grills on their lockers were broken so that they could easily mutilate themselves on the wire; the cell windows were often broken; and the inmates had only one blanket each.

When the youths brought food or milk from their canteen, the only way they could keep the food from spoiling in the summer was to float it in the toilet bowl.

The guards did not appear to relate to the inmates. They sat on a viewing balcony and watched them milling about in a type of bullpen.

Some states create work camps for their antisocially disturbed young:

When in 1982 a part-time nurse finally was hired in one such camp in upstate New York, she found the boys to have head and body lice. The mattresses had not been turned on their beds for three years. When a boy was sick, he would not be seen until at least 10:00 A.M. by any professionally trained person.

In another camp, 12- and 13-year-old children who were adjudged delinquent were placed some 200 miles from their impoverished parents, thereby further exacerbating their sense of isolation.

It has been said that "the deflating and controlling techniques used by adults with adolescents are generally not the ones they employ in personal relationships with other adults or even children. The shaming, reproaching, guilt provoking and stereotyping techniques have a particularly disruptive and sadistic element to them" (Anthony 1975, p. 492).

In addition to moral and ethical issues, as the number of young people, relative to that of the older adult population, declines, society will no longer be able to afford to waste young people's abilities because of poor schools, poor correctional facilities, and inadequate psychosocial care.

REFERENCES

Anthony, E. J. (1975). Adults' reactions to adolescents. In *The Psychology of Adolescence*, ed. A. H. Esman. New York: International Universities Press.

Diagnostic and Statistical Manual of Mental Disorder. (1980). 3rd ed. Washington, D.C.: American Psychiatric Association Press.

Lewis, D. O., Lewis, M., Unger, L., and Goldman, C. (1984). Conduct disorder and its synonyms: diagnosis of dubious validity and usefulness. *American Journal of Psychiatry* 141:516–519.

Miller, D. (1967). *Growth to Freedom: The Psychosocial Treatment of Delinquent Youth.* Bloomington: Indiana University Press.

Stunkard, A. (1972). New therapies for the eating disorders: behavior modification of obesity and anorexia nervosa. *Archives of General Psychiatry* 26:391–398.

1

Developmental Issues Influencing Treatability

INFANTILE PRECURSORS OF ADOLESCENT EXPERIENCE

Adolescents' capacity to respond to treatment depends on their ability to make emotional investments in others and to handle frustration in a way that others find tolerable. Treatability also depends on an accurate diagnosis and on effective intervention.

Especially important are those developmental issues that influence adolescents' capacity to make trusting relationships and to tolerate frustration. Without such relationships, adolescents are at the mercy of their impulses and cannot develop a loving, empathic personality or genuinely cooperate in their treatment.

A child's developmental history should note the presence or absence of those factors that enable him or her to develop the capacity to be trusting. This in turn requires the ability to make an attachment (Bowlby 1984), which includes both bonding and dependence.

Bonding is the means through which a mother and her child learn about each other in an intuitive and nonintellectual way. It is a biopsychological process, the beginning of the strong attachment between a mother and her child. Bonding behavior in mothers consists of en face fondling, caressing, kissing, looking at, and smiling. Long before conscious perception, there is a cascade of reciprocal interactions between a mother and her baby (Klaus and Kennell 1976). In mammals, vaginal-cervical stimulation has been shown to play a role in the onset of maternal bonding behavior. Imprinting thus seems to depend on an intact sense of smell (Keverne 1983), and the integration of sensory and endocrine mechanisms can then produce highly complex behavior. Similar processes may be present in humans.

Dependence implies the capacity to see others as separate from the self and to rely on them for emotional and physical necessities. We hypothesize that if a child does not become dependent on individuals to whom he or she has bonded, the attachment process will be inconsistent. It is reasonable to assume then that a sense of genuine trust will be more difficult to develop, and without a lasting internalization of a sense of trust, emotional support from the parents is likely to offer only temporary solace. An internal image of a loving contact with others will then need the constant reinforcement of their presence.

When an infant perceives the mother as a separate person, he or she projects tension into her, and she in turn returns comfort and nurture. Thus, the mother–child interaction contains infantile tension: the child projects bad experiences into its mother, these are contained by the parent, love is then experienced, and thus the tension is resolved (Winnicott 1955). The capacity to bond and be dependent also involves the father, siblings, and others with whom the child has consistent relationships. The child's dependence on the father is different from his or her dependence on the mother but is of equal significance (Lamb 1975). Furthermore, the way in which the infant becomes attached to the father is different than to other adults (Yogman 1982). Fathers provide greater excitement than do mothers, without the holding quality (Winnicott 1955) that is present in the infant's relationship with the mother, and fathers also allow a safe experience away from the mother. Fathers thus facilitate the infant's first steps toward autonomy (Abelin 1975). Through the relationship with the father, as the child begins to crawl and walk, he or she moves into "an exhilarating environment outside the safer but quieter maternal sphere" (Ross 1984, p. 378).

By the age of eighteen months, all toddlers can recognize a picture of their father and understand his similarity to other male adults (Brooks and Lewis 1975). During this same age, the father begins to serve another role. A girl now begins to feel loved for herself, irrespective of her sexuality, by a figure whom she recognizes as different from her mother. When a boy identifies with his father, he is able to see himself as separate from his mother.

The father's physical presence, both actually and emotionally, thus is necessary for the child's development of a firm sense of sexual identity (Socarides 1982). The father is also a significant disciplinarian and helps protect the child from both his or her fantasy of projected destructiveness (Herzog 1982) and the real dangers of the external world. The child thus ideally incorporates into his or her own personality this perception of the father as a person concerned with play, environmental mastery, and benign control.

A father who actively supports and participates in the mother's care-giving role influences the infant's capacity to be trusting and make attachments. If the quality of parenting is impaired, therefore, the attachment mechanisms will probably be similarly affected. Infants who are not securely attached to their mothers show a variety of syndromes: anxious avoidant infants often do not seem to mind leaving their mothers when they explore their environment, and they may avoid their mothers upon reunion. If children are expected to form multiple relationships without a firm parent–child attachment, they may be able to form only superficial relationships, and their sexual and vocational sense of self may be tenuous. Human beings probably go through a sensitive period (Klaus and Kennell 1976) during which contact between mother and child is highly important but a single event probably cannot cause a lifelong problem. A person's capacity to establish trusting relationships thus depends on very early infantile experiences, but attachment problems may be influenced by factors other than physical separation.

Along with emotional dependence, bonding can continue throughout life, between adults in a marital relationship. It can be pathological. For instance, a victim of a terrorist attack may emerge from a hijacked plane and announce that the terrorists were decent and kindly. Such a statement implies that the victim has abandoned his or her judgment and has sought safety through a psychological surrender—an internalization of the terrorists' values.

The child's security is mediated for many years, from infancy onward, by the parents' socialization patterns, by the extended social system in which they live, by the child's genetically inherited biological sensitivity, and by the possibility of biological and psychological trauma. The need for parenting, from both the mother and the father, thus continues well into adolescence (Esman 1982). Early adolescents, in particular, still need nurturing, mothering, and external control, even though they deny them (Miller 1974). Indeed, their response to a perception of parental rejection or abandonment is often disturbed behavior, which may be manifested by intense passivity, ranging from watching too much television, to academic and social non-productivity, to drug abuse. Some adolescents become antisocial, and their behavior ranges from difficulties in school to wanton destruction, theft, violence, and promiscuous sexuality.

The one-parent family, whether it be because of illegitimate birth, divorce, or death, poses particular developmental difficulties for children. Besides possible problems of economic and emotional deprivation, the absence of a father impedes the development of identity. The child's initial emotional distancing from the mother, which is necessary for further emotional growth, becomes even more complicated. For instance, the child identifies with a fantasy figure, as his or her image of the father may be of a person who does not have a real relationship with the mother but merely impregnates her and then disappears.

Either death or divorce causes especially complex problems for children. A fatherless home deprives the children of a role model, and so they have fantasies about their absent father, which may spoil their relationship with their mother (Feinstein and Davis 1984). Such children are likely to feel potentially intolerable anger toward the remaining parent, especially if it is the mother. Mothers are seen as all-powerful and, in a magical way, should have been able to prevent the disaster produced by separation. This anger is particularly likely to surface at adolescence, when the turbulence of that age period attenuates the capacity for denial, and it may appear as outer-directed violence or inner-directed depression.

With a single parent and without a network of caring adults, one of whom occupies the role of the missing parent, personality maturation probably will not be satisfactory. Many children brought up without shared parenting—often in isolation from loving extraparental adults—seem to retain until adulthood certain attitudes that are phase appropriate for early adolescence. In particular, their self-esteem seems overly dependent on their perception of what others think, an experience that is normative for early adolescents in Western culture.

A marital divorce is not the same as a parental divorce. In a marital divorce, the parents may not live together, but both are actually and potentially available to the child. But in a parental divorce, the child is effectively abandoned by one or other parent. Divorce, however, almost always implies an absence of shared parenting. If young people have no internalized image of intrafamilial relationships that include two parents, the resolution of both internal and external conflict with either parent will be difficult, as there is less reality with which fantasy can be compared. Finally, the development of a capacity for ambivalence—loving and hating the same person at the same time, which is necessary for mature adulthood—becomes difficult. In a two-parent family with many multigenerational and emotionally meaningful relationships, anger with one person may be attenuated by relationships with others.

THE VALUE OF PUNISHMENT

Appropriate punishment, apart from assisting in the development of controls, assists in the development of the capacity to be ambivalent. Because parents are bigger, more clever, and more emotionally mature, their children can be controlled on the strength of interpersonal relationships and appropriate firmness. When a parent punishes, apart from conveying the important idea that it is all right to express anger, he or she also demonstrates that one's feelings can be mixed. Thus in order to understand the adolescent's capacity to handle violent feelings and to contain anger, one must understand the controlling techniques of the nuclear family and the social system in which the child lives. An angry parent still loves the child, and the child knows this. With loving parents who offer appropriate punishment, therefore, the child has a model of ambivalent behavior. The issue, however, is not just whether the parent punishes; it is also how this is done. If in response to perceived misbehavior, the parent abuses the child or if the punishment seems to bear no relationship to the act—in time, quality, or intensity—the child will feel and internalize the punishment as coercive.

A child will feel punished when the parents control the child's unacceptable wishes. A parent who never becomes overtly angry will, however, make the child feel that overt anger is particularly dangerous. So in order for children to learn that ambivalence is possible, they must know that anger too is possible as well as permissible, can be contained and attenuated, and does not destroy love.

When a child is punished by those who do not love him or her, such punishment may carry a message about reality that can influence children in appraising the consequences of their behavior. It does not help the development of ambivalence and, depending on what is done, may teach children to use abusive techniques themselves.

This is a developmental and therapeutic issue. Social systems that offer clear consequences for behavior have effects different from those whose consequences do not seem to relate to the behavior and thus are felt only as coercive. In order to deal with the tension experienced when wishes are thwarted, the child identifies with the controlling individuals and their techniques of control. If these are felt as unduly coercive, incomprehensible and unfair, the child will identify with those techniques. If coercion is not actually present, then the child's perception of it can be modified as the child develops the capacity to appraise reality. But if the result of behavior is not directly related to the incident, no amount of intervention can disprove the child's belief that it is coercive.

VIOLENCE

The likelihood of violent behavior is lessened if an adolescent can form meaningful emotional relationships with individuals and systems that do not condone violence. The adolescent's abilities to be ambivalent and to feel loving toward another person also interfere with his or her ability to play out such angry feelings in action. Violent behavior can be modified by the capacity to empathize with the other person and by the way the individual has experienced the violence of others. A positive internal image of the object of one's anger automatically diminishes its intensity.

The way that anger is expressed may be cultural. In some ethnic groups, children remain very polite to their parents but take their anger out on others. Samoan children, for example, do not express their anger directly to their parents but go behind their hut and take it out on one another (Bateson and Mead 1927). In lower socio-economic groups, especially for deprived children in deprived neighborhoods, a gang provides a special area of emotional if not actual safety for the child; it also provides excitement and the possibility of peer acceptable projection of violence. For children who have not been well nurtured, the gang can also provide them with an outlet for their anger, a means to externalize their hatred. Withdrawal from the gang is made difficult by its members so in order to rescue themselves safely from such settings adolescents need to develop a high degree of psychological maturity.

A highly delinquent boy who had multiple episodes of cruel behavior including violence and robbery was finally admitted to an adolescent psychiatric treatment program. There he was diagnosed as suffering from a mood disorder which would respond to Lithium Carbonate. His antisocial behavior was also related to unresolved mourning around his father's death. The boy was a member of a powerful street gang which would not allow its members to leave.

As the boy slowly matured, he projected less and began to withdraw from gang activity. He carefully did not announce that he was leaving. When he finally began to live in the community he removed himself from the gang neighborhood, dropped wearing the clothes that indicated gang membership, and effectively dropped out of the gang's sight.

HUMANIZATION AND DEHUMANIZATION

Whether or not violence is directed towards other people seems to depend on the capacity to perceive them as warm, human, feeling and alive. Humanization is that quality by which others are seen as human; human qualities are also ascribed to animals and things.

Humanization is an essential quality of life. It relieves anxiety about the unknown by offering explanations in terms of human behavior. For example, primitive people explained the violent forces of nature in human terms. Even today, hurricanes are given the names of people. When the cultural assumption in the United States was that women were submissive, the names of hurricanes were female, presumably with the unconscious wish that the violent storms could be tamed as women were. Nowadays, female and male names alternate. This type of anthropomorphic thinking also helps explain the inexplicable; for example, animals become human, and the earth becomes a mother. This capacity to humanize depends on appropriate nurturing and stable attachments in the first years of life. In children it indicates the beginning of a capacity to be empathic, and it is seen intermittently first when children are about three years old. This capacity may be lost with the experience of frustration:

A three-year-old child was waiting for his mother to collect him from a hospital waiting room. While the child was waiting, he picked up a cockroach from the floor; he began talking to it and stroking it as if it were a person. Then his mother hurried in and grabbed the little boy by the hand; he dropped the cockroach on the floor and stamped on it.

Dehumanization, on the other hand, relieves painful internal tension by making projection easy, as it removes the human element from people. A decrease in a person's perception of others' human qualities also is a decrease in a person's sense of his or her own humanity. The ability to dehumanize first appears in children from about the age of six. It has its own language: for example, Jews are "kikes"; black people are "niggers"; and whites are "honkies." In wars, this language is common: most recently, to the British, the Argentinians became "Argies"; to Americans in the Vietnam War, the Vietnamese were "gooks" (Gault 1971). In street gangs, outsiders are given special names, and especially under conditions of economic and emotional deprivation, these groups may be exploited for material or instinctual satisfaction. So Latino street groups in Chicago hunt the "Unknowns," or vice versa, and in correctional centers, the weak and young are sexually abused as if they were objects rather than people.

It is clear from such sexual abuse as gang rape that the dehumanization of others also involves the self, and the two sides are mutually reinforcing. As a boy who took part in a gang rape explained, "I don't know what happened; I became an animal"; and a boy who was raped in prison said, "They didn't care; all they wanted was my ass; I was a thing."

Dehumanization may vary in intensity: sometimes individuals are perceived as subhuman, and sometimes they become inanimate, despicable objects (Barnard et al. 1965). Dehumanization also includes a number of psychological defense mechanisms, especially denial, repression, and depersonalization. Pathological dehumanization is responsible for people's ability to tolerate mass homicide, and it was clearly a factor in the Holocaust, when the Germans exterminated six million Jews and other groups. But the coldness of pathological dehumanization is more apparent in adolescents than in other age groups, especially when adolescents engage in homicidal or sexually aggressive behavior (Szymuiska and Lesniak 1972). That is, adolescents do not disguise their capacity to dehumanize and are more vulnerable to group contagion than are adults.

Dehumanization may be intermittent, and some types of behavior demonstrate the rapidity with which conscienceless pathological behavior can appear:

> Among the violent gangs of Chicago, it is not uncommon for one group member to cross another's turf and be caught. He may be murdered in an apparently inconsequential way. However, an alien gang member may take his girl friend home in absolute safety. It is only after he leaves her house that he may be "wasted."

Sometimes intermittent dehumanization is a function of stress; one boy became homicidal only when sexually stimulated:

> One seventeen-year-old said, "Sometimes I see a lady in the supermarket and she turns me on. Then I follow her home and try to get into her apartment if she's alone. I like to have her give me a blow job, and I like to bite her tits. If she refuses, I hit her, and if she yells, I'll kill her."

Projective identification requires partial dehumanization. This is also an important determinant of prejudice, in which an unacceptable part of the self is split off and projected onto others who, because they are the recipients of the projection, become nonhuman. For example, adolescents in normative conflict about their own sexual identity may use derogatory words to describe others, such as "fag" or "faggot" for individuals whom they do not like or with whom they are angry. A late-maturing boy may, however, be constantly taunted as a "fag," because his lack of masculine qualities poses a threat to postpubertal youths, particularly in the intimacy of locker rooms. This is a transient phenomenon, but adults in conflict about their own sexuality may see homosexuals more definitively as the cause of their country's decline in status and influence. That is, they dehumanize those who are homosexual and wish to have them isolated or eliminated. The current epidemic of AIDS in which some demand, quite irrationally, that those with positive blood tests be isolated, demonstrates this. Such individuals are apparently projecting intolerable anxiety and an unacceptable part of themselves onto dehumanized others, and then they demand their elimination.

Partial dehumanization is often used as an excuse to ignore situations that would otherwise be intolerable; that is, it allows empathy to be sidestepped. Thus poverty as an abstract situation can be discussed without considering what it must be like not to have adequate food and shelter. Partial and intermittent dehumanization may therefore temporarily remove the humanity from groups and individuals so that they need be considered only in the abstract. Such partial dehumanization is beginning, furthermore, to be adaptive for society at large.

Adaptive dehumanization is part of all complex social systems: from hospital emergency rooms when a physician does not give prime attention to the patient's pain if analgesics make diagnosis impossible, to prison systems in which guards may work in conditions that ignore both their own and the inmates' humanity, to high school systems in which teachers and pupils are transferred from school to school in pursuit of goals that ignore the here-and-now experience of the children and staff. The boundary between adaptive dehumanization and pathological dehumanization is blurred: when predatory violence toward others is present in peacetime, dehumanization is pathological, whereas the same attitudes in wartime are adaptive.

The more that persons are dehumanized as children, the more likely they will be as adolescents and adults to dehumanize others. Compared with nonabused siblings, abused children are more likely to have been separated from their mothers in the first forty-eight hours after birth, as they are often products of abnormal pregnancy, labor, or delivery (Lynch 1975). These individuals also may themselves become child abusers, often because they really wish their infants and children to look after them. "Most, perhaps all, parents who expect their children to care for them, have experienced very inadequate parenting themselves" (Bowlby 1984, p. 281). When adolescents become the victims of dehumanized violence, as in correctional centers, they are likely to be more violent when they leave than when they were admitted.

The assessment of treatability thus includes the capacity to make a meaningful emotional investment in others, a capacity that is based to a considerable degree on the adolescent's developmental experiences. It requires an understanding of the way that frustration is handled and the individual's capacity for violent behavior. Those who commit violent acts in hospital wards are said to have been severely disturbed in childhood, to have committed previous acts of violence, and to suffer from bipolar illness (Yesavage 1983). Slowly, psychiatry is coming to realize that there are predictors for violence, a viewpoint that some have held for more than a decade (Miller and Looney 1976).

Depending on how children have learned to express their anger, they may handle it in adolescence by withdrawal from reality and into fantasy, by projection onto others or by actions that constructively or destructively try to alter the situation.

The existential support that the child feels from the family and others, the strength of the child's own personality, the unconscious internalization of loving parental figures, the stresses that the child experiences, the intensity and quality of the mood shifts, and how much these are a function of neuroendocrinological vulnerability all influence the appearance of violent outbursts.

REFERENCES

Abelin, E. (1975). Some further comments on the earliest role of the father. *International Journal of Psychoanalysis* 56:293–302.

Barnard, A., Ottenberg, P., and Redl, F. (1965). *Dehumanization: a Complex Psychological Defense in Relationship to Modern War*. New York: Science and Behavior Books.

Bateson, G., and Mead, M. (1927). *Balinese Character*. New York: Academy of Science.

Bowlby, J. (1984). Caring for the young: influences on development. In *Parenthood, a Psychodynamic Perspective*, ed. R. S. Cohen, B. J. Cohler, and S. H. Weissman, pp. 269–284. New York: Guilford Press.

Brooks, J., and Lewis, N. (1975). Person perception and verbal labelling: the development of social labels. Paper presented to the Society for Research in Child Development. New York: Eastern Psychological Association.

Esman, A. H. (1982). Fathers and adolescent sons. In *Father and Child: Developmental and Clinical Perspectives*, ed. S. Cath, A. Garwitt, and J. Ross. Boston: Little Brown.

Feinstein, S. C., and Davis, M. (1984). The parental couple in successful divorce. In *Parenthood, a Psychodynamic Perspective*, ed. R. S. Cohen, B. J. Cohler, and S. H. Weissman. New York: Guilford Press.

Gault, W. B. (1971). Some remarks on slaughter. *American Journal of Psychiatry* 128:4, 82–86.

Herzog, J. (1982). On father hunger. In *Father and Child: Developmental and Clinical Perspectives*, ed. S. Cath, A. Garwitt, and J. Ross. Boston: Little Brown.

Keverne, E. B., Levy, F., Poundron, P., and Linsay, D. R. (1983). Vaginal stimulation: an important determinant of maternal bonding in sheep. *Science* 219:81–83.

Klaus, M. H., and Kennell, J. H. (1976). *Maternal-Infant Bonding*. St. Louis: C. V. Mosby.

Lamb, M. (1975). Fathers: forgotten contributors to child development. *Human Development* 18:245–266.

Lynch, M. (1975). Infant health and child abuse. *Lancet* 2:317–319.

Miller, D. (1974). *Adolescence: Psychology, Psychopathology, Psychotherapy*. New York: Jason Aronson.

Miller, D., and Looney, J. (1976). Determinants of homicide in adolescence. *Adolescent Psychiatry* 4:231–254.

Ross, J. M. (1984). Fathers in Development: An overview of recent contributions. In *Parenthood, a Psychodynamic Perspective*, ed. R. S. Cohen, B. J. Cohler, and S. H. Weissman. New York: The Guilford Press.

Socarides, C. (1982). Abdicating fathers, homosexual sons. In *Father and Child: Developmental and Clinical Perspectives*, ed. S. Cath, A. Garwitt, and J. Ross. Boston: Little Brown.

Szymuiska, L., and Lesniak, R. (1972). Juvenile homicide and sexual behavior. *Psychologica Polska* 62:143–149.

Winnicott, D. W. (1955). *Collected Papers*. London: Tavistock.

Yesavage, J. A. (1983). Bipolar illness: correlates of dangerous inpatient behavior. *British Journal of Psychiatry* 142:554–557.

Yogman, M. (1982). Observations on the father-infant relationship. In *Father and Child: Developmental and Clinical Perspectives*, ed. S. Cath, A. Garwitt, and J. Ross. Boston: Little Brown.

2

Development in Puberty and Adolescence

Maturational age is based on both chronology and the level of physiological and psychological development. A prepubertal fourteen-year-old thus differs physically, cognitively, and emotionally from a postpubertal peer of the same age. A negativistic, rebellious pubertal youngster may become adolescent—that is, reach the appropriate maturational age—in the course of treatment: the behavior may not change, but its developmental significance does. For example, the acting out of conflict may have become a necessary developmental acting up.

PSYCHOLOGICAL RESPONSES TO PUBERTY

In all cultures, people have psychological responses to puberty. The way in which people handle such stress is related to the particular culture and social system, but the gratifications and basic anxiety of puberty are the same everywhere.

Physiological puberty starts with an increase of follicle-stim- ulating hormone (FSH) and luteinizing hormone (LH) and ends with a stabilized adult androgen/estrogen ratio. Puberty is as- sociated with changes in physical appearance, behavior, cognitive functioning, and mental life: Puberty has been said to denote the physical and morphological changes that accompany sexual mat- uration (Blos 1974).

Many young people show behavioral changes before physi- cal changes are apparent. In parallel with the initial changes in endocrine balance—which occur before any physical changes are visible—girls may temporarily become more "seductive" with their fathers, and boys may become interested in their mothers as women.

Physical development in puberty is initially felt as inexplica- ble, and it creates, along with a sense of gratification at both pleasurable new sensations and growth, physiologically driven anxiety about the loss of control: When bodily changes come too fast or too slow, too soon or too late, or just at the time one would expect, they are a source of exquisite self-consciousness (Stone and Church 1957).

In the West, a major psychological issue in puberty is the wish for environmental mastery. This initially may be regarded as a reaction formation to deal with the youngster's feelings of helplessness associated with the loss of control. This helplessness has many determinants, including a physiologically driven up- surge in aggressive and sexual drives, a rapid change in bodily shape and size produced by the spurt in growth, frequent erec- tions in boys, and menarche in girls.

Many behavioral techniques are used to gain a sense of control. For example, pubertal boys may masturbate not only to gratify themselves but also to gain a sense of control over their bodies. The psychological mechanisms that young people may use to cope with their now-unfamiliar bodies include denial, isolation, repression, and projection. If these do not offer relief, individuals may then act out their conflicts and excessive feelings of helplessness.

Helplessness carries with it a feeling of being vulnerable to external criticism, which may be misperceived. For instance, parents find that comments that their children earlier did not resent now have become tormenting.

The physiological changes of puberty lead to overinvolvement with the self. If this self-involvement becomes excessive, it will become a pseudoinfantile regression with petulant irrational responses to the external world. This outcome is especially likely if the boy or girl has neither sociopsychological nor cultural supports or cannot internalize them because of previous psychological damage. Infantile positions may then take precedence over the mastery of current reality, and culturally and socially appropriate adaptive responses become impossible.

Strangely, along with their feelings of helplessness, pubertal boys and girls may feel quite omnipotent. The two contrasting perceptions do not, however, counterbalance each other but, rather, exist in parallel. Young people's sense of time is impaired, so they often are "prisoners of the present." For example, adults' warnings of the future consequences of behavior are relatively meaningless, and if before puberty children have begun to think abstractly (Piaget 1975), they may temporarily stop doing so. There are remarkable variations in their capacity to pay attention. Adolescents may spend hours on desired activities, but if they become frustrated, their attention may wander, and they may turn to restless daydreaming.

Most adolescents unconsciously use these physiologically driven changes. That is, their wish for environmental mastery becomes a search for autonomy, and their rebellion mixes with their striving for independence. They may use inattention to defy certain authority figures, but this may also help the abandonment of childish dependence.

One conscious goal is to control the environment and make it more gratifying. If adolescents' complaints are excessive or their behavior is intolerable, they may actually achieve not environmental gratification but, rather, environmental persecution. The more disturbed the adolescent boy or girl is, the more negative will be the response of other persons and the social systm. The result of this dilemma for behaviorally disturbed adolescents is an emotional position of helplessness, hopelessness, and omnipotence. Thus they continue to behave with little thought of future implications, but internally they may be filled with empty despair.

PUBERTY AND THE DEVELOPMENT OF COGNITION

Accompanying the physical changes of puberty are shifts in adolescents' cognitive capacities. Formal abstract thinking is said to develop between the ages of eleven to fifteen (Piaget 1975), but the development of abstract thought depends on maturational rather than chronological age. Not everyone who becomes pubertal develops this capacity, but without puberty, it is doubtful that it can fully develop. During early adolescence, particularly at times of maximum physical change, there may be periods in which the capacity for abstraction seems to be lost, but then it is regained. Furthermore, shifts from abstract to more concrete thinking are likely to take place during periods of stress.

For six months during early adolescence, children may also become difficult to teach (Miller 1974). Teachers who have children over a two- or three-year period regard this as a developmental shift. Those teachers who keep pupils for only one or two semesters may mislabel those undergoing physical change as underachievers. This may lead, at best, to family anxiety and, at worst, to the development of a false identity as an academic failure.

Those children who do not learn before puberty to value language as a significant communication become extremely action oriented during this phase. But in all children, the physiological changes of puberty revive infantile drives, which the children usually express through activities that release physical tension. The changes in body boundaries mean that adolescents must also reposition their sense of self in space. In order to adjust to these boundaries, which lead to changes in body image, action is required. For those who are psychologically deprived and to whom this is culturally acceptable, sexual intercourse may become the only significant heterosexual communication, and violent behavior may become the only way of expressing anger.

EARLY ADOLESCENCE

Adolescence traditionally is divided into three subperiods: early, including puberty; middle, the era of identity consolidation; and late, the period of coping (Miller 1974). Early adolescence, which has also been described as a period of secondary separation-individuation (Blos 1967), can be damaged by environmental deprivation, just as primary separation-individuation in an infant can be disrupted by inadequate nurturing.

At the onset of adolescence, the environment is either growth promoting or growth impeding. Our society, for instance, often does not meet adolescents' general developmental needs. Many adolescents are not given opportunities for physical sublimation in age-appropriate activities; their creativity and imagination are often not valued; and many educational and social systems encourage passive conformity.

Stable peer groups are developmentally necessary for adolescents, as they provide both special friends and means of entry into small social systems. Early adolescents are highly sensitive to what they perceive as peer attitudes; they may defy parental norms but conform closely to their peers in their language, music, dress, and behavioral expectations. When adolescents do not receive appropriate psychosocial nurture from their parents and extraparental adults, they then become overdependent on their peers for a sense of worth. They may excessively defy parental norms; they cannot risk peer disapproval; they then may fail to develop an appropriate sense of inner direction.

Early adolescents are normatively outer directed. They crave support from others in the environment. Their dependence on what others say about them mediates their self-concept of how they stand in the world (Stone and Church 1957).

Shifts in the self's inner experience are influenced by changes in the early adolescents' perception of their bodies, and they then require validation from the world that they are acceptable. Thus, the pubertal girl calls attention to herself by covering her breasts with her hands when in the swimming pool, and the pubertal boy anxiously compares the size of his penis with those of the other young males in the locker room.

Adolescents whose developmental needs are not appropriately met are likely as adults to remain highly outer directed. Their sense of worth may continue to depend on their feeling valued by others, a nonspecific "they" who determines what is acceptable.

The maintenance of this attitude in later adolescence and adulthood helps create an individual who is overconformist and who has difficulty being creatively different. This is understandable, because an individual who demonstrates a special ability must produce some degree of envy in others. This envy, in turn, cannot be tolerated by those who need the good opinion of others to maintain their self-esteem. Thus adolescents must develop a sense of personal worth, a concomitant of a firm sense of self. This process is made more difficult, however, if prepubertal children cannot modify the normal idealization of their parents. This process requires many extrafamilial supports of the children's personality functioning, including satisfactory hero figures and stability in interpersonal relationships.

Early adolescents seek to control the world and be controlled by it. If they cannot appropriately master their world, then they will withdraw from reality, sometimes into fantasy and sometimes in reality. For example, in the early 1980s, a hero figure for many adolescent groups was Jim Morrison, the lead singer of the popular group the Doors. He had killed himself with drugs, and the adolescent fantasy was that he was not really dead but was hidden away "in Africa or somewhere" and would return. This kind of fantasy is part of adolescents' omnipotent perception of death, that it is not really final. This is a view often manifested by adolescents who attempt suicide.

Asceticism and intellectualization in early adolescence (Freud 1958) also have many uses, as defenses against emotional withdrawal from the real world, intense involvement with the physical self, and the transient abandonment of trying to master the environment.

Early adolescents, especially, manifest the greatest amount of turmoil (Baittle and Offer 1972). The emotional crises traditionally associated with adolescence, with the fluctuations in the capacity to tolerate frustration, and with a high growth potential, (Erikson 1959) are most evident at this time. During early adolescence, girls are maturationally two years ahead of boys of the same age. Thus at the same age, girls appear to be better students, have a greater capacity for introspection, develop a greater sense of the past and the future, and have a greater capacity for empathy.

All early adolescents, because of the rapid shifts in their physiology and psychology and their inevitable regression from time to time, have some difficulty separating themselves from other people who are important to them or from things in the world outside themselves. This can help explain the attachment of young teenagers to clothing, record players, and their best friends. One intellectually retarded boy put into words the needs of all such young people: "I must have my red shirt as that makes me a groovy teenager." A more sophisticated youth would have merely reached for the shirt.

The combination of the psychophysiological turmoil induced by puberty, along with the early adolescent necessity to resolve oedipal conflicts before developing a more valid sense of autonomy, means that parents alone cannot completely contain splitting (Klein 1946). Thus, there will be projective spillovers.

A social organization to which adolescents can belong is now needed to offer emotional supports so that they can continue to resolve their psychic tensions. If the society's social systems do not provide this, adolescents will have difficulty continuing their emotional development. Appropriate support means that parents, peers, and extraparental adults all belong to a social network in which they have significant positive emotional involvements. No one group is isolated from another. If this network does not exist and there is little or no interrelationship among these groups, the adolescent peer group will then reinforce splitting and the adolescents' perception that the external world is only bad. Thus they will find it easier to dehumanize both themselves and others and will be more likely to behave in antisocial ways in regard to sex, drugs, and violence.

THE ROLE OF THE HERO
IN ADOLESCENT DEVELOPMENT

Maturation in early adolescence also necessitates a change in the primitive, overidealized concept of the parents. A common way that this is done is for adolescents to project the image of an ideal person onto a public hero. It is as though adolescents project onto their hero the concept of an ideal self based on their original idealization of their parents. Adolescents then identify with this ideal and reintegrate it into their own personalities. Not being consciously aware of this process enables adolescents to begin to feel like separate persons.

Nowadays adults look upon adolescent heroes with mixed feelings, and such heroes are often not those of society at large. This in turn means that adolescents' heroes may be essentially countercultural. An example is the current androgynous stars of popular music. As our society no longer offers hero figures who represent its best values, it is more difficult for adolescents to modify the overidealization of their parents. The recent tendency in the West has been for adolescents to look up to individuals with a highly regressive, often impulse-ridden way of life or to join cult religions. Thus young people often perceive society as communicating a contradictory message about their hero figures; that is, society encourages the idealization of individuals whose way of life is often seen as regressive.

All adolescent disturbances have been said to reflect the existence of a developmental impasse of the early stage of adolescence (Blos 1974). If an individual reaches psychosocial adolescence, as distinct from merely showing the psychological reactions to puberty, this is true. Thus, a study of the normal and abnormal psychology of early adolescence is likely to help in understanding the personality development of those individuals who are exposed to excessive psychosocial stress and who show unresolved disturbances in the chronological middle and late stages of this period.

An early adolescent may frequently be described as being self-centered, having little or no capacity for empathy, being eager to obtain admiration and approval from others, being unable to experience depression but filled with anger and resentment, and having strong conscious feelings of insecurity and inferiority. This is actually a description of a pathologically disturbed, self-centered, "narcissistic" personality (Kernberg 1969), but it can also be applied to one aspect of the early adolescent's personality. However, the early adolescent, unlike the individual with serious psychological disturbance, also shows a capacity for altruism and love and an ability to be creative and imaginative.

Early adolescence is that stage of life in which children begin to withdraw their emotional dependence on their parents. The self-involvement of this age period can be explained partially because the parents' emotional support can no longer be used by adolescents as it was when they were infants and latency-age children. This, along with puberty, threatens a temporary impoverishment of personality functions. Although internal turmoil is always present, some cultures, the Chinese, for example, insist that persons internalize their conflicts and show compliant behavior. In all ethnic groups, peer approval at this stage becomes crucial. Self-esteem depends to a considerable degree on the opinion of friends of both sexes and also on a diffuse perception of what others of the same age might think. Almost for the first time, an unknown "they" becomes significant in assessing self-worth.

Human personality development continues throughout life, with some obvious nodal points (Levinson 1978). At each stage of development, there are social, psychological, and biological needs that must be met. Periods of rapid physical change—infancy and childhood, adolescence and early old age—are of particular significance for future competence.

EARLY ADOLESCENCE AND ACTION COMMUNICATIONS

Pubertal children who are, developmentally, also early adolescents, begin to detach themselves emotionally from the loved objects of their childhood. A concomitant increase in their preoccupation with the self is produced by physical change. Because early adolescents have not yet acquired new love objects, they may have difficulty both feeling emotionally supported by and emotionally involved with others and understanding their feelings.

The need for action is based not just on relieving the tension associated with an upsurge of sexual and aggressive drives.

Rather, action is one way of obtaining a sense of oneself in space and confirming a sense of body image. It also is a way of contacting people and things outside the self. Because early adolescents find difficulty in verbalizing emotional involvement with others, they can best express their feelings through action. They will reach out for stimulation and reinforcement of their imagination and creativity. So, appropriate external stimulation from both the school and the community will help diminish the feelings of boredom and emptiness that occur as part of early adolescent sadness. This type of depressive response is a result of the loss of childhood and the infantile attachment to the parents. If children's creativity and imagination are not reinforced during early adolescence, they are more likely to form an emotionally impoverished adult personality.

The communication implicit in action can be understood by the concepts of acting up and acting out. Acting up is behavior designed primarily to produce an environmental response. For example, authority figures may dislike early adolescent behavior that seeks to elicit a response of appropriate external control. When this response is reasonable and not denigrating, it relieves the tension for both parties; when it is not, the tension rises and the misbehavior increases. Thus acting up is developmentally necessary.

Acting out is an attempt to resolve conflict by manipulating the self and the environment. Individuals may act out to recreate an earlier experience of being loved. Especially when they cannot perceive more age-appropriate caring in reality, they may have to look for it in fantasy.

Regressive involvement in drugs, particularly marijuana and alcohol, is a typical way of trying to recreate the earlier experience of being fed and loved by the mother. Indeed, the expression on the face of a well-fed infant can be aptly compared with the facial expression of an adolescent "stoned" on drugs or alcohol.

Young people may also act out a type of repetition compulsion to gain a sense that they can control painful experiences. They arrange and rearrange the world in reality as well as in fantasy, so as to repeat earlier traumatic experiences, usually of separation from emotionally meaningful adults. Individuals are consciously and unconsciously prompted to behave as traumatically as emotionally significant individuals did in the past. But this time the adolescents avoid the experience of helplessness with its concomitant sense of persecution, because they, in a sense, have arranged the trauma.

ENVIRONMENTAL STIMULATION
OF ACTING OUT

People act out because external stress and the way that the stress is perceived have stimulated biopsychologically induced internal conflicts. Stress may be produced by the behavior of authority figures in the society at large, by the family, and by therapeutic systems. The ethos and conflicts of the larger social systems that impinge on adolescents may also affect the appearance and form of acting out behavior.

The family ethos was recognized by Aichorn (1984) as important in influencing the frequency and manner of adolescent acting out. He believed that parents may vicariously gratify their own poorly integrated, forbidden impulses through their child's acting out, which is encouraged by the parents' unconscious permissiveness or inconsistency. Antisocial children in fact often identify with their parents' gross ethical distortions. Indeed, in almost all delinquency syndromes, parental permission can be seen as stimulating their children's antisocial behavior (Johnson and Szurek 1956, Miller 1958). The parents' words are by no means their only influence on the child; their ideas, hopes, interests, fears, and frustrations are also perceived by the child in the parents' gestures, intonations, body movements, and provocative smiles, as well as in their manipulation of events (Liten, Giffin, and Johnson 1954).

The psychotherapeutic situation may also precipitate acting out, affecting both its form and its intensity. Therapists themselves may inadvertently provide sanctions for acting out by their patients: that is, warnings of or questions about acting out, without factual justification, may be interpreted by patients with sexual perversions or serious antisocial tendencies as stimulation and permission (Johnson and Szurek 1956). When a patient's acting out behavior is not forbidden by therapists, their silence may be taken as permission. This is quite evident in adolescents who abuse drugs and come in drugged to their therapist's office. If the therapist only briefly comments on the drug abuse or, worse, does not even notice it, the patient may interpret this as permission.

When dealing with action-oriented youngsters, every nuance of the therapeutic situation and process, as well as the therapist's interventions and spoken and unspoken attitudes, may influence both the process and the content of acting out (Blum 1976). Acting out may also be prompted by misunderstanding, mismanagement, and the patient's identification with the therapist's irrational actions (Greenacre 1969).

The goal of disturbed adolescents is to avoid stress, to seek a consistent environmental response, and to maintain a position of minimal tension. When appropriate emotional support or action does not achieve this goal, adolescents may, at first, try complying with perceived consistent environmental demands. If they perceive authority figures' wishes as inconsistent and conflictual, disturbed adolescents will seek to find and obey that which is consistent.

Young people, however, receive many contradictory communications. For example, society at large disapproves of marijuana use, and yet the movement not to penalize those who use the drug is seen by concrete-thinking adolescents as permission to use it. Within family structures, when parents shout at their adolescents that they should not shout, they are not telling them that shouting is unacceptable but, rather, that one should be bigger and better at it in order for it to be accepted. In some institutions for delinquent youth, the staff uses violence to control adolescent brutality; for example, when adolescents bully one another, they may be physically chastised by a staff member. The essential message then is not that bullying is wrong but that the bullying must be more efficient.

Because implicit messages tend to be consistent, they are the ones that an adolescent seeking to avoid stress may obey. If the consistent implicit message contradicts an explicit one, it may represent a conflict either within the system or within the personalities of its authority figures. So when adolescents obey conflicting implicit messages in order to try to avoid stress, the environmental response may be highly negative. On the one hand, this reinforces the stress, but on the other hand, potentially helpless adolescents can use this negative response as a second line of defense.

The adolescents' obedience to consistent implicit communications leads to a situation in which the overt attitude of those in the environment becomes negative, and perhaps even coercive and persecutory. The adolescents' initial confusion about the reality of this perceived torment—which is felt by those who experience intense helplessness and increases their experience of stress—is now partially resolved, when the torment is actually occurring.

Adolescents may also use the conflicting responses of authority figures to gain a perverse sense of mastery. One can often see a triumphant expression on the faces of many pubertal young people when they make authority figures lose control. Sometimes, too, an internal experience of potential persecution is converted into a real persecution:

> A 15-year-old boy perceived his mother as constantly devaluing him. She seemed to be always rejecting him by going away on trips. Actually, she was a seriously depressed individual who could not meet his needs. Despite the boy's superior intellect, he was placed in the special education class of his high school because of his consistent underachievement. This boy also perceived the school as telling him that he was "a dummy." Eventually the school rejected him because of his vague suicidal threats, and thus he created in reality the rejection and devaluation that he felt as always present in his human relationships.

It is often difficult for children to perceive their family system as consistent because of the children's own changing demands, caused by their continuing growth and development. These changes peak during periods of maximum turbulence in early adolescence. At this time young people are particularly likely to respond in ways that adults perceive as negative. Adolescents' obedience to the obvious wishes of a social system requires them to tolerate a degree of confusion. Clearly, the less tolerant the adolescents are in this regard, the more likely they are to respond in an unacceptable way.

ADOLESCENT DEVELOPMENT
AND ITS DISTORTION

Various biopsychosocial stress situations, including the trauma produced by the symptoms of psychological illness, may retard emotional development (Parnas et al. 1982). If emotional development is held back, then what is normal for one stage of adolescence may still be at the forefront many years later. This has therapeutic significance, as external control has different implications in early adolescence than it does in later adolescence. For example, sometimes in family therapy, parents are taught behavior modification techniques to help control a child's disturbed behavior. Perhaps the parents will use a system of rewards and punishments to control the eating disorder of their fifteen-year-old daughter. This constraint, however, need not be antithetical to the girl's personality development at that age. But if the parents use the same techniques when their daughter is seventeen, such methods will reinforce the daughter's enmeshment in the family and weaken her attempt to become autonomous.

Certain syndromes reflect the transience of adolescent processes. A common picture is of an adolescent who appears on the surface to be bewildered, disinterested, dissatisfied, sexually undifferentiated, and seeking peace at any price (Esman 1977). Such young people complain of boredom and emptiness and may seek solace in the regressive world of drugs, in impulsive and sometimes self-destructive gestures, or by creating excitement and turbulence in those around them; thus they gain a feeling of being alive.

Another typical individual is one who is amiable when his or her wants are gratified but coldly dehumanizes others when these wants are frustrated. This adolescent boy or girl—whose personality is usually severely damaged—lives on impulses, seeks gratification at any cost, has no capacity for empathy, and divides the world concretely into good and bad on the basis of what is immediately gratifying.

Another group includes those who attempt to gain a sense of self and a feeling of mastery in sexual activity, among whom

are the adolescents who produce illegitimate children or unwanted pregnancies.

Finally, adolescents who find it difficult to deal with the
helplessness of not being able to control either themselves or
their world may attempt to resolve this by developing eating
disorders or abusing drugs.

Traditionally, adolescence has been considered to encompass
two broad types of psychological changes: those changes that can
be attributed to the psychosocial reactions to the processes of
puberty and those that are necessary to develop a sense of an
autonomous self.

Early adolescence begins with the onset of puberty, and late
adolescence ends with the onset of young adulthood, though this
last phase of adolescence is not necessarily associated with physical growth. Adolescent phase-appropriate behavior may appear
at a chronologically abnormal stage—even in, chronologically,
young adulthood. Furthermore, because of contemporary
changes in child-rearing practices, it is now common to see a
continuation of early adolescence phase-typical behavior. For
example, many 30-year-olds continue to live according to their
impulses and to remain chronic marijuana smokers. Nevertheless, this behavior does not make such individuals adolescent, and
so they should not be treated as such.

PSYCHOSOCIAL STRESS AND IDENTITY

Identity development in adolescence may be obstructed by pre-
adolescent personality disturbances, and psychosocial stress during this age period may prevent the personality from maturing.

We live in a world filled with chaos. In 1979, there were over
1 million divorces in the United States, involving 1.2 million children, and over 10 million children now live in one-parent families
(Jellenek and Stark 1981). In such situations, children will have
difficulty establishing an acceptable male or female role and a
firm sense of sexual and intrafamilial identity. In a divorce, the
father typically is the absent parent, and so many children grow
up with little awareness of what a male parent actually does.

Furthermore, such children are not able to internalize how husbands behave with wives, and vice versa. Indeed, a pervasive omnipotent fantasy for such children is that traditional masculine and feminine roles can be changed to suit the current situation.

Society's implicit, if not explicit, attitudes often appear to devalue human life. Thus, society's awareness of sixteen-year-old adolescents' proneness to automobile accidents does not raise the driving age. The casual way in which the political establishment talks of megadeath is not lost on the intelligent young who read or listen to the news. A youth unemployment rate of 25 percent is apparently considered acceptable. Society thereby threatens and, at the same time, devalues young people. A person's sense of worth is based on the perception that his or her life and productivity are valued. It is not surprising, then, that sometimes society's failure to meet young people's developmental needs produces a picture of disturbance similar to that produced by severe early deprivation (Miller 1978). But normally, adolescents who weather the early part of this developmental phase are, by the middle and late stages, conforming to the norms of their ethnic or social group (Offer 1969, Baittle and Offer 1972).

ADOLESCENT OMNIPOTENCE

Intensely greedy and self-centered young people cannot obtain support for their infantile demands. They then, therefore, seek magical solutions and may perceive adults' helpful attempts as an implicit promise that such solutions are forthcoming. Such adolescents thus project their imagined omnipotence and inevitably are disappointed, to which they respond with rage. For example, a well-intentioned adult may offer to a very deprived adolescent real gratification, such as taking him or her home because the young person has nowhere else to go. The adolescent perceives this as a promise of ultimate caring, and when this cannot be delivered, the response is to steal from the benefactor. Similarly, adolescents may appear to reintegrate dramatically after one therapeutic interview but then withdraw because the "magical" solution is not delivered. If nothing is said about this, they may assume that the interview had some usefulness, which also does not materialize. Likewise, if medication is given, the implication of magical solutions will reinforce the expectation of the therapist's omnipotence.

NEGATIVE IDENTIFICATION

Adolescents may deal with their anxiety about being persecuted by identifying with their persecutor and deciding that the persecutor's behavior is in fact acceptable:

> The principal of a British school for delinquent boys was investigated for brutality after his behavior was exposed. He would beat the boys for disciplinary infractions, and pictures of their bruised and bleeding backs and buttocks appeared in the national press. The defense that he offered was that the boys agreed that their behavior was wrong and that their punishment was justified. Indeed, as the boys made such statements, they looked admiringly at their tormentor.

The perception of being persecuted is thus attenuated, and the acceptability of such behavior is internalized, becoming part of the individual's sense of self. Such young people, however, then commonly become brutal, rejecting, and hostile.

This problem is particularly important in the treatment of violent young people. For example, in most correctional centers, it is now difficult, if not impossible, to control the inmates' verbal or physical violence toward one another, and this the inmates see as permission to behave in this way. Thus the young inmates internalize the system's implicit violence, and they leave more violent than they were when they entered the institution.

Previously well adjusted children who are brutally treated during childhood or adolescence may later identify with the brutality in order to deal with the stress. As adults, they may then replay with their own children some of the experiences that they themselves had:

> A 35-year-old Jewish woman had hidden for three years during the Nazi invasion of Holland. As she knew at the time, other

Jewish people were being taken by train to unknown destinations and were told they were to be "resettled."

Her 14-year-old son stayed at home from school for two years. She felt quite unable to get him to return, and so she finally arranged for him to enter a psychiatric hospital. Her plan was to tell him they were going for a drive in the country. She would then stop at the hospital, and then the staff would force him to enter.

When parents inflict excessive physical punishment on their children, the children in turn may do the same when they become parents. Furthermore, it is not just the behavior that is imitated but also the implicit dehumanization. Sometimes the family adopts the brutal actions of the larger community, and they may pass them on through the generations. For example, in most African tribal cultures, children are not whipped, and therefore violence is not a significant presenting issue for immigrant black youths seen in psychiatric clinics in Britain. American black youth, however, are commonly whipped by their parents, and violence is a common presenting symptom among young blacks admitted to psychiatric clinics in the United States. One theory for this phenomenon is that the young black youths were the ones who survived the slave ships and were later whipped by their owners. They then internalized the whipping as acceptable behavior, and so it has now been passed on through the generations.

In conclusion, to understand an adolescent's difficulties, one must consider the following issues: Besides chronological age, the therapist should determine whether the youngster is pubertal and whether the growth spurt has occurred. If turmoil is present, the therapist must decide whether it is developmental acting up, or acting out to resolve internal tension. Of special importance is the adolescent's ability to be empathic and the situations that prompt humanization and dehumanization. Finally, whether the adolescent can think abstractly and the conditions under which he or she is likely to do so should be determined. Likewise, the adolescent's hero figures and identification models and the way that he or she attempts to gain environmental mastery are developmentally significant.

Identifying the adolescent's available support systems includes understanding the role of the father and possible substitutes, the adolescent's friendship networks and family, and the family's ability to reinforce creative and imaginative learning. The family's and society's ethos and their implicit and explicit techniques of communication also help in assessing the adolescent's developmental stress.

REFERENCES

Aichorn, A. (1984). *Wayward Youth.* Evanston, IL: Northwestern University Press.

Baittle, B., and Offer, D. (1972). On the nature of the male adolescent rebellion. *Adolescent Psychiatry* 1:139–161.

Blos, P. (1967). The second individuation process of adolescence. *The Psychoanalytic Study of the Child* 22:162–186.

———. (1974). *The Young Adolescent.* New York: Free Press.

Blum, H. P. (1976). Acting out and interpretation. *Annals of Psychoanalysis* 4:163–184. New York: International Universities Press.

Erikson, E. (1959). *Identity and the Life Cycle.* New York: International Universities Press.

Esman, A. H. (1977). Changing values—their implications for adolescent development and psychoanalytic ideas. *Adolescent Psychiatry* 5:18–34.

Freud, A. (1958). Adolescence. *Psychoanalytic Study of the Child* 13:255–279.

Greenacre, P. (1969). *Training Growth and Personality.* New York: International Universities Press.

Jellenek, M. S., and Stark, L. S. (1981). Divorce: its impact on children. *New England Journal of Medicine* 305:557–560.

Johnson, A. M., and Szurek, S. A. (1956). The genesis of antisocial acting out in children and adults. *Psychoanalytic Quarterly* 22:323–343.

Kernberg, O. (1969). Failures in the treatment of narcissistic personalities. *Journal of the American Psychoanalytic Association* 18:51–107.

Klein, M. (1946). Notes on some schizoid mechanisms. In *Developments in Psychoanalysis,* ed. J. Rivere. New York: International Universities Press.

Levinson, D. J. (1978). *The Seasons of a Man's Life.* New York: Knopf.

Liten, E. M., Giffin, M. E., and Johnson, A. M. (1954). Parental influence in unusual social behavior. *Psychoanalytic Quarterly* 25:37–55.

Miller, D. (1958). Family interaction in the therapy of adolescent patients. *Psychiatry* 21:277–284.

——. (1974). *Adolescence: Psychology, Psychopathology, and Psychotherapy.* New York: Jason Aronson.

——. (1978). Early adolescence: its psychology and implications for treatment. *Adolescent Psychiatry* 6:434–448.

Offer, D. (1969). *The Psychological World of the Teenager.* New York: Basic Books.

Parnas, J., Teasdale, T. W., and Schulsinger, H. (1982). Continuity of character neurosis from childhood to adulthood. Prospective Individual Study, *Acta Psychiatrica Scandinavia* 66:691–698.

Piaget, J. (1975). Intellectual development of the adolescent. In *The Psychology of Adolescence*, ed. A. H. Esman. New York: International Universities Press.

Stone, L. J., and Church, J. (1957). *Childhood and Adolescence.* New York: Random House.

Winnicott, D. (1955). *Collected Papers—Through Paediatrics to Psycho-Analysis.* New York: Basic Books.

3

The Individual and
the Family

Whatever kind of relationships the nuclear family may have, they are a basic socializing agent for the children (Campbell 1969). Historically, the family has been viewed as the central institution of human society to which belongs this major responsibility. One role of the family is to help the child develop ambivalence, and another is to become the repository of the child's anger before the ambivalence is developed. In infancy, when a child cries—for whatever reason—the mother's immediate response is to hold her child. In this situation the mother physically absorbs her infant's tension and returns love (Winnicott 1965). In older children a similar process occurs. Parents may listen to stories about the child's current, rageful experiences, and by being appropriately supportive, they can absorb the child's tension and the child can resume functioning. Thus the family becomes a psychosocially acceptable repository for a child's angry feelings.

A child's or adolescent's learning socially and psychologically acceptable behavior depends on the interactive processes in the family, between the family and society, and, finally, on the internal dynamics of the child's or adolescent's personality. This learning also is produced by the interaction between the child and society in its larger and smaller social systems and the individual's genetic vulnerability to stress, particularly various neuroendocrine disturbances. In the etiology of psychological disturbances, the effects of the nurturing experiences in childhood and adolescence on the development of an adult personality are crucial.

The conflicts of the social system to which young and old belong influence the way that significant authority figures respond to adolescent behavior, and nowhere is this more evident than within the family. The role that parents occupy in reinforcing or reducing their children's aggressive or regressive behavior is often related to their own conflicts, although the way that parents react to their adolescent children is also partially determined by the parents' stage of psychological development.

A healthy adult's identity will change as he or she grows older (Levinson 1978). For example, while they both are aging, wives may become more dominant than their husbands, a phenomenon apparent in both primitive tribes and more sophisticated societies (Guttman 1972). People try to maintain an acceptable minimum of psychic tension. The members of a nuclear family do this by adopting predictable roles and offering one another support. Despite this, however, the family constantly receives stress, because of both maturational shifts within its members and strain inflicted by society at large. The family influences society and the society influences the family, just as parents may influence their children and vice versa. Adolescent children may be delegates from society to the family; they may act for the family and perform actions in society that individual family members would like to do but dare not (Sterlin 1976). Thus, the family affects the way that their adolescents' emotional disturbances show themselves.

Adolescents assume that if adults know of an action and do nothing, then they must approve. For instance, many young people believed for a time that a "natural high" was acceptable. This attitude permeated society and was reinforced by it because so many parents and their offspring appeared to have been convinced by campaigns for the legalization of marijuana that the drug must be harmless. Indeed, society's increasing tolerance of adolescents' abuse of drugs and alcohol forces those families that oppose their use to adopt extreme positions in order to justify their attitudes; that is, they may insist that marijuana is as dangerous as is a chemical hallucinogen.

FAMILY STYLE AND DISTURBED BEHAVIOR

Behavioral disturbances often reverberate both within the child's personality and within relationships in the family. An adolescent may gain instinctual satisfaction from problem behavior and is therefore reluctant to abandon it. On the other hand, the parents may have the subtle, if unconscious, gratification of keeping their child dependent and thus capable of only pseudo-maturity.

The life-styles of families—nuclear, extended, and even social networks—differ markedly. In some ethnic groups in the United States—Appalachian groups, for example—some women may implicitly hand over to their husbands the care of their daughters when they reach puberty.

Families' overt attitudes can be broadly conceptualized as belonging to two main types. Families that control impulsive behavior may be called *controlling families*, and those that tolerate more impulsive behavior, both aggressive and regressive, *impulsive families* (Miller 1980). These represent extremes. That is, for controlling families to be adequate vehicles for mutual loving and the personality growth of all their members, they must tolerate some impulsive and regressive behavior, and impulsive families need a variety of controlling techniques.

The psychological significance of aggressive or regressive behavior differs according to the type of family to which a youngster belongs. One kind of violent behavior, predatory violence, is the equivalent in modern urban society of the hunting behavior of people and animals. In adolescents who come from families and social systems that reinforce such antisocial behavior, predatory violence is not necessarily indicative of emotional disturbance. Nevertheless, the adolescent who shows behavioral responses that accord with his or her family style may also be psychologically disturbed. Such techniques may be used to try to reduce tension. For example, persons with biologically determined mood disorders may respond to frustration with excessive rage but may also use learned techniques. Therefore, although the successful treatment of such a mood disorder may not change the behavior, it may change the reason for it. Furthermore, if adolescents use a certain type of behavioral response that is not acceptable to their family and social system, it will almost always be a sign of severe emotional difficulty.

CONTROLLING FAMILIES

In Western society, controlling families generally are members of the middle class, and they teach their children to resolve conflicts by means of words (Goode 1969). Such families generally value the capacity to tolerate psychic pain and frustration without an immediate recourse to action or magical solutions, or this may be their outward attitude. But privately, such families may treat headaches with analgesics, anxiety with mild tranquilizers, sleeplessness with sedatives, and daily tensions with ritualized drinks. Thus the implicit message that coping with psychic pain and tension by means of sedatives is acceptable contradicts the explicit credo that frustration must be tolerated. Indeed, adolescents who abuse drugs often come from families that use medications to deal with minor difficulties but that outwardly decry their acceptability.

Generally, controlling families value a compulsive life-style, that is, socially acceptable environmental mastery and conformity to a puritan ethos. When such controlling families unwittingly make it difficult for their late adolescent children to become autonomous, these young people may seek out pseudomaturity with drug abuse (Williams 1970). This may be a problem especially in the first year of college and is a fairly common reason for students to drop out at that time—particularly from large schools that offer little emotional support to their students.

Controlling families may also "use" their children to act out conflicts over gratification, especially in regard to sex and food. This is particularly common when the family deals with such conflicts by making overly rigid demands on the children, which may mean that the necessary expression of the parents' and the children's instincts has been frustrated.

Controlling families do not normally tolerate promiscuous sexuality, but one or both parents may use their adolescent's promiscuous sexual acting out to gain unconscious gratification (Johnson 1949):

A 14-year-old girl who lived in the suburbs of a large city was seen in consultation. She was constantly running away from her parents to the inner city. The area was dangerous, and logically, upon her return, one might have expected her parents to be concerned about her safety. Instead, they would demand a blow-by-blow description of her sexual activity.

The implicit message they gave their daughter was a high degree of interest in this behavior, though their explicit message was, of course, disapproval. It was this implicit request that encouraged her promiscuous behavior.

Although the family had tried therapy for two years, the husband's impotence was not disclosed to the family therapist. Thus is is reasonable to assume that their adolescent daughter was acting out the parents' need for sexuality.

Because of the differing attitudes of society at large, conveyed through their children, controlling families may become confused about their own attitudes, which may appear in their response to their children's heterosexual behavior:

One father remarked, "When I was a boy of 17, my father said, 'No girls in the house.'" His son's reply was, "I'm horny; why shouldn't I bring a girl to the house and screw her?" The father then indicated that it was acceptable if, when he and his mother were home, his son took the girl to the basement. However, he described how his wife would ring the doorbell when she returned to the house if she thought their son was there with his girlfriend.

The father perceived the pressure from his son's report of local attitudes as implying that his insistence on "moral" behavior at home was ridiculous. However, the father saw nothing wrong in his son's taking his girl friend to a motel, which was indicative of the father's conflicted feelings.

The children of controlling families show mood disturbances in a way that is consistent with the family's style of relating. For instance, a boy who recalled having been slapped by his mother only twice in his life, as his family generally expressed anger only through words, demonstrated his disorder as follows:

> Aged 15, he was admitted to a hospital with a history of severe drug abuse. He had a history of temper tantrums for which no organic cause was found and which had persisted until puberty. At that time, he began to use marijuana excessively, and the tantrums subsided. In the hospital, some three to four weeks after his admission, when the breakdown products of tetrahydro-cannibinol had presumably cleared from his nervous system, he began to stage rage attacks. When frustrated, he would swear and shout. He never struck anyone, although he threatened to "kill them." He was diagnosed as suffering from a mood disorder, and his symptoms subsided after therapy.

Adolescents who starve themselves commonly have parents with conflicts concerning either the type of food that they eat or how it is prepared. The latter is seen more often when both parents are working (Miller and Carlton 1985). In other situations, the family may use the adolescent's behavior in subtle ways to alleviate an excessively strict family conscience. Parents who cannot tolerate any defiance within the home may have children who behave in unacceptable ways in the community at large. In such families, the parents may have an excessively strict conscience and may force their children to behave at home in highly conformist ways. Such families may produce adolescents who are highly conformist within the nuclear family but antisocial within the community at large.

Sometimes parents who implicitly contradict overt demands for conformity may help produce antisocial behavior in their adolescents, who may act out in society the subtle techniques that their parents have taught them in the past:

A 17-year-old boy had an excellent educational and social record, never giving a moment's trouble until he reached his junior year. Then he was involved in three successive car accidents associated with speeding. At the same time, his school work rapidly deteriorated in both quality and quantity. Interestingly, when the boy was younger, his rigid, demanding, apparently scrupulously honest father had always had him look out the rear window of the automobile to check that there was no patrolman following the car when it was exceeding the speed limit.

Controlling families are found in a variety of ethnic groups, and their family style is related more to social class than to ethnocentricity. The middle-class black family, for example, may be more like its white counterpart than like a lower-class black family.

IMPULSIVE FAMILIES

Impulsive families may not consciously approve of violence; yet in this type of family, the parents may often behave violently toward their children. These families often use words as a preface to a physical attack, rather than as a technique of mediation. Indeed, the amount of yelling, scolding, slapping, pinching, hitting, and yanking produced by impulsive families and acted out by the parents against their very small children may appear shocking to people from controlling families (Steele and Pollock 1968). Historically, such families have internalized the concept that violence toward children is acceptable, and so their mood disturbances may typically involve violent behavior, particularly if it is reinforced in the local community and culture. Not surprisingly, adolescents who have mood disorders and who come from impulsive families almost automatically use physical violence:

A 14-year-old boy came to a psychiatric unit because he had violently assaulted his probation officer. He was suffering from an episodic dyscontrol syndrome which eventually responded to lithium carbonate in therapeutic dosage.

His rage attacks had been homicidal in intent and involved much physical brutality. He came from a family that controlled the children by inflicting pain. The mother would beat him with a belt, and before deserting the family, the father would use his fists. The boy also lived in a deprived neighborhood in which survival required one to be "streetwise."

Besides his "affective" violence, this boy attempted to control the other adolescent boys in the hospital by a variety of "strong arm" methods. He had trouble understanding that this was not acceptable behavior in the adolescent program in which he was residing, as for him, the use of violence to control others was an internalized behavioral technique.

In impulsive families, violence may become excessive when their members suffer particular stress, typically because of socioeconomic conditions. It is well known that in times of high unemployment, the incidence of alcoholism, child abuse, and wife beating increases. Although estimates of the incidence of child abuse continue to be inaccurate (Newberger, Newberger, and Hampton 1983), the rising unemployment rate in the United States in the early 1980s led to a reported increase in interfamilial violence, and the number of children reported as having been abused was said to have risen. Apparently, the less socially valued by the community is the head of an impulsive family, the more likely is the family to become both internally violent and socially deviant. This, then, produces deviant problem behavior in the children and adolescents.

FAMILY STYLE AND SEXUAL, VIOLENT, AND DRUG-ABUSING BEHAVIOR

Controlling families are less tolerant than are impulsive families of their adolescent children's experimenting with sex. Impulsive families may be more willing to accept their children's heterosexual relationships, and by the time their children reach the middle stage of adolescence, the parents may not find distressing their children's sexual activities.

Impulsive families disapprove of masturbation as being infantile, whereas controlling families are generally more tolerant of it. Impulsive families may also allow their children to have extramarital sexual relationships in the family home. They may also readily take in their daughter's illegitimate baby, although later, the child's mother may have to compete with her own mother to rear the child. Incestuous relationships within these families, between brother and sister or father and daughter, are not uncommon, particularly in more isolated areas of the country.

Whenever impulsive families suffer psychic pain, their immediate response is to take action to relieve it. Such action may be either drinking alcohol or initiating some sort of physical action. Such families generally project the cause of their difficulties, soothing themselves with the belief that the enemy is without.

Impulsive families are likely to be overtly prejudiced and to dehumanize other groups with apparent ease. Prejudice in controlling families, on the other hand, is more clearly related to unconscious psychological conflict within its individual members. Thus when white controlling families are antisemitic or anti-black, they can think of a variety of illogical reasons for not liking these minorities, reasons that clearly relate to unconscious conflicts over their own family norms. Thus Jews are said to be "pushy," and blacks are said to be "oversexed" or "too violent." In impulsive families, prejudice is more simplistic: "They take our jobs and our houses, and the government gives them preferential treatment."

Families that use violent punishment encourage violence in their offspring. Violent behavior that controlling families may regard as antisocial may be seen as acceptable by impulsive families.

All symptoms of adolescents' psychological disturbances can be seen in problem behavior, even if such behavior does not arouse social concern, for example, overconformity and emotional withdrawal. Both controlling and impulsive families may have illnesses in which psychological pain is largely internalized, although impulsive families are more likely to have adolescents who "act out" their conflicts in ways that society defines as delinquent. Symptoms of behavioral disturbances do not just preserve an individual's psychic equilibrium; they also come to develop meaning in the life of the individual's family. The goal of symptoms is to maintain or restore emotional balance, or psychological homeostasis, when the personality is exposed to stress (Menninger, Mayman, and Pruyser 1963). Within the family the symptomatic behavior of an emotionally disturbed child may create, or help preserve, an equilibrium around which the family can maintain a consistent pattern of involvement with its individual members and society at large.

THE FAMILY'S PSYCHOLOGICAL SUPPORT

Some families are able to offer their adolescents enough support so that they do not need to behave antisocially in order to feel appropriately masculine or feminine. But when such a family lives in a neighborhood with a high delinquency rate, its attitudes may contradict those of its immediate society. The offspring of such a family are constantly exposed to conflicts. For example, if the local adolescent group has an "acceptable" mode of antisocial behavior, such as becoming illegitimately pregnant or being placed on probation, those adolescents with good relationships with parents who condemn the neighborhood norms will not behave in this way.

The family becomes a less-effective socializing agent when it is isolated geographically from a group of caring adults or when it is isolated intellectually and emotionally. During adolescence, when the child begins to move psychologically from the family, conflicts will arise that the family may not have taught the child how to handle. Without such extrafamilial psychosocial supports (Miller and Carlton 1985), the child may then cope with such conflicts either by regressing into the family—often by abusing drugs and/or alcohol and thus not being able to become autonomous—or by becoming more antagonistic to the family's mores.

When a single-parent family is psychologically isolated, it is particularly vulnerable to the production of a disturbed offspring. On the other hand, if a single-parent mother instills in her son a value system that overrides the neighborhood's antisocial norm, she may be able to prevent overt delinquency, although her son will still probably need to defy his mother in some significant area of living in order to prove to himself that he can be free of his mother's domination:

John, aged 15, was the son of a hard-driving, ambitious, bright, black woman who was determined that he would not be like his ne'er-do-well father who had abandoned her when the boy was three. John did not take part in neighborhood delinquency; he did use some marijuana, and although sexually active, he always used a contraceptive. He was very bright, but for a year he had been intermittently cutting school to spend time in the video game store, although he knew this distressed his mother. He would never directly contradict her: when, for example, she bought a picture for his room that he neither wanted nor liked, he would place it on the wall and tell her how much he enjoyed it.

In therapy, John began to see that his irresponsibility in school was similar to his father's behavior and that presumably this behavior had been attractive to mother. John's behavior also ensured some emotional separation from his mother, thus, he could feel more independent.

Sometimes when a family lives in a community in which antisocial behavior is a generally accepted norm, the family may eventually adjust to this behavior. Many parents then appear to agree with their offspring's antisocial actions; that is, they may not notice when their children steal things or they may choose to believe untrue stories:

A 16-year-old boy broke into a local school and stole all its audiovisual equipment. He took it to his room at home, dismantled it, and sold many of the components. But his parents did not notice that he was spending excessive amounts of time in his room or that he was spending more money than was usual for him.

When adolescents live in areas where antisocial behavior is acceptable to the peer group, the type of problem behavior that they may adopt often will modify their families' norms. Similarly, adolescents may adopt their own family's style in dealing with the larger society. For instance, when adolescents from families to whom making money is particularly important become drug dealers, they may rationalize this by reasoning that making money is the family style:

> In the suburban area of a large midwestern city, a 17-year-old boy was reputed by his peers to be making $30,000 a year dealing drugs. This was clearly an exaggeration, but he did buy an expensive automobile and, from time to time, flew on "vacation" to various parts of the United States. His father was a stockbroker and accepted the son's story that he made enough money as a checker in the local supermarket to support his life-style.

Adolescents with sexual difficulties may carry them into the family, reinforce a previously implicit communication, and make it explicit. This can be seen in adolescents' sexual acting out (Newman and San Martino 1976). Violent sexual behavior may also mimic behavior that the adolescent observed in the family when he or she was a child and may represent parental behavior of which the adolescent was, in a sense, a childhood victim:

> Kenneth was arrested at the age of 17 for violent assaults on women, whom he would rape while threatening them with a knife. He would indicate to them that if they resisted, he would cut off their breasts. After he had finished with his victims, he would slap their faces, call them foul names, and leave. Each attack was preceded by a hallucinatory experience.

> One aspect of Kenneth's etiology was temporal lobe epilepsy, and another was in his child-rearing experience.

> Kenneth had lived with his natural parents until he was five, when he was removed from the family because of child abuse. Apart from being a direct victim of violence himself, he had observed his drunken father having sexual relations with his mother on the floor of their living room. On these occasions, the father would threaten to mutilate his mother and then would beat her.

> Both Kenneth and his mother independently described these episodes without knowing that the other had told a similar story.

Adolescents' problem behaviors may meet an important family need. Runaway behavior, for example, is not uncommon just before or just after a family move. Such an adolescent may actually be a scout for the parents. Even though the parents may disown the child's behavior, the child may be scouting out the new home for the parents or may be returning to the original home from which both the parents and the child may have felt unfairly torn away. Sometimes an adolescent runaway may act as a delegate of the family to society at large, and the behavior may be, in a sense, for the sake of the family. Adolescents who run away may do this partly to satisfy a parent's angry demand to "get out of my life." They may also provide excitement for the family, who must live in a state of tension while the adolescent is on the run. Finally, the runaway may be seeking information for the family about the world at large. Thus, as with much antisocial activity, running away may demonstrate the interplay between the adolescent's intrapsychic conflicts and the family's interpersonal dynamics.

PERSONALITY DISORDERS AND THE FAMILY

Both antisocial and drug-abusing behavior in adolescents may accompany a characterological disturbance that has been produced by nurturing deficits. Personality disorders are enduring, inflexible, and maladaptive (DSM III 1980). Adolescents who suffer from these disorders are unable, to a greater or lesser degree, to make trusting relationships. Such individuals cannot handle frustration, and so they rarely consider the future implications of their behavior, and they do not learn easily from experience. Such persons' emotional life tends to be empty and desolate, and they may appear to others to be cold and uncaring and not empathic. In their attempts to gain environmental mastery, they often ignore reality. Their personalities are rigid, and they foreclose their identity at an early age so that they are not able to deal easily with society's changing demands.

These individuals are so frustrating to others that they

make them repeat a cycle of coercion, rejection, and despair. Not surprisingly, in response to the behavior of their personality-disordered offspring, the parents, in order to gain a sense of controlling the seemingly uncontrollable, may ultimately condone and even provoke their child's behavior. Such behavior may be violent and antisocial or regressive, often drug-abusing behavior.

When an adolescent behaves in antisocial ways, he or she may be made a scapegoat by a family that cannot tolerate the acting out of its implicit needs. Or the problem behavior may hold the family together (Erickson 1962). An adolescent who behaves antisocially may give the parents a common focus both for concern and for the projection of their own anxieties. It is not unusual when children are successfully treated for antisocial difficulties—whether regressive or aggressive—for a marriage that has been precarious to then fall apart.

Again, the scapegoated adolescent may become the repository of parental projections but also may represent a common bond for the family. The parents may invite the behavior and then attack it. But when the adolescent's regressively and aggressively disturbed behavior helps the family stay together, the child may be aware that his or her actions are providing a bond for the parents.

DRUG AND ALCOHOL ABUSE

Parents often buy kegs of beer for parties given by 17- and 18-year-olds at which they know youngsters of 15 and 16 will be present. Thus they reinforce the likelihood of alcohol abuse. Two or three decades ago, most middle-class families, for example, would have regarded intoxication in their children as deplorable, and most school systems would not have tolerated intoxicated adolescents in the classroom. But now it is not uncommon for some youngsters to drink before school, and seemingly no one notices their flushed faces and slurred speech. The use of nonprescription drugs, such as Visine, to clear conjunctival injection may not adequately hide the fact that an adolescent is "stoned," but even this, too, may not be observed.

The message of drug acceptability is further reinforced by the failure of some of society's authority structures. Schools, for example, rarely prevent young people from using drugs and alcohol and even provide cigarette-smoking areas in which marijuana is almost always discussed and sometimes is used. Sometimes the parents of a child who uses drugs obtained from another youngster either are unable to withstand either their own child's rage if they indicate that they will speak to the friend's parents, or may fear being told that they are interfering. Thus the parents may rationalize that they need not be concerned, provided that their children do not use drugs too often, "too often" varying, of course, from individual to individual.

An important cause of drug and alcohol abuse is thus family relationships. An early study of cigarette smoking in boys demonstrated that it was associated in a statistically significant way with their mothers' use of cigarettes (Emery 1967). In some Western societies, adolescents were introduced to the use—and abuse—of diet pills prescribed to overweight parents. In impulsive families, something "good" prescribed for the mother may be used by the whole family. For example, when adolescents are "bored," their mothers may offer them pills from their own medical prescription. In controlling families, medications prescribed for the parents may be left lying around, and the adolescent may steal them. Indeed, doctors' households are notorious drug dispensaries, as the adolescent children of physicians may identify with their parent and "prescribe" stolen samples for their friends.

Often an adolescent's drug abuse is reinforced by the parents' unconscious wish to have the child remain sick, dependent, or immature. It is not unusual for drug-abusing adolescents to be unable to break dependent, if hostile, ties to their parents. Some parents who have difficulty expressing their feelings have a powerful need to infantilize their child. Therefore, alcoholic and marijuana-abusing adolescents may, by means of their gross incompetence, bolster their parents' sense of worth.

Mothers often play a dominant identification role in their children's drug abuse. A child's passivity may be reinforced by drugs, and furthermore, passivity is still associated with the role of women in our society. Children who abuse drugs thus may in some ways be seeking both to be nurtured and to identify with a nurturing mother. For instance, the adolescent who looks after his or her peer who is on a drug trip is, to some extent, adopting a pseudomothering role (Williams 1970).

The prognosis for those adolescents who abuse drugs as a result of developmental difficulties is considerably better than that for those who, because of earlier characterological difficulties, have become physically pubertal but not psychologically adolescent. To some extent, drugs hold out the promise of magical solutions, and their use is clearly related to the mixed feelings of both the child and the parent about separating from each other. Drugs offer a fantasy of autonomy, and within the family, drug use may reaffirm and preserve an infantile object constellation.

There is evidence that drug abuse has a significant physiological cause when it is used to self-medicate mood disorders, schizophrenia, and the helplessness produced by attention deficit disorders. In some types of alcoholism, and perhaps with marijuana, there may be a specific reinforcing response to the drug that is physiologically produced in the genetically vulnerable drug taker. This problem, furthermore, has been compounded, because in our society, experimentation with drugs has become almost as common as an early adolescent's experimentation with minor theft.

The successful treatment of adolescents' antisocial behavior requires the parents' active cooperation; if the adolescent lives with the parents or is to return to the family, the treatment of the family will be crucial to the successful treatment of its children. If the child's antisocial behavior is preserving the parents' psychological equilibrium and the family members' interpersonal balance, then the treatment will become difficult, if not impossible. That is, families whose survival depends on an aggressively or regressively disturbed child may find it inordinately difficult to allow the child to give up this behavior.

The principal issues in any antisocial behavior are the nature of the act, its frequency, and its significance regarding future personality development (Miller 1974). One must also understand the developmental stages of adolescence in order to recognize the biopsychosocial roots of antisocial behavior. Of equal importance is the way that parents relate to their children, which partly depends on the children's personality growth. In a sense, the parents are instructed by their children when to give them more freedom and responsibility. Because an isolated or impulse-ridden adolescent cannot signal that he or she is ready to take more responsibility, this may lead to the parents' becoming over-protective or negligent. This, however, is often a result of their child's difficulties rather than its cause.

DELINQUENCY

As socially and legally defined, delinquency may be included with all problem behavior that inflicts pain and frustration on the self and others. The abuse of drugs and alcohol may or may not be considered delinquent. In some states, alcohol can be sold to eighteen-year-olds, but in others, it cannot. Some drugs, especially marijuana, are effectively tolerated by many segments of society. Although marijuana use is considered illegal, it is essentially condoned; that is, usually no legal action is taken when marijuana use is discovered.

Many causes are relevant to the treatment of those exhibiting antisocial behavior, whether regressive drug abuse or delinquency. The relationship between the family and its social system, or the infrastructure within which the individual and his or her symptomatic behavior interact, may be as significant as the social organization of the family itself, the psychology of the individual involved, or his or her biological vulnerability. Usually, society reinforces the ethos of the nuclear family as a "tribal" ethos. If the nuclear family's attitudes conform to the neighborhood's antisocial behavior, its children's behavior, even though antisocial, will not be related to social conflict, which explains one aspect of socially determined, so-called cultural delinquency.

REFERENCES

Campbell, J. S. (1969). The family and violence. In *Law and Order Reconsidered*, ed. J. S. Campbell, J. R. Salud, and O. F. Stang. Washington, D.C.: U.S. Government Printing Office.

Diagnostic and Statistical Manual of Mental Disorders III. (1980). Washington, D.C.: American Psychiatric Association.

Emery, F. (1967). *Affect Control and the Use of Drugs.* London: Tavistock Institute of Human Relations.

Erickson, K. T. (1962). Notes on the sociology of deviance. *Social Problems* 9:307–314.

Goode, W. (1969). Violence among inmates. In *Crimes of Violence,* ed. D. Mulvihill and M. M. Trimin. National Commission on the Causes and Prevention of Violence. Study Series 13:954, app. 17. Washington, D.C.: U.S. Government Printing Office.

Guttman, D. (1972). The cross cultural perspective: Notes toward a comparative psychology of aging. In *Handbook of the Psychology of Aging,* ed. J. E. Birren and K. Warner. New York: Van Nostrand Reinhold.

Guttman, D., and Krohn, A. (1972). Changes in mastery style with age: a study of Navaho dreams. *Psychiatry* 34: 289–301.

Johnson, A. M. (1949). Sanctions for the super-ego lacunae of adolescents. In *Searchlights on Delinquency,* ed. K. Eissler. New York: International Universities Press.

Levinson, D. J. (1978). *The Seasons of a Man's Life.* New York: Knopf.

Menninger, K. A., Mayman, M., and Pruyser, P. (1963). *The Vital Balance: The Life Process in Mental Health and Illness.* New York: Viking.

Miller, D. (1969). *The Age Between: Adolescents in a Disturbed Society.* London: Hutchinson.

———. (1970). Parental responsibility for adolescent maturity. In *The Family and Its Future,* ed. K. Elliot. London: Churchill.

———. (1974). *Adolescence: Psychology, Psychopathology, Psychotherapy.* New York: Jason Aronson.

———. (1978). Early adolescence: its psychology and implications for treatment. *Adolescent Psychiatry* 6:434–448.

———. (1980). Family maladaptation reflected in drug abuse and delinquency. In *Responding to Adolescent Needs,* ed. M. Sugar. Jamaica, N.Y.: Spectrum Publications.

———. (1983). *The Age Between: Adolescents and Therapy.* New York: Jason Aronson.

Miller, D., and Carlton, B. (1985). *The Etiology and Treatment of Anorexia Nervosa.* Adolescent Psychiatry 12:219–232.

Newberger, E. H., Newberger, C. M., and Hampton, R. L. (1983). Child abuse: current theory base and future research needs. *Journal of the American Academy of Child Psychiatry* 22:262–268.

Newman, M. B., and San Martino, M. R. (1976). Adolescents and the relationship between generations. *Adolescent Psychiatry* 4:60–71.

Steele, B. F., and Pollock, C. B. (1968). A psychiatric study of parents who abuse infants and small children. In *The Battered Child*, ed. P. E. Helfer and C. H. Kempe. Chicago: University of Chicago Press.

Sterlin, H. (1976). The adolescent as a delegate of his parents. *Adolescent Psychiatry* 6:72–83.

Williams, F. S. (1970). Alienation of youth as reflected in the hippie movement. *Journal of the American Academy of Child Psychiatry* 9:2.

Winnicott, D. (1965). *Maturational Processes and the Facilitating Environment.* New York: International Universities Press.

4

Preventing and Diagnosing Adolescents' Emotional Disturbances

Drug abuse, sexual disturbance, poor school performance, antisocial and violent behavior, excessive withdrawal, and family and social turbulence may appear among those who have become psychosocial adolescents as well as those who are only pubertal. Epidemiological studies indicate that many emotional disturbances are automatically corrected, that many adolescents come to terms with earlier traumatic experiences, particularly those associated with parental separation (Wallerstein 1985). At any one time some 15 percent of a high school population show behavioral symptoms, although only about 3 percent are seriously disturbed (Feinstein and Miller 1979). The larger percentage includes those who appear to recover by either the chance appearance of psychological support or increasing maturation. Sometimes brief supportive therapy may put the youngster back onto an acceptable developmental track.

Those adolescents who are caught in delinquent acts in early adolescence are not likely to be still involved in this behavior in early adulthood (Gibbons 1970), but those who first become delinquent at fifteen are more likely to continue to behave in this way. A number of early adolescents who begin intermittent drug abuse that does not seriously impair their development may be able to abandon it at the end of middle adolescence. But the abuse cannot be so great that they cannot form meaningful emotional relationships:

Seventeen-year-old Will had a progressive falloff in his grades for three months before he was brought to see a psychiatrist. His parents recognized that their toleration of his "occasional" pot abuse had allowed him to become a daily user who also drank alcohol (beer) on weekends. After talking to some friends whose sons' similar problems had been resolved, Will's parents referred him for help. They felt helpless because their techniques of grounding their son, withdrawing privileges, and not allowing him to use the family automobile had made no difference.

When Will was seen, he was told that if he could not stop smoking and drinking in order for a diagnostic assessment to be made, he would have to come to the hospital. He was able to relate well enough to see this not as a threat but as a determination to take his situation seriously. So Will was then able to dry out and to make a relationship with his psychiatrist. After some 20 sessions of supportive treatment over ten weeks, Will had stayed dry; at a two-year follow-up, he continued to have a good adjustment.

Nevertheless, at the present time, one should assume that regular and intermittent abusers of drugs are unlikely to abandon their use spontaneously. Furthermore, many are unlikely to receive treatment, because adequate resources to resolve this and other adolescent problems are relatively hard to find. Even brief interventions, when they work, require sophisticated diagnostic and therapeutic skills, and so prevention is clearly better.

The unrealistic goal of most preventive techniques is to provide quick answers, especially to violence and suicide, drug abuse, promiscuous sexuality, eating disorders, obesity, and self-starvation. The search for instant solutions is also implicit in the actions of those adolescents who seek immediate tension relief.

To be successful, attempts at prevention need to take into account both the child's emotional development and his or her relationships with the family and the larger society. Knowledge of the effects of specific syndromes is helpful to adults and healthy adolescents who are able to recognize reality, but it is of little help to those who are unable to accept their own vulnerability.

The reinforcement of some aspects of child and adolescent development should help decrease the amount of later maladjustment. In child rearing, parents need to understand their children's needs, especially for emotional stimulation and stability. A working mother who has initiated a satisfactory bonding/dependent attachment between herself and her child needs to be able to spend quality time, that is, when she is not tired, relating to her child. The importance of both stimulating the child's play and talking to the infant needs to be understood.

There is a serious question as to whether our current child-care social policy is providing satisfactory emotional supports. In day-care centers, the continuing reinforcement of a trusting relationship with the parents and other adults is often not considered a central issue.

While the parents' emotional support is available and acceptable to their child, usually up until puberty, any impairment of the child's capacity to be trusting does not necessarily produce problem behavior. But at adolescence, the stress of emotional separation from childhood dependence begins. Then, those who have not internalized a sense of security in relation to authority figures are more likely to manifest disturbed behavior.

Problems may also be created in families by modern technology. Television watching may or may not induce violence in children (Rubenstein 1983), but it does tend to isolate them from their parents. At best, parent–child relationships may be mediated via television; at worst, the child relates to a screen and not to people. Television viewing also carries the implicit message that entertainment is possible with minimal effort, that all that is required is to press buttons or switch channels. Thus there is clearly some virtue in limiting the amount of time that infants and children watch television and in restricting the types of programs they watch.

The boredom experienced by many adolescents appears to

be related to the loss of the many opportunities in childhood for creative play and interaction with others. For example, living in a high-rise apartment may prevent children from playing with one another. Nowadays schools often do not value equally with the acquisition of cognitive skills time spent on the arts, vocational activities, and creative expression.

Even though American schools have the potential to teach more subjects than do their British counterparts, during any one semester American children cover fewer subjects than do their British peers. Indeed, American children's choices are restricted, as it is thought that all children should be taught the same subject at the same time every day. Convergent rather than divergent thinking is preferred, thus producing excessive conformity in the acquisition of knowledge.

Some people's concern about the lack of prayer in school is an attempt to deal with some of the educational system's failures to teach ethical and moral values. These are, however, best taught by enabling children to identify with adults who have these values and with whom they have a continuing positive emotional involvement. Sports, which also offer sublimations of and outlets for aggression, tend to be restricted in schools to only a talented few.

Children exposed to a social system that offers them meaningful and consistent relationships with emotionally significant extraparental adults and peers may avoid serious developmental and behavioral disturbances (Miller 1983). Nuclear families need to be helped to break down their isolation from one another, which perhaps may be done by church and other groups that can provide social relationships.

Adults should understand the necessity for children to be brought up by two parents who are involved in the child-rearing process, that isolation from extraparental adults is developmentally inappropriate, and that stable peer groups are vital. Indulging either the parent or the child is not helpful, and parents need support in tolerating their children's anger. Insufficient sleep, the absence of adult supervision, the provision of drugs and alcohol at parties, and excessive television viewing all need to be controlled. Furthermore, parents' overuse of analgesics and regular use of alcohol to relieve tension imply to their children that magical solutions are possible.

In addition, the deleterious effects of divorce should be made clear (Hetherington 1978). A ten-year follow-up study of 113 children from a largely white middle-class population of divorced families in northern California suggests that some psychological effects of divorce are long lasting (Wallerstein 1985). Even though siblings in divorced families may act as an emotional support for one another, it is generally agreed that divorce increases the likelihood of problem behavior in both boys and girls (Hetherington and Cox 1985), and in girls, it lowers self-esteem (Kalter, Reimer, and Brickman 1985). It seems reasonable to suggest that married couples with children should be discouraged from seeking divorce as an easy solution to marital frustration.

Some believe that the children of single parents are more mature than are those from intact families, because the single-parent mothers use their teenagers as confidants. But there is little or no evidence to suggest that if parents attempt to weather their marital crisis and stay together that they will harm their children more than they will if they divorce. Unfortunately, society's preoccupation with supporting single parents suggests that divorce is a satisfactory solution to an unhappy marriage.

We should attempt to rebuild the networks of society within which children grow (Miller 1969). If generations are isolated from one another, for example, by putting grandparents, at best, in isolated apartment dwellings or, at worst, in inadequate nursing homes, the communication between children and older adults will be lost. Foster grandparents, although indeed helpful, do not substitute for society's failure to consider social and developmental needs in long-term planning.

PREVENTING DRUG AND ALCOHOL ABUSE

If society wishes to preserve the health and well-being of its competent youth, drug abuse must be stopped. No society can afford to impair the effectiveness of perhaps 20 to 30 percent of its adolescents. It is apparent, from clinical observation, that the children of drug-abusing parents are likely to behave in a more extreme way, and that a marijuana-smoking parent may produce a cocaine-addicted adolescent.

The first issue of prevention is whether the syndrome can be dealt with directly, that is, whether the supply of such intoxicants can be stopped. Drugs reach the population through large dealers and a network of small distributors, but little is done to deal with either. When adolescents are picked up with small quantities of marijuana, little or no attempt is made to discover from whom they bought it. On the other hand, in Singapore, drug dealing is a capital offense, and so the supply has effectively dried up. In the United States, through the Comprehensive Drug Abuse Prevention and Control Act of 1970, some effort is now being made to confiscate the property of dealers who introduce younger people to drugs. In Illinois, the Narcotics Profit Forfeiture Act of 1984 has enabled dealers' possessions to be seized unless they can prove that they were not obtained by means of the profits of their trade.

A preoccupation with civil liberties forbids an adequate search of school lockers and the use of urine tests to diagnose drug abusers in school. Further, without improvement in the correctional system, middle-class parents are likely to go to great lengths to protect their own drug-abusing children from the consequences of their illegal behavior. The failure to control drug abuse among adolescents encourages succeeding generations of young people to become involved themselves.

It is true that the media do influence the types of drug abuse. In some movies, it is clear that the actors are smoking marijuana, and many pop stars and football and baseball players have abused, and do abuse, drugs. To behave as if this is acceptable, by allowing these individuals to continue to perform, is as antithetical to prevention as is the collusion of law enforcement in the drug abuse that takes place during rock concerts. Nonetheless, it is questionable whether this is a prime cause of adolescent drug abuse.

Some parents are timid about informing other parents that drugs and alcohol are being abused in their homes, and thus they are effectively colluding with both the dealing and the abuse. Some school teachers know which students both abuse and deal, but they are unable to act because suspicion of drug abuse is not legally a category of child abuse. In the case of child abuse, in most states, the child's welfare takes precedence over the possibility that an informant has provided inaccurate information. Therefore, the incidence of drug abuse is likely to decrease when parents inform their neighbors when they catch their children smoking marijuana with their own offspring and when influential citizens insist that the schools, police, and legal authorities take such use seriously. Such parental behavior has the additional advantage of recreating a network of concerned adults, which is a prerequisite for healthy personality development.

Closing the known distribution points should not be a token gesture. One boy told his therapist:

"Do you know the dam? It's where all the drugs are distributed in my neighborhood. Two or three cars are there all the time, and cars line up so people can buy. A guy comes to the window, asks what you want, money changes hands, and there it is. Two years ago the police made a drug bust, but that only stopped it for a few days. I guess they don't really mind that we use drugs."

Around high school graduation in an affluent school district, another boy reported:

"It's prom night next week. The school seems full of coke. Seniors and juniors are selling it. They buy $300 worth and get $100 free."

If intra- and extrafamilial determinants of drug abuse have been dealt with, then drug education may have a place in prevention, although the evidence from the early efforts was that it did not lessen abuse. A slight dip in 1984 in the incidence of marijuana abuse was almost certainly due to other factors, and alcohol abuse is still rampant.

Raising the age at which alcohol can be bought, from eighteen to twenty-one, has already reduced the incidence of automobile accidents among sixteen- to eighteen-year-old youths (Highway Research Institute 1982). But retaining a drinking age of 18 in one state when it is 21 in another leads to the production of death alleys; the highway between Wisconsin and Illinois was one example of this. In 1984, however, Congress brought pressure on recalcitrant states to raise their drinking age to 21.

SEXUAL PROMISCUITY AND DELINQUENCY

Illegitimate pregnancy in adolescents is a major public health problem. Some people disapprove of abortion performed for essentially economic and social reasons, but psychologically immature mothers find it difficult, if not impossible, to rear emotionally healthy children. The outcome of adoption is also often unsatisfactory. Sex education, in hopes of preventing illegitimate pregnancy, may fail, partially because society is reluctant to provide contraceptive assistance. Little note is taken of either the psychology of young males who will not practice birth control or that of females who are the willing victims of impregnation. Some people believe that informing parents of their adolescents' wish to receive birth control information will in some way induce chaste behavior, and others believe that widespread sex education in schools will stimulate adolescent sexual behavior.

Except in some high schools with "Teen Clinics," sex education is rarely offered to adolescents in the context of human relationships in which they feel valued. Only then would they implicitly and explicitly be taught to value both themselves and the integrity of others. Perhaps because of this failure, there is no evidence that sex education has been helpful in reducing the illegitimacy rate among adolescents. The availability of contraceptives does help reduce the incidence of illegitimate conception, as is shown by a comparison of incidence between those countries that make available such knowledge and the United States. Some people feel that the availability of contraceptives may suggest permission for adolescent sexual intercourse, although this belief has not been validated. However, extramarital intercourse has been the norm among many from the time that early marriage was abandoned. Therapists still see large numbers of young people who have little or no knowledge of sexual and reproductive biology.

The prevention of delinquency seems to rest on the idea that if an example is made of one adolescent, then the others will "listen." This idea may have relevance to healthy adults, but antisocial, omnipotent adolescents not only do not easily learn from their own experience, but they also do not seem to care about the fate of others.

Urban violence among adolescents is usually controlled because the police can contain those angry deprived unemployed youths who are most likely to engage in such behavior in the urban ghettos. Although this does not stop violence within such areas, it helps to control its spread. This is important, as when violent youths leave their own, deprived turf, their random violence spreads into more affluent areas. This occurred in Los Angeles in 1980 and 1981. It appears that the widespread availability of drugs of abuse, particularly marijuana, among deprived ghetto youth helps contain violent behavior. So in those societies in which these drugs are not easily available, explosive outbreaks of urban violence are common.

Society usually incarcarates those adolescents whose antisocial behavior is deemed delinquent. Correctional centers, even if they know what they should be trying to do, are often ill equipped to carry it out. Therefore, adolescents are more likely to commit violent crimes after they leave such centers than they were before they entered them (Miller 1966).

TREATING AND DIAGNOSING DISTURBED ADOLESCENTS

Resources are not available for the adequate treatment of disturbed youths, partly because of the complexity of the problem, the way professionals are trained, the preoccupation with the treatment of symptoms, and society's unwillingness to make such resources available. This has led to an approach to intervention in which patients are clustered on the basis of what is likely to be reimbursed.

Although a number of diagnostic issues need to be understood before satisfactory treatment is possible, diagnosis and treatment essentially start together. The severity of the patient's symptoms must be assessed in regard to their danger to the self and others and to their destructiveness to the patient's personality development. One important issue is whether total control of symptomatic behavior is immediately necessary, and another is the ease with which the symptoms can be controlled and whether or not any spillover into the patient's behavior is tolerable. To some extent, the seriousness of the problem behavior depends on what the world has made available. For example, a driver's license at sixteen may make the automobile a destructive weapon. Marijuana, cocaine, and alcohol must be available in order to be used. Finally, children who have episodic dyscontrol syndromes caused by grand mal, temporal lobe epilepsy, or neuroendocrine vulnerability may become members of violent gangs only if they are in their neighborhood.

Both the youngster's developmental state (Thoma 1953, Freud 1962) and the effect of the child's symptoms should be assessed. An acute disturbance, apart from that associated with toxic drugs, generally has less effect on development than does a chronic disturbance, as the psychosocial feedback produced by a chronic symptom may secondarily reinforce developmental distortion. Symptoms can become intractable when they provide so much pathological gratification that they cannot be abandoned. For instance, it may be so satisfying to smoke marijuana that despite an awareness of short-term memory impairment and social disinterest, there is no reason to desist. Adolescents may not be able to stop tormenting their parents, to abstain from gratifying the greed associated with theft, or feeding the omnipotence associated with violence and suicidal threats.

ASSESSMENT OF INTERPERSONAL RELATIONSHIPS

In the initial interview, the primary goal is to establish whether or not youngsters can perceive the interaction in a sufficiently positive way so that they will consent to abandon, even temporarily, their destructive behavior. Within two or three sessions at the most, the therapist should assess the adolescent's further capacity to make a positive relationship with the helping person, and within the context of such a relationship, the therapist should determine the adolescent's capacity to contain his or her symptoms while living in the usual environment. If the patient has difficulty in making such relationships, this may apply only to one-to-one situations, with their potential intensity, but not to groups, which may provide a supportive network that is not so emotionally threatening.

There is a difference between a clinging relationship and one that represents a genuine development of positive feeling. The former is the equivalent of that of a deprived child who clings to the clothing of any adult because of the fantasy that the grown-up represents security, and the latter involves the adolescent's positive appraisal of the interviewer's qualities, both personal and professional, and a perception that the interviewer's opinions are to be valued.

Wherever an adolescent is treated, all the prerequisites of successful intervention require a capacity to make relationships with others that are felt as positive and meaningful.

Standard psychiatric history taking, which means asking the youngster to answer several questions, implicitly asks the adolescent to be agreeable and compliant. The possibility of assessing the youngster's capacity for spontaneity, honesty, and emotional attachment is then made more complex. The purpose of the initial interaction should be to help the adolescent feel as comfortable as possible, to help him or her perceive the therapist as interested and interesting and on the child's side but not against the parents and society, and, finally, to help the adolescent feel like a valued individual.

The dilemma is that a history of the patient's difficulties must be obtained, which requires posing specific questions, perhaps about symptoms that may not be mentioned spontaneously. A mental status examination also is necessary, to assess the patient's psychological state. If the interviewer sees the collection of these data as taking precedence over understanding the patient's capacity to make relationships, then all that he or she may have accomplished will be to have determined the patient's capacity to accept medical authority and to be obedient. The therapist may, however, infer evidence about the patient's capacity to make judgments, ability to control behavior, and stated attitudes toward various relationships. When the initial primary task is seen as the assessment of the adolescent's ability to make a meaningful emotional relationship, the way that the interview is structured will be different. Essentially the goal is to go from what the adolescent knows and currently experiences to areas that may be less clear to him or her. This means that the therapist should find out how the referral took place, what the experience of professional intervention was in the past, and what might be family and societal attitudes. The adolescent's verbal and nonverbal communications are both highly significant. It is our practice to find out beforehand minimal information about the youngster, because the omission of significant data can be a problem in communication between the interviewer and the adolescent patient. The clinician should display an attitude of "do what I do" rather than "do what I say." Thus, if the clinician has prior knowledge about an adolescent patient, he or she should state immediately what is known. If the clinician does not do this, the adolescent will then be put in the difficult position of not knowing what is known. But if the therapist has too much knowledge, then the retelling will become excessively time-consuming.

If the adolescent becomes increasingly comfortable in an initial interview or responds positively to a reality clarification about the current situation or his or her current feelings, this is likely to signify an emotional involvement. If the therapist makes an interpretation that leads to a change in affect or content, then a relationship is under way.

An adolescent's failure to form a meaningful relationship in one interview does not mean that this cannot be done. The failure may be due to previous experiences with therapists, unresolved anxiety about the current situation, drug toxicity, or concern about confidentiality. In regard to the last item, adolescents should not be promised absolute confidentiality; rather, the stance should be that nothing hurtful will be done. Trust will not magically appear, its appearance will partly depend on the adolescent's experience with other professionals as well as with other adult authority figures, such as parents, teachers, and physicians. The therapist's general attitude here should be that he or she would like to be *useful*, as the idea of being *helped* is often felt by young people as infantilizing.

It is clear that the way the youngster is handled before the interview—by secretaries, receptionists, probation officers, and other mental health professionals—will affect the ease with which he or she can form relationships. An adolescent previously exposed to multiple diagnostic interventions, with no positive results, is likely to show at least a guarded wariness in a new diagnostic and therapeutic intervention. A previous, worthless invasion of the adolescent's privacy may induce a profound distrust of professionals.

Adolescents under the age of 16 or 17 are rarely consciously motivated to seek assistance and often state their objection to being interviewed. But the fact that they have come to the interview indicates that the stated objection is not the final word. Adolescents communicate through their actions: the verbal denial of a wish for assistance often represents a striving for autonomy. When a boy or girl of 15 or 16 or even younger agrees that help is needed, this may represent a surrender to uncontrollable forces. Legal intervention, which demands verbal consent for treatment and purports to protect young people from a coercive intervention, may thus be disastrous. Those adolescents who express a wish for assistance are either in very severe psychological pain or come from psychologically sophisticated families.

The immediate goal of the initial interventions is to give the youngster a feeling of inner freedom, to demonstrate that his or her current behavior represents a type of imprisonment, even if it seems desirable. The implicit message is that the youngster does control his or her own destiny and that a sense of helpless torment is not inevitable.

The adolescent needs to look at the realistic implications of his or her behavior and be shown why its consequences, some of which he or she may have chosen not to see, are inevitable.

A significant issue is the magical expectation of the difficulty's rapid resolution. If the interaction in the initial interview is felt as positive, the adolescent is likely to project his or her own sense of omnipotence onto the therapist. But if the therapist does not make clear that there will be no magical resolution, the adolescent may not wish to return, perceiving, after having left the office, the interaction as having been useless.

The interview clearly needs to be open-ended. Putting a priority on the youngster's capacity to make relationships means that data will be collected during a diagnostic phase of treatment. This usually involves three to four psychiatric interviews; psychological and educational testing; and a physical examination, including clinical and biological assessments of possible organic central nervous system pathology.

The therapist, besides determining the adolescent patient's capacity to form a trusting relationship, must make some decisions about his or her symptomatic behavior. It is improbable that an outpatient intervention will stop all symptomatic antisocial behavior, and so the diagnostic issue is what type of behavior is tolerable both to society at large and for the continuation of treatment. In regard to drug use, the adolescent should be told by the end of the first interview that nothing particularly useful is likely to happen unless he or she stops using drugs. If the adolescent cannot or will not stop, then an inpatient evaluation will be necessary.

The issue with violence and suicidal behavior is whether or not it is controllable, a decision that has to be made quickly. Any type of dangerous behavior is not tolerable. When an outpatient psychological assessment allows the symptomatic activity to continue, then the clinician is implicitly giving permission for such behavior. In the adolescent age group, not to act is to act; silence and noninterference give consent. The adolescent's capacity to tolerate frustration and to understand the implications of his or her behavior, along with the ability to take some responsibility for what has occurred and not merely to project this responsibility onto others, are factors that are evaluated in the initial diagnostic assessment. The relevant issues are, then, as follows:

1. How dangerous is the symptom? Can it be contained within the interpersonal situations created by the treatment intervention? If not, how frequently is it likely to occur? In any case, homicidal, suicidal, antisocial, and drug-abusing behavior must be contained, but there is more leeway with adolescents who, for example, intermittently refuse to go to school.
2. Does the symptom interfere with the adolescent's capacity to form meaningful emotional relationships?
3. If the behavior is antisocial, does merely listening to the

adolescent seem to be collusive? If so, this may impede the success of the intervention.

Whatever the severity of the behavioral symptoms, those adolescents with a capacity to make meaningful emotional relationships, given adequate specific and nonspecific therapeutic intervention, probably have a good prognosis. But those young people, even with relative minor symptoms, who cannot do this have a much worse outlook.

DIAGNOSING PERSONALITY DISTORTIONS

Some boys and girls reach their teenage years, become physiologically mature, show the psychological responses to this process (Miller 1978), but fail to develop an autonomous sense of self. These are individuals who have had significant nurturing deficits, brain disorders, or chronic physical illnesses. They have become pubertal but not adolescent.

Personality distortion that occurs before puberty makes improbable the secondary separation-individuation (Mahler 1972) necessary to become adolescent. When such individuals become postpubertal and chronologically adult, it is clear that they often have the same personality as they did before puberty. They may have coped with some of the psychological issues of puberty, and they may recognize the changes in their body image. Their efforts at dealing with issues of helplessness and hopelessness have failed, and so angry dependency and the projection of responsibility onto others may become such persons' central emotional position. Characterological difficulties that existed before puberty tend to be reinforced at this time.

Children who suffer from neuroendocrine disorders may be diagnosed before puberty as being characterologically disturbed. After puberty they become more turbulent; more serious characterological disturbance is apparent; and the unacceptability of their behavior may lower the likelihood of an accurate diagnosis. This problem is more prevalent in lower-socioeconomic-class groups, whose children tend to be seen in a less adequately staffed area of the mental health, educational, and correctional systems.

Adolescents who suffer from a borderline personality disturbance cannot distance themselves emotionally from their parents and may then develop behavioral problems that confirm their distorted view of the world as intensely persecutory. These are young people who continue to give emotional power to their parents. Often they perceive their parents as insufficiently caring and insist that they are unloving and inadequate. Such adolescents experience inordinate distress about this at a chronological age when they should feel less involved. Each episode of parental mishandling is felt as so intolerable that these infantile young people attempt to master the experience by constantly provoking their parents. They hang around their parents apparently waiting for love to turn up, but instead they induce and receive even more torment and rejection. These young people reach puberty but do not move past the psychological responses of this age period. They are trapped in a cycle of helplessness and persecutory experiences and alternate between omnipotent grandiosity and hopeless despair.

The adolescent's developmental history may reveal the cause of this type of disorder. They are often children who were traumatized by early inappropriate parent–child separation, by an early physical disability, or by a genetic vulnerability. Their initial attachments were inadequate, and they did not develop a capacity to make trusting relationships. If a family is able to provide sufficient emotional support before puberty, such disturbances may not become obvious until the turbulence of that age period appears. Furthermore, adolescence carries with it a demand for emotional separation. Behavioral symptoms may also appear toward the end of middle adolescence, when there is an expectation of becoming emotionally involved with others, particularly with members of the opposite sex. Sometimes an actual separation, a change of schools, going to college, or the expectation of this may reveal a borderline personality disturbance.

Another group of disturbed young people may become adolescent, but the psychosocial processes required to support development through this age period are not available. Traumatic separation from emotionally significant others—from parents, peers, or extraparental adults by divorce or death or family moves—means losing a stable network of people. Early adolescents exposed to these experiences may seem as though they are suffering from a borderline personality disorder. But if this is a secondary rather than primary event, it will have a better prognosis for rapid recovery.

FAMILY INTERVENTION AND DIAGNOSIS

The treatment of adolescents who live with their parents is impossible unless the parents want help for their child (Miller 1969). This is most significant in early and middle adolescence, when young people are still intensely involved with their parents. The behaviorally disturbed adolescent often sees the therapist as being on the parents' side, and so the diagnostic and therapeutic process should involve a number of professionals. It is difficult for a therapist working alone to help both adolescents and their families unless the syndrome is intrafamilial rather than a function of personality disturbance.

Treatment of early and middle adolescents who live with their parents and those of all ages suffering from a borderline personality necessitates that help be offered also to the parents and the family. In some borderline syndromes, the instinctual tie between the parent and child may be so negative that outpatient therapy cannot work, as the family environment has become too psychonoxious.

Because adolescents are seeking a sense of autonomy, there is an advantage in having the initial clinical contact with the boy or girl rather than with the parents. When the parents talk with another professional, at the end of their first interview, they should usually be seen also by the child's therapist, together with their son or daughter. Apart from allowing the parents to meet their child's therapist, the therapist will then be able to see the child's problems from the parents' viewpoint, and the family interaction will become more apparent. At the end of these initial meetings, the parents and the adolescent should be told what the diagnostic process might involve (Schwartzberg 1979), how long it is likely to take, and what other individuals will be part of it. The therapist should obtain permission to contact the child's school, the referring agency, and the child's pediatrician. If the law is involved, the therapist's relationship with the legal authorities should be explained.

Particularly for adolescents who still live with their families, parental involvement is essential. Marital and family functioning, the parent's own problems, and the family's relationship to the adolescent's symptomatic behavior need to be understood in order that treatment can be planned.

The relevant history of the patient's life is not restricted to just the traditional concept of developmental milestones. In addition, the mother's memory of her first interaction with her child is important, and unlike the remembrance of developmental milestones, this is usually accurate. Those mothers who were not able to bond satisfactorily to their infant may forget this episode; also, mothers usually remember who looked after the child in its first year of life and during significant parental absences. The father's role and memories of the infant's capacity to relate to its parents and others are important.

The therapist should ask about the parents' techniques of control and punishment, how the family handles frustration, their attitudes toward learning, and their capacity to be empathic with one another. Sibling relationships and the family's social network are as significant as the parents' own upbringing. Separations from loved individuals because of horizontal and vertical social mobility, death and divorce, and the youngster's capacity to mourn losses should be noted.

Typical family histories tend to stress the parents' experience with their own families, and this is helpful in determining how parents are likely to replay their own conflicts. Because of our now-greater awareness of the significance of genetic vulnerability to mood disorders and sensitivity to tension, a medical and psychological history of the parents and their collateral relatives is helpful, as is information about alcoholism, depression, phobias, and "strange behavior."

A family diagnostic session will demonstrate their current

communication techniques. The roles of the parents and the siblings and how various members of the family handle interpersonal stress especially may be revealed. Disturbed behavior does not exist in isolation and it comes to have meaning in the life of the family.

There are many means by which parents and siblings can be included in the diagnostic and therapeutic process. Some therapists like to have an initial family diagnostic conference at which the parents and child (not siblings) are seen together. The timing of this has meaning to the adolescent, as, if this is the first therapeutic contact, the patient may feel that the issue is for him or her to be an integral member of the family unit. Indeed, the child may feel that this is more significant than are issues of autonomy. But if the adolescent is seen first, this more traditional approach will help the adolescent understand whose agent the interviewing therapist is to be.

THE ROLE OF THE PARENTS IN THE TREATMENT

In most states, parents have no legal power to insist that their children over the age of sixteen or seventeen seek assistance. The laws demanding that such young people be told that they have "the right to refuse treatment" can mean that they may never get to talk to a therapist. This is a problem particularly in drug abuse. Parents may have no legal recourse for children in this age group to insist that they seek help, and their threatening to eject the children from the family is a most unsatisfactory attempt at control:

> Karl, the 16-year-old son of a successful restaurant owner, would appear regularly drug toxic in his father's restaurant and solicit the staff for illegal drugs. This was particularly hostile behavior because the father had always fired any staff whom he caught abusing drugs. Karl was out of his parents' control: he did not go to school; he spent many hours of the day in bed; and he spent his nights in the less salubrious parts of the city.

Karl adamantly refused to see anyone. His parents could not obtain help from law enforcement authorities: First, they would find his drug abuse difficult to prove. Second, the routine needed to convince the police and courts to intervene was almost impossible. In the state in which they lived, the possession of a small quantity of marijuana was a misdemeanor, but the attitude of the local police was really that they could not be bothered.

This is a worst case. Parents can usually invoke their child's positive feelings for them or their anxiety about what the child might do to persuade him or her to visit a therapist.

BEHAVIOR AND TREATMENT PROBLEMS

Danger to the self or others is an indication for commitment under most mental health laws, but developmental danger is recognized by only a few states. Especially for the lower socioeconomic groups, antisocial behavior and violence are usually within the purview of juvenile justice.

Violent and antisocial adolescents inside or outside the legal system are generally the most reluctant to be honest. An adequate treatment recommendation is then more difficult to make. Young people who direct their violence toward themselves in self-mutilating or suicidal behavior commonly show a massive denial of their difficulties. Often their initial insistence is that the behavior will not be repeated, that they have learned their lesson, and that therefore intervention is not necessary.

Adolescents who show suicidal behavior are not always referred for assistance. Thus it is quite common, when help is sought for such youngsters, to hear of two or three previous attempts about which nothing was done. Sometimes these children have been seen in hospital emergency rooms, and because the technique of self-destruction seemed so inadequate, the child was not referred to a psychiatrist. The boy or girl who takes three aspirin may be as suicidal as one who takes fifty barbiturates. Further, parents may accurately regard their child's suicidal behavior as an attack upon themselves and so may deny it.

Because the youngster may also deny the significance of the action, the parent and child may cooperate in deciding that nothing need be done. The denial of a suicidal intent is similar to the denial of death in incurable illness (Kübler-Ross 1970).

When violence takes place within the home, help may be sought only when the violence is perceived as excessive, uncontrollable, and long lasting:

> Peter was finally referred for treatment by his probation officer because he had attempted to kill a friend in a fight, by strangling him. He had not killed him only because the group of adolescents watching the fight had, with difficulty, managed to pry Peter away from his victim. Peter had a long history of rage attacks directed against his peers: He had beaten one boy unconscious with a hammer, attempted to drown another, and on one occasion threw a cousin down the stairs in his home, fracturing his leg.

Peter's mother, who had beaten Peter with an electric light cord when he misbehaved, belittled the significance of these violent events. She was thus surprised, although agreeable, when the probation officer referred Peter for a psychiatric opinion.

Sometimes parents do not refer their violent adolescents for help because of their own fear; that is, sometimes their children's violence is directed toward the parents themselves:

> An elderly couple came to see a psychiatrist to ask for help for their daughter, aged 28. She lived in their house with her dog, who was not housebroken. She refused to work and for ten years had been assaulting her parents to obtain money and goods. It had never occurred to them that indeed it was reasonable to seek to have their daughter leave their house.

In cases of patricide or matricide, the murder is sometimes performed for the other parent. Such episodes sometimes follow a long period of parent–child or family brutality. A brutal father may be killed by a son or daughter in order to "protect" mother, or a child may kill a member of the extended family to carry out the covert wishes of the parents:

A 17-year-old boy, while high on amphetamines, bludgeoned to
death his affluent grandmother. She had "controlled" his parents
by using her money as a threat. Both his parents clearly were
pleased that she was dead, and neither expressed the slightest
sorrow at her demise. They seemed concerned only that an insan-
ity defense might not be possible for their son.

Borderline adolescents, who feel their parents as intolerable per-
secutors, may brutalize or kill them.

Young pregnant teenagers are often seen in obstetric clinics,
but are seldom referred for psychiatric assistance, except in some
clinics in which psychiatrists have helped their colleagues understand that this may be justified. Likewise, sexually promiscuous
girls are nowadays rarely referred for psychiatric help, but such
behavior is always indicative of emotional difficulties.

Psychosomatic illnesses and eating disorders may cause parents and children to become enmeshed with each other (Minuchin 1977). Girls with anorexia nervosa often become competi-
tively involved with their mothers, and issues of control over
themselves and others may dominate their lives.

The diagnostic process thus includes an assessment of the
type and severity of the problem behavior and an understanding
of its biopsychosocial causes. Apart from the diagnosis of the
specific illness and personality disorders, this includes an awareness of the family's functioning in relation to the child and the
child's place in the larger social system. The individual study of
the child includes an understanding of his or her ability to make
meaningful emotional relationships with others and an assessment of the child's personality difficulties (GAP 1957), which
may underlie or be present with biological pathology and educational and cognitive deficits. Because a diagnostic intervention
may require several interviews and take some two to four weeks,
its goal should always be therapeutic as well as diagnostic.

REFERENCES

Feinstein, S., and Miller, D. (1979). Psychosis in adolescence. In *The Basic
Handbook of Child Psychiatry*, vol. 2, ed. J. Noshpitz. New York: Basic
Books.

Freud, A. (1962). Assessment of childhood disturbance. *The Psychoanalytic Study of the Child* 17:149–158.

Gibbons, D. C. (1970). *Delinquent Behavior*. Englewood Cliffs, N.J.: Prentice-Hall.

Group for the Advancement of Psychiatry, Committee on Child Psychiatry. (1957). The diagnostic process of child psychiatry. New York: G.A.P. Report 38.

Hetherington, E. M., and Cox, R. (1978). The aftermath of divorce. In *Mother-Child, Father-Child Relations*, ed. J. H. Stevens and M. Matthews. New York: National Association for Education of Young Children.

——. (1985). Long-term effects of divorce and remarriage on the adjustment of children. *American Academy of Child Psychiatry* 24: 515–518.

Highway Research Institute. (1982). *Incidence of Automobile Accidents*. Ann Arbor, MI: Highway Research Institute.

Kalter, N., Reimer, B., Brickman, A., and Chen, J. W. (1985). Implications of parental divorce for female development. *Journal of the American Academy of Child Psychiatry* 24:538–544.

Kubler-Ross, E. (1970). *On Death and Dying*. New York: Macmillan.

Mahler, M. D. (1972). A study of the separation-individuation process and its possible application to borderline phenomena in a psychoanalytic situation. *Psychoanalytic Study of the Child* 26:403–424.

Miller, D. (1966). A model of an institution for treating adolescent delinquent boys. In *Changing Concepts of Crime and Its Treatment*, ed. H. J. Klare. Oxford, England: Pergamon Press.

——. (1969). *The Age Between: Adolescents in a Disturbed Society*. London: Hutchinson.

——. (1978). Early adolescence: its psychology, psychopathology and implications for therapy. *Adolescent Psychiatry* 6:434–447.

——. (1983). *The Age Between: Adolescents and Therapy*. New York: Jason Aronson.

Minuchin, S. (1977). Input and outcome of family therapy in anorexia nervosa. *Adolescent Psychiatry* 5:313–322.

Rubenstein, E. A. (1983). Television and behavior: research conclusions of the 1982 NIMH report and their policy implications. *American Psychologist* 38:820–825.

Schwartzberg, A. Z. (1979). Diagnostic evaluation of adolescents. In *The Short Course in Adolescent Psychiatry*, ed. J. R. Novello. New York: Brunner/Mazel.

State of Illinois, Narcotics Profit Forfeiture Act. (1984). *Revenue Statistics* 56:1505.

Thoma, H. (1953). Besbachtung und Beurteilung von Kindern und Jugendlichen. *Psychologicsche Praxis* 15:1–64.

United States Code Annotated. (1970). Comprehensive Drug Abuse and Control Act, 5848, app. 2.

Wallerstein, J. S. (1985). Children of divorce: preliminary report of a followup of older children and adolescents. *Journal of the American Academy of Child Psychiatry* 24:545–554.

5

The Planning
of Treatment

Emotional disturbances have biopsychosocial causes, and if the biological problems are not treated, any psychosocial intervention may be almost useless.

Psychosocial treatment requires that the therapist decide what interventions will resolve the adolescent's psychological difficulties and the conflicts of the family and the social organizations that affect the youngster's behavior and self-esteem. The resolution of some problems may automatically resolve others; for example, if a behavioral symptom is abandoned, the environment may become less coercive and persecutory, and adults will then become more benign identification models.

Neuroendocrine and conduction disorders in the central nervous system (Miller 1978a) require psychopharmacological intervention, although this may not resolve the problem behavior. That is, medication alone will not remedy the almost inevitable developmental distortion and consequent behavioral problems produced by biological sensitivity, but without it, they cannot be adequately helped.

Before any neuroendocrine disorders are treated, an adolescent may understand his or her hypersensitivity to stress and tolerate it better, but the stress response will remain:

> Dave was a 16-year-old schoolboy who, when provoked, would injure himself and lash out at others. He was a big boy, and people became fearful of him. Dave's behavior was more frequent and more violent at home than in school or with friends. He tended to feel miserable in the morning, and from time to time during the day, his mood would change, without reason. He would feel fine and then suddenly get depressed.
>
> Dave saw an excellent psychotherapist who treated him twice weekly for two years. Dave developed some awareness of the causes of his anger, and this reduced the frequency of his attacks. There was, however, no change in the quality of his rage or in his labile moods.
>
> There was a family history of depression. Dave's natural father, unknown to Dave, committed suicide when the boy was one-year-old, and his mother's sister had been treated for depressive illness.
>
> When Dave received appropriate medication, all of the therapeutic interventions became more effective. At his follow-up four years later, he had made a good psychosocial adjustment and was free of symptoms.

Treatment requires both specific and nonspecific intervention. Nonspecific care (Knesper and Miller 1976) meets generalized biopsychosocial needs that depend on the individual's developmental situation. But if the behavioral syndromes determine the type and location of the treatment, then the patient's developmental needs may often be met only by chance. If the diagnostic heterogeneity underlying the behavior disorders is ignored, the outcome is likely to be unsatisfactory, though some patients may show some improvement because, by chance, their developmental and etiological needs have been met.

Specific biopsychosocial interventions based on the disorder's causes are more effective when nonspecific needs are met. Current therapeutic examples demonstrate the difficulty of successful intervention if developmental needs are ignored. When early adolescents are treated in special centers for drug abuse or eating disorders or antisocial behavior, successful outcome is less likely. For example, a 13-year-old delinquent boy, in a treatment center located miles away from his impoverished parents, to whom he will return, cannot possibly resolve his beginning struggle with them for autonomy. A 16-year-old girl treated as an inpatient in an eating disorders program, whose other participants are women of 25 to 30, will almost certainly develop an identity in which she sees herself as anorectic. These adolescents are likely to answer the question "Who am I?" on the basis of their symptoms and thus come to regard themselves as, say, a freak, a burnout, an anorectic, or a delinquent.

DEVELOPMENTAL NEEDS

Developmental needs are biopsychosocial and always are present. Biological needs include the provision of adequate food, sleep, exercise, light and air, warmth, and physical care. It might appear that in Western society these are satisfactorily met for adolescents, but this is clearly not always the case. For adolescents living in the community, both diagnostic and therapeutic issues are a concern in regard to hearing, sight, teeth, skin, and general physical health. Acne tends to be ignored; eating habits are often poor; and general hygiene and physical fitness are often not satisfactory.

In institutions these problems may be even worse. Surveys of correctional settings indicate gross deprivation of nonspecific needs: youths are kept with insufficient exercise, poor food, and bad hygiene. In psychiatric hospitals, adolescents may have long periods of physical passivity, during which they may watch television; the food may be impersonally served on trays or badly served and cooked; and snacks may not be offered or may be high-calorie junk food. The registered nurses on duty are not always trained in child care so the importance of clean clothes, clean bodies, clean teeth, and adequate sleep is often ignored. The institutions' staff often do not understand that the early adolescents' needs differ from those of older adolescents. Irrespective of diagnosis, younger adolescents need to have their behavior appropriately monitored, whereas older boys and girls may be better able to organize themselves. Most 13-year-olds will not organize their own laundry and do not normally keep their rooms neat, but a 17-year-old may be able to do this.

In almost all treatment settings, nonspecific care is the hardest to provide. Institutions may have to be persuaded that children need a snack in the evenings, and in some centers, if it is offered, it may be withdrawn as a punishment.

It is common nowadays for adolescents not to have a good breakfast. Many will therefore have a low blood-sugar level and feel hungry by 9:30 or 10:00 A.M. and if they cannot have a snack then, their blood sugar will drop even more. They then will become irritable and find it more difficult to pay attention. Thus in most schools, the class period before lunch is not one in which the most learning takes place. In many institutions, because of staff and administrative convenience, the last meal of the day is offered between 4:30 and 5:30 P.M. Then if adolescents are not given a bedtime snack, they are more likely to become difficult at bedtime, sleep badly, and have disturbed nights.

CONTINUITY OF CARE

The capacity to involve oneself with other human beings requires maturation on the part of the patient and also the availability of consistent human relationships. The premature loss of loved individuals before a child is psychologically ready is a major traumatic insult and is a significant cause of many of the major disturbances of adolescence. Unfortunately, the models of care delivery typically repeat for the child the pain of separation from significant others.

In hospitals the move from open to closed wards breaks relationships. If partial hospital program centers attached to an inpatient hospital setting exist, they commonly have a staff different from the inpatient staff. The move to outpatient care also usually means a change of therapist. Thus the constant trauma of separation can become a major bar to adequate treatment.

The inner turbulence of adolescence is such that the interruption of important external relationships becomes more traumatic than it is in either an earlier or a later age period. Before puberty, children's major emotional involvement is with their parents, and by early adulthood, young people should have formed extraparental relationships. Adolescence implies an emotional withdrawal from involvement with the parents, and thus relationships outside the family become especially important. Therefore a diagnostic intervention should be followed by therapy that does not require a change of therapist.

Residential and hospital social systems provide varying levels of care. All should have a conceptual framework for returning young people to a healthy developmental track. High-intensity care may be needed at first and may be followed by a less-intensive special support system, such as a partial hospital program. This may also provide the opportunity to live in a small group home and should include the same specially designed school that is required during high-intensity care. Many adolescents in such partial programs may, of course, live with their parents. Low-intensity care, that is, outpatient therapy with the same therapist, is the final step before discharge from treatment.

If the therapeutic social system divides the typical care program into separate administrative areas—inpatient, partial hospitalization, and outpatient, each with its own chiefs and support staff—the care generally will be disrupted as the patient moves from turf to turf. But if such a program has only one administration, then the continuity of relationships with the therapeutic personnel can more easily be preserved. Systems that are close to one another geographically or administratively generally do not provide genuine continuity of care. If this can be provided, a medium-intensity care program can shorten the length of the stay required in the most intensive care program, and it should be a substitute, not an addition. Adolescents require stable adult and peer relationships for optimal personality development and the loss of such relationships may be as traumatic as the loss of a parent (Miller 1974). Open and closed wards, which in usual psychiatric hospital practice mean changes in therapeutic personnel as well as, sometimes, changes of psychotherapist, are antithetical to the best care.

In the correctional system, consistent relationships are generally not possible after the youngsters leave the residential settings, although a few such centers now have therapeutic group homes in the community. These homes unfortunately do not produce consistent relationships as many correctional and residential treatment centers are placed well away from local communities.

When adolescents are treated while they are living with their parents, the availability of meaningful stable relationships outside the nuclear family is an important issue. If individual psychotherapy is recommended and the therapist becomes the child's only significant person other than the parents, the resolution of his or her difficulties is less likely. The child's recovery also will mean losing the therapist, with whom the child will have formed a significant, extraparental relationship, and the price may be too high. Alternatively, the dependence implicit in the situation may be so great that the therapy cannot get off the ground.

CREATIVITY AND INTELLECTUAL GROWTH

One common side effect of serious behavioral disorders is the failure to develop the ability to be creative. It is well known that academic potential is often impeded by emotional and behavioral impairment, although some young people, especially those who cannot make emotional investments in others, may become hyperintellectual. Girls with anorexia nervosa are often those who make profound emotional investments in academic success. To them, a high grade is almost as important as an androgynous, starving body; their intellectual prowess must be demonstrated to the world and themselves. Such young people need to be helped to develop their creative capacities as well as their formal thinking (Piaget and Inhelder 1958).

The resolution of problem behavior and its underlying causes precedes the restoration of age-appropriate emotional, cognitive, and creative development. Families may become so preoccupied with a child's disturbance that they become conditioned to accept the failure to meet these needs. It is rare that the parents of disturbed adolescents try to induce their child to be involved in other than academic, and perhaps physical, education; the idea that parents can teach their children to be creative is not now popular.

The idea that children can be taught and encouraged to be imaginative and creative and that they must always strive to do their best is reinforced by how the adults around them behave. If the adults in their environment are passive, then children and adolescents will identify with them. So if television watching is encouraged, noncommunication will generally be reinforced:

> An affluent family complained that their 13-year-old son would not read or do his homework. He was said to spend most of his time watching television. The family had six television sets in their home, and the father's preferred activity was watching football games.

In institutions for the care of disturbed youth, if the staff do not perform socially valuable tasks but, instead, passively watch their charges, this will become the valued activity.

In treatment settings, the compartmentalization of staff skills often impedes their creative use. Occupational therapists, for example, may be often reluctant to share their skills with other staff members. Youngsters should be offered remedial and age- and grade-appropriate education and physical activities such as sports, swimming, gymnastics, aerobic exercises, and weight lifting. Such activities should be both remedial and therapeutic and should offer normal sublimations. Creative subjects such as art, ceramics, philosophy, music, woodwork, acting, and constructive games should be available on a daily basis.

Sometimes adolescents who suffer acute and chronic mood disorders and schizophrenic syndromes and those who abuse drugs may become temporarily less academically competent (Feinstein and Miller 1979). When such young people recover from such syndromes, however, they do not automatically return to their previous level of competence, and their teachers may expect too much, or too little, from them. This expectation, too, may become an additional stress, which may cause the disturbed behavior to return. That is, the adolescent may feel devalued either by being unable to cope or by being put in an inappropriate special class.

A sense of personal worth depends on many factors, and an important and sometimes neglected issue is a sense of continuity with one's personal, familial, and cultural past. Finding out about one's past thus can be a crucial psychological intervention:

A 15-year-old Japanese American boy suffered from acute identity confusion, in particular, being doubtful about his own sexual identification. He had no knowledge of either his family's or his cultural group's historical past, and he felt no loyalty to other Japanese Americans. Perhaps because his parents had themselves been interned during World War II, he perceived Caucasians as vaguely hostile.

He knew nothing of the way in which his own group lived, although he himself was preoccupied with not losing face. When admitted to an adolescent treatment center, he had been refusing to go to school for a year, was violent with his elderly father, and was scornful of his mother.

His recovery was hastened as he learned about his own heritage, as all that he had understood before was that his parents expected behavior from him that did not agree with that expected of his Caucasian peers. His parents, holding many traditional Japanese values, were themselves isolated from Japanese American contacts, and their son needed to learn more about Japan, its history and culture, his own family's historical past, his extended family, and Japanese people's experience in the United States.

NONSPECIFIC SOCIAL NEEDS

All social systems appear to have implicit and explicit ways of life which should be compatible. Apart from this consistency, the system is best if it is small enough for adolescents to identify with its ethos. If, for example, schools have more than 500 to 600 pupils, they cannot become significant organizations with which young people can identify (Miller 1974). Such large high schools cannot convey messages about productivity, ethical behavior, and a responsive moral code. As teachers change yearly and adolescent groups change for each class period, the process of identification is impeded, and the system conveys that consistency in human relationships is unimportant.

The goal of residential treatment should be to help the young person find the right developmental track: age-appropriate educational mastery, the capacity to tolerate frustration without action that obstructs future goals, the ability to care for others and respect their integrity, and the ability to care for one's own body through constructive physical activity. Long periods of inertia produced by staff shortages, poor staff training, or a shortage of resources can make difficult the achievement of these goals. It is easy to see how few treatment and correctional systems are able to be therapeutic, and they then are likely to create institutionalization, which can be defined as an "emotional deficiency disease" (Bettelheim and Sylvester 1946). This also teaches a socially aberrant way of life (Miller 1954). For example, adolescents' loss of responsibility for a sense of time is produced by the failure to provide watches and clocks, and thus the adolescents' attendance at school, getting up in the morning, and going to bed at night are no longer their personal responsibility. They may be denied contact with the opposite sex, and the quality and amount of their school and other work may be unacceptable to the larger society. In many psychiatric hospitals, one hour of formal education a day is all that most children receive.

Often, in psychiatric hospitals the physical environment is ugly and barren. In 1984, the New York State Psychiatric Institute had hardly any furniture for their adolescents, and watching television became almost the only way that the patients could pass time.

A problem for both education and psychiatric treatment is that conformist behavior is often seen as an acceptable norm. In treatment settings, this may mean that neither necessary adolescent acting up nor acting out is understood. Additional problems are created when staff are treated by their superiors in a way that suggests that they have no creativity, and so they treat their charges likewise. When trouble occurs, the staff blames a scapegoat, and so the inmates will probably do the same.

Residential care should have definite goals and techniques. The therapeutic environment should contain disturbed behavior so that it will seldom appear during treatment. There is, however, no way that all excessive tension can be contained, and acting out and acting up are inevitable. But they should not involve physical violence, property destruction, or the refusal of education and self-care. Ideally, excessive tension should be contained with any necessary biological interventions and with specific therapeutic interpersonal relationships. If emotionally disturbed young people feel excessive anger, the more that it can be contained in individual and group therapy, the less it will spill over into the larger social system. The way that it appears will depend on what the social system will implicitly allow.

In social organizations, adolescents consider freedom and personal responsibility as rewards and regard their withdrawal as a punishment. Although this may be the adolescents' observation, punishment deliberately applied is not acceptable. The institutional use of chemical containment, isolation, and strap restraints to contain disturbed behavior represents a failure to provide adequate resources for care. They are never used at Northwestern Memorial Hospital in Chicago, although potentially violent adolescents are admitted. People and property are nevertheless not damaged.

SPECIFIC BIOLOGICAL INTERVENTIONS

Specific biological interventions are still not sufficiently available, especially for those diagnosed as suffering from conduct disorders. Many children, particularly lower-socioeconomic-class violent adolescents, do not see psychiatrists, and many professionals treating disturbed adolescents are not educated in psychopharmacological indications and may not even understand the psychological changes produced by the physiological effects of puberty.

Current diagnostic criteria indicate the appropriate use of psychotropic drugs. But minor tranquilizers and sedatives are not indicated in the care of emotionally disturbed adolescents, one reason being that physicians should not reinforce drug abuse by prescribing nonspecific mood changers. Many of these drugs are habituating and thus reinforce the likelihood of the behavior's reappearing.

Medication may facilitate psychotherapy (Karasu 1982), but in young people it may also reinforce their projection of omnipotence onto a therapist, enhance magical thinking, and make the therapist feel more authoritarian (Gutheil 1982). Furthermore, medication does not resolve the developmental impairments often produced by neuroendocrine disorders. Such medications increase the effectiveness of psychosocial interventions, but they cannot replace them, and this should be made clear to the adolescent and the parents.

A failure to deal with the therapist's perceived omnipotence is one reason that many adolescents become reluctant to continue to use medication. Those who cannot bear to feel helpless and externally controlled are also omnipotent, and such young people project both omnipotence and helplessness onto their therapists. Thus medication may inappropriately reinforce both the clinician's perceived omnipotence and the patient's pervasive sense of helplessness, and the adolescent may flee the situation. On the other hand, if a clinician refuses to accept any projection of omnipotence, the adolescent will perceive him or her as helpless. This also is likely to make the patient more anxious and thus more likely to act out. In summary, then, medication reinforces therapeutic omnipotence if it helps the adolescent feel calmer and more effective but the very success of the intervention may make the adolescent feel helpless because of the therapist's power.

Postpubertal youngsters who never reached psychosocial adolescence may refuse medication. In this case, a combination of biological and psychosocial interventions should produce adolescence. The youngster may then perceive the therapist as a parental equivalent, and his or her refusal to take medication becomes a way of establishing autonomy.

MOOD DISORDERS

Particularly significant are attention deficit and mood disorders and the schizophrenias. Attention deficit disorders are characterized by an impaired ability to pay attention, particularly in the classroom; impulsive behavior; and sometimes diffuse hyperactivity. Such disorders affect approximately 200,000 children in the United States (Hunt, Mindexcai, and Cohen 1985) and are often underdiagnosed in adolescence and adulthood. Behavior disorders are commonly caused by attention deficit disorders (Eyre et al. 1982), and failing to treat them in childhood may lead to serious problems in adolescence, especially drug abuse, delinquent behavior, and school difficulties.

Many children respond well to methylphenidate and d-amphetamine, and adolescents are often helped by the stimulant pemoline. Unfortunately, these have side effects such as insomnia, explosiveness, and lack of appetite (Cantwell 1975). Recently, however, in a clinical trial, clonidine was reported as helpful (Hunt et al. 1985) without these side effects. Some children and adolescents may also suffer from a mood disorder, usually a type that responds well to lithium carbonate. Such medications, however, are symptomatic and not curative: they may facilitate learning but do not automatically improve classroom behavior or academic achievement (Gittleman-Klein and Klein 1976). After a long history of not being able to pay attention, children must be taught the habit of learning or reading.

When attention deficit disorders are either present with or secondary to learning disabilities, medication alone may not be helpful. A learning disability may produce a secondary disorder of attention that may not be easily treated if the former is not helped.

Adolescents manifest mood disorders in a variety of ways and require intervention with lithium carbonate and/or tricyclic and nontricyclic antidepressants. Some young people have the core symptoms—which are basically culture free—of sleep difficulties, intermittent wakefulness, morning irritability, and a lack of appetite until noon or later. These symptoms, which indicate a mood disturbance as a significant cause, are rarely volunteered and are not unusually asssociated with conduct disorders (Work 1982), including drug abuse and self-starvation.

Another type of mood disorder involves rapid mood fluctuations that cannot be explained and that arouse feelings of helplessness. Youngsters may then use marijuana in order to manipulate this mood, that is, to seek a posthigh depression that can explain the inexplicable. Finally, various rage responses are associated with biologically based mood disorders, a particular problem in violent children.

The specific drugs used for adolescents' mood disorders are the tricyclic antidepressants, particularly imipramine, whose usual dose should not exceed 5 mg per kilogram per day. Nontricyclics such as bupropion (Feighner et al. 1984), alprazolam, (Feighner 1983) and s-adenosylmethionine (Lipinski et al. 1984) are also helpful. Lithium carbonate is used most effectively in young people whose violent behavior has a strong affective explosive component (Campbell, Perry, and Green 1984), and it should be given to produce a serum level of 0.6 to 1.8 milliequivalents per liter. In our experience, as with slow-release imipramine, slow-release tablets are not as effective. Propranolol (Ratey, Morrill, and Oxenberg 1983) has also been used for adults and is useful with resistant rage attacks in adolescents.

Organic brain syndromes, including mental retardation, may require specific medication, especially in the presence of epilepsy. Approximately 1 to 3 percent of the population meet the diagnostic criteria for these (Szymanski 1980). Multiple neurological abnormalities are common with these syndromes.

Toxic hallucinogens, such as LSD, marijuana, amphetamines, barbiturates, opium derivatives, and a variety of street drugs all may produce chronic organic brain syndromes that generally do not require specific psychotropic medications.

Schizophrenic syndromes that appear during and after puberty are often underdiagnosed in behaviorally disordered youths. A long period of behavioral deviance may be present before frank schizophrenic symptoms appear, although a careful clinical examination can almost always reveal the presence of a thought disorder. Schizophrenic syndromes are caused by biological vulnerability and probably are not homogeneous. The biological vulnerability may be due to abnormal prenatal or neonatal development of the central nervous system, a specific functional abnormality with a genetic component, or a defect in synaptic elimination genetically programmed to occur in adolescence (Feinberg 1983).

The phenothiazines have different specific actions in schizophrenia. Haloperidol (Haldol) is particularly useful for hallucinatory experiences, but it may not be used in combination with lithium even for those young people who suffer from schizophrenic syndromes with a strong affective component. Thioridazine (Mellaril) is helpful for schizophrenic syndromes with a marked depressive overlay and can be used with lithium in those diagnosed as suffering from schizoaffective disorders.

Developmental issues are important in the use of these and other antipsychotic drugs. Chlorpromazine should almost never be used for adolescents because of its muscle-splinting action; physical activity is an important way for this age group to release tension. Thioridazine sometimes has the side effect of inhibiting erections and/or ejaculation, and if concrete-thinking adolescents are told of this possible side effect, they may be convinced that it will happen to them and will then refuse to take the drug.

All of these biological syndromes, if they are of long-standing duration, will produce a developmental impasse, which is significant in the production of personality disturbances. Individuals lose part or all of their capacity to make identifications, have difficulty in handling frustration, and do not learn by experience. Their emotional lives tend to be desolate, and they experience the world as boring. Often such patients' capacity to recognize reality is impaired. Behavior disorders are often indicative of both personality impairment and biological disorders of the central nervous system.

PSYCHOLOGICAL INTERVENTIONS

Specific psychological interventions include individual, group, and family psychotherapy and the provision of relationships to enable the formation of extraparental and developmental models.

Because therapists have often disagreed as to when various therapeutic techniques should be used, this may have led to a widespread use of often ill conceived new theories, ideas, and techniques (Applebaum 1982). The reason for a specific therapy, who should be present, how often the therapy should take place, how long the sessions should last, and how long the treatment probably will last are often not clear.

Psychotherapy is both cognitive and affective, and which is given more weight depends on individual needs. Expressive psychotherapy seeks a cognitive and emotional understanding of oneself; supportive psychotherapy uses the positive emotional interaction between the patient and therapist to modify experience, attitudes, and behavior; and behavioral therapy tries to change learned behavior and attitudes. Expressive and supportive psychotherapies require that the patient have the capacity to make trusting relationships, although such a capacity is also important to behavior therapy. Without it, therapeutic interchanges are futile. Likewise, drug toxicity hinders the use of therapy, and those whose capacity to make relationships has been destroyed by early deprivation and abuse also cannot be helped by psychotherapy. Without the capacity to trust, one must consider what one says rather than say what one thinks.

SUPPORTIVE THERAPY

Supportive therapy is designed to help the patient interpret reality and adapt to it. It thus reinforces those parts of the human personality that are able to appraise reality accurately. It should help the individual act in the present with an awareness of the future, be sensitive to the feelings of others, and be both vocationally and sexually productive. All of the psychotherapies require learning, but the emphasis in supportive therapy is on learning that it is permissible to express one's feelings and ideas and on understanding—through reality confrontation and clarification—that the projection of responsibility onto others is not appropriate. So one must also understand the implications of one's own behavior.

Supportive therapy may include direct reassurance, although this should not infantilize the patient. It may also include advice on current living problems and active organization of the patient's environment (McGlashan 1982). Empathy, the ability to place oneself in another's place (Basch 1983), is a necessary part of human interaction, for without the capacity to be empathic, individuals will behave with little or no concern for the experience of others. The therapist who empathizes with the patient thus provides a model, and discussing the affective experiences of others in relation to the youngster and his or her actions helps wean the adolescent from self-centeredness. The therapist can also talk with the patient about his or her (the therapist's) emotional experience which represents a communication from the patient. For example:

> "When you tell me what you are still doing to yourself, I get angry and feel helpless. Perhaps you feel this way about yourself?"

A particular issue in supportive therapy is to help the youngster accept responsibility for his or her own actions and feelings, and to cease to blame them on others. The patient should eventually internalize this idea:

> One 17-year-old boy who had abused drugs for four years before treatment said after he had been dry for four months, "I used to think my father was an 'asshole.' He's not. He really cares about me, and I don't know how he put up with me the way I used to be."

A therapist should recognize how behavior may differ during the phases of adolescence in different social classes and cultures:

> In discussing with a delinquent boy of 15, who was the father of an illegitimate child, his need for sexual restraint, the therapist remarked, "It must be difficult to have to make love in a secretive way." The boy looked at him as if he were totally stupid (accurately) and replied, "I don't know what you're talking about. I always take her to my own bed, and no one at home minds."

It is entirely appropriate for the supportive therapist to reinforce the patient's interest in new ideas, concepts, and roles. This has been called *communicative marking* (Mahler 1965).

Cognitive therapy is a variety of supportive therapy, designed to train patients to correct "negative thinking" (Teasdale et al. 1984).

During supportive therapy the adolescent should make the therapist an ally and begin to recognize problem areas of living. Often the improvement produced by supportive therapy is dramatic. Apart from obtaining more realistic satisfactions, adolescents begin to identify with the perception of the caring qualities inherent in their interaction with their therapist. The adolescents also internalize the way the therapist behaves, and it becomes a part of their own sense of self. After their psychological defenses of denial, projection, avoidance, and acting out have been resolved, some return to a normal developmental track and do not seek therapy again. Others, as young adults, recognize internal difficulties and return to therapy seeking their resolution.

The therapist needs a constant and consistent expectation that the patient will act in a realistic, healthy, mature fashion, combined with an attitude of consistency, concern, and investigation when the patient does not (Masterson 1976). The therapist should spell out what is acceptable. Situations in which therapy becomes an intellectual game, in which understanding may be present but with no significant feeling, should be avoided.

EXPRESSIVE PSYCHOTHERAPY

Expressive therapy may follow or be included with supportive therapy. It clarifies the patient's patterns of relating in the context of his or her life experiences and in relation to his or her current interaction with the therapist. The goal of expressive therapy is to enable the individual to understand, both intellectually and affectively, the reason for his or her behavior and current experiences, as determined by both the historical past and the present reality. Such insight alone will not produce change, but it will help the patient do so, and it will modify the patient's approach to current conflicts.

The goals of expressive therapy are for the individual to be able to relate to other people, to develop a capacity to be loving and empathic, and to develop constructive mastery. Expressive therapy requires the development of a transference neurosis, and one of the elements of cure is resolving this (Dewald 1983). This therapy also means bringing into the relationship with the therapist the patient's current experiences and clarifying with the patient their meanings in the present and the past. The patient is also expected to speak freely, to say what he or she thinks. Clarification often precedes interpretation, in which the therapist offers to the patient a hypothesis as to how and when the patient's present feelings are communicated and how they may relate to the patient's personal history:

> A 16-year-old boy who had profound problems with intimacy brought in a poem for his therapist, which included:
>> Fuck you mother.
>> Fuck you father.
>> Fuck you death.
>> Fuck you fear.
>> Fuck you people.
>> Fuck you life.

The therapist explained (clarified) to the patient that he had listed anxieties that he felt he had. The therapist also commented that it was remarkable that the only way the boy mentioned sex was in the word *fuck*. The boy blushed and explained, "I have always wanted to talk about sex. I learned everything on the street. Others in our group seem to know much more than I; I have wanted to talk about sex for weeks."

Unusually, the boy wore tight pants and a shirt open to the navel. The therapist thought that the boy's poem combined with his dress had a homosexual meaning, but the issue was one of timing. The therapist did not interpret the boy's appearance, as he thought that this might produce an intolerable level of anxiety.

Expressive therapy should take place at least two to three times weekly. The frequency depends on the adolescent's capacity to tolerate anxiety without destructive acting out. The ability to retain, even if unconsciously, a knowledge of what occurred in previous sessions is also pertinent. *Working through* is usually taken to mean that the content of therapy is taken over by free association, dreams, fantasies, and memories. It is not the same as the process of *working out* conflicts when the therapy is not actually in process. Working out occurs between sessions and is impaired when the patient uses alcohol and drugs, especially marijuana.

Adolescents find it difficult to use expressive therapy if they cannot think abstractly (Piaget and Inhelder 1958), or such thinking has been interrupted by physical or emotional illness. Concrete-thinking adolescents may regard an interpretation as denying the validity of their communication, and it may then become a futile, tormenting, and alienating experience.

Interpretations that explore motivation or bring to consciousness unconscious feelings should be made only by trained psychotherapists in formally structured settings. If seriously disturbed adolescents in hospitals are told by child-care workers about the possible unconscious meaning of their communications, they will become anxious and confused. The staff should understand the meaning of an adolescent's verbal and nonverbal communication so that they can respond appropriately. Their role is therapeutically counteractive, as it does not require verbal interpretations:

A child-care worker in an adolescent unit took a 16-year-old boy for a walk through a nearby arboretum. They saw two male students who had climbed a tree and were sitting on one of the branches. The patient said, "Are they gay, do you suppose?" The staff member replied, "Two males can go out together without there being any sexual feelings between them."

This staff member well understood that the question was about his own motivation and was also expressing some of the boy's own anxieties about himself.

BEHAVIOR THERAPY

Behavior therapy tries to modify the interaction between a person and his or her environment. The goal is to alleviate symptomatic behavior; unconscious conflicts are not considered. Behavioral techniques may, however, be used to control destructive symptomology, and then as this happens, other psychotherapies can be used.

Adolescents ultimately should appreciate the consequences of their antisocial behavior as authoritative rather than punitive and coercive. If a child cannot get up on time, the therapist should assume that the child is not getting enough sleep, and so his or her bedtime should be earlier. When a patient's room is untidy, even though he or she can organize this activity, it is reasonable to assume that there are too many personal possessions and that the number can be reduced.

Behavior therapy is particularly helpful for the symptoms of eating disorders, drug abuse, or violence, as these do not just interfere with psychosocial development but they also reduce the value of medications. For instance, patients with bulimia may vomit their medications, and those who abuse marijuana and alcohol may, at best, forget to take their medications, or at worst, these substances may interfere with the efficacy of imipramine and lithium.

The behavioral technique of systematic desensitization (Wolpe 1958), or progressive relaxation, is valuable for phobias (Jacobson 1938), and implicit and explicit rewards for adequate control are useful for antisocial behavior of all types. Token economies are widely used to treat adolescents (Ayllon and Azrui 1968), although when universally applied token economies obviously ignore adolescents' varying maturational levels. Such an approach may, however, be helpful when applied individually to those who cannot involve themselves with others in an emotionally meaningful manner so that other therapeutic maneuvers can work.

Aversive therapy has no place in adolescent treatment, as adolescents often identify with the coercion implied by this approach and may then become more coercive individuals themselves.

Behavioral therapy is particularly useful for concrete-thinking adolescents with a limited attention span who communicate largely by action and have difficulty making meaningful one-to-one relationships. Supportive therapy may implicitly be behavioral, as it suggests special interest and attention from a valued adult. If this aspect of supportive therapy is ignored, reducing the frequency of the therapeutic interaction as the patient's behavior improves will not be a satisfactory reward. In some probation services whose probation officers may accept the stated reluctance of many antisocial young people to come for counseling, when they do improve, the officers will change the frequency of the adolescents' appointments. But the message may then be that unacceptable behavior produces attention.

Because behavior therapy also rewards acceptable behavior but makes no effort to ameliorate patients' hostile feelings toward the therapist or to deal with their idealization, the patients' behavior is then less likely to be acceptable after the patient leaves the therapeutic system. When there is no longer any behavioral pressure on the patient, he or she tends to ignore its lessons. Besides general deprivation, this is one of the correctional system's problems. A behavioral approach may create conformist behavior, but unless the patient feels positive about his or her behavioral counselor, permanent change is not likely.

ADMINISTRATIVE PSYCHOTHERAPY

Administrative psychotherapy is a type of in-hospital supportive therapy. The therapist plans a therapeutic day with the patient and the staff, including the balance between therapeutic and grade-appropriate education; the location and frequency of parental visits; recreational, occupational, and therapeutic off-unit activities; the patient's level of responsibility; and the patient's involvement in creative, physical, and intellectual pursuits. The level of responsibility that the patient can handle is manifested by whether he or she needs staff to carry out such activities, whether the patient needs constant staff observation, which adults should help the adolescent meet special needs, and when the patient may visit his or her home.

The patient's behavior, relationships with staff and other patients, and interactions with the family are seen both as a communication to the therapist and as an involvement with the real world. Because of his or her psychotherapeutic expertise and understanding of the adolescent's personality dynamics, the administrative therapist is actually an extremely powerful person in the patient's life. This reinforces the patient's omnipotent projection, which in any case occurs between the patient and therapist when the patient makes the therapist a narcissistic extension of the self at the beginning of treatment. In expressive therapy this must be interpreted, but in supportive therapy it is used to reinforce the healthy parts of the patient's personality functioning.

The projection of omnipotence helps control the patient's violent or unacceptable behavior. Furthermore, the administrative therapist becomes a significant positive identification model for the patient as the patient's hostility is interpreted and understood. Control by means of identification is particularly helpful for these who abuse drugs and engage in predatory behavior, but it is of little help for inner confusion. Disturbed adolescents who are unable to return to an acceptable developmental track by identifying with their therapist, who cannot progress without resolving their internal conflicts, may require administrative therapy from one therapist and expressive therapy from another. Examples of this are histrionic personalities with symptoms of anorexia nervosa, those with histrionic or borderline personality disorders, and those with sexual perversions.

Histrionic personalities, in particular, attempt to find out what their therapist wants and then defend themselves by compliance. They cannot be helped if a psychotherapist has actual control over their lives.

Individual, group, or family intervention all use the above techniques of therapy, but their labels are meaningful only in that they indicate who is present. Individual therapy refers to one patient with one therapist; group therapy may mean only that several patients are being treated by one or two therapists; and family therapy indicates that a whole family is being treated.

Psychotherapeutic techniques may be used for long- and short-term intervention. Brief therapy (Malan 1963), which may also be used with groups (Raubolt 1983) and families, uses an expressive supportive interaction focusing on an individual's primary conflict. Many diagnostic interventions include a brief therapeutic approach. For many disturbed adolescents, six to seven psychotherapeutic sessions focused on autonomy and identity struggles are sufficient to restore them to an appropriate developmental track.

FREQUENCY OF THERAPY

One goal of the diagnostic process is to assess the adolescent's capacity to use, alone or in combination, an expressive, supportive, or behavioral intervention. The therapist should decide, both in the diagnostic phase and later, the frequency of the sessions and the best length for each therapeutic contact. The sessions may be shorter or longer than the usual 45 or 50 minutes.

The frequency of the initial interviews is partly determined by the patient's ability to cooperate. For an anxious, concrete-thinking early adolescent, if the gap between sessions is more than two or three days, the significance of the interaction will be lost, and a gap of a week may be felt as a rejection by both the parents and the patient. It may also make the interaction meaningless because the emotional contact has not been reinforced.

The frequency of contact in the treatment's diagnostic phase depends on

1. The patient's and family's conscious motivation to seek assistance.
2. The need to reduce or stop symptoms of drug abuse, violence, and self-destruction.
3. The patient's level of anxiety.
4. The intensity of pain inflicted on others.
5. The pain felt by the patient.

6. The patient's capacity to make a positive meaningful emotional relationship.

A once-weekly intervention based on factors other than the patient's need makes it difficult to perform an adequate assessment. Furthermore, the fairly prevalent opinion that the parents should be seen only once a week tends to ignore that the type and frequency of the therapeutic intervention are family as well as individual issues.

The time spent in sessions may also vary. Clearly, for those who cannot pay attention for that time period, the 50-minute hour is too long.

Adolescents suffering from schizophrenia, affective disorders, and attention deficit disorders may be able to use only brief 15- to 20-minute sessions during the acute phase of their illness. Medications may also change the length of each session.

Decisions about the frequency of psychotherapy are made during the diagnostic phase and are based on the following:

1. The intensity of anxiety that the therapy produces in the patient, how long the patient can bear tension without support from the therapist, and the likelihood of the patient's antisocial acting out.
2. The time that a patient can maintain an internal image of a therapeutic session. Although conscious remembering is important, the process of therapy should be internalized, for too-infrequent contacts seem to have little value.
3. The more frequent the sessions are, the more likely the patient is to feel emotional support, although serious illness or excessive dependency may be implied by too-frequent interventions.

SPECIFIC SOCIAL INTERACTIONS

The therapist may recommend the type of education a youngster should receive. The socially isolated offspring of a rigid family who goes to a rigid school may need to be put into a more tolerant social system with easier staff–pupil relationships:

A 14-year-old boy with only one friend, who had moved away, was referred by his anxious father because the boy had refused to continue to attend a military school after being there for only one week. The boy had been sent there because of failing grades during the previous year in a local private school. He was an extremely isolated, withdrawn boy with no conscious motivation for psychological help. He was found to have a learning disability in areas that involved mathematics and spelling, which had surfaced when academic demands changed and he could no longer automatically readjust to them. The social recommendation was that he go to a small private school with excellent interpersonal relationships which could also address his disability.

Youth clubs that provide art classes, sports activities, and adult interactions or job placement may be recommended to enhance a sense of worth. Some adolescents may need placement in specially designed social systems. Settings that are overrestrictive, do not respect individual integrity, and do not meet nonspecific developmental needs are of little value.

Some adolescents need intensive care in a therapeutic system away from their parents. This should be recommended as a diagnostic indication, not because outpatient treatment, applied as a least-restrictive alternative, has failed. The indications for such inpatient care are as follows:

1. Symptomatic behavior that is dangerous to the self or others and appears as a response to perceived frustration. This frustration cannot be contained, even with medication, by interpersonal relationships with the family and a therapist.
2. Developmentally destructive behavior, which includes chronic drug abuse, alcoholism, and sexual promiscuity.
3. Psychic pain of such intensity that it precludes age-appropriate functioning.
4. A psychonoxious environment that either prevents the patient from accepting therapeutic intervention or produces excessive external stress.
5. Biological assessments that cannot be provided on an outpatient basis.

Sometimes residential treatment centers may be recommended for young people who need long-term care over years. These vary in the quality of their social organization and their conceptual model of care. Some are run on behaviorist principles and devise levels of responsibility granted on the basis of points earned for a variety of acceptable behaviors. Others may use isolation to induce acceptable behavior. Still others use group approaches, including peer-group techniques of control. Some believe that older adolescents can offer controls to younger adolescents. All of these systems create a way of life with which the adolescent can identify, but the influence of such social systems on the personality development of the adolescents in their care is unclear. With some exceptions, many such centers do not meet their patients' biopsychosocial needs.

Behavior does not exist in isolation, and the concept of behavior or a conduct disorder may be destructive to adequate specific intervention, as it does not consider causes. It also allows the projection of adult anger regarding such behavior onto the young people who act in this way. This is understandable but does not justify the subsequent massive attack on the adolescent's personality development that is caused by the failure of both outpatient and residential care to meet the adolescent's developmental needs and to provide the specific treatment that each syndrome requires.

REFERENCES

Applebaum, S. A. (1982). Challenges to traditional psychotherapy from the "new therapies." *American Psychological Association* 37:1002-1008.

Ayllon, T., and Azrui, N. H. (1968). *The Token Economy.* New York: Appleton-Century-Crofts.

Basch, M. F. (1983). Empathic understanding: a review of the concept and some theoretical considerations. *Journal of the American Psychoanalytic Association* 31:101-126.

Bettelheim, B., and Sylvester, E. (1946). Principles of care. *American Journal of Psychiatry* 18:191-206.

Campbell, M., Perry, R., and Green, W. H. (1984). Use of lithium in children and adolescents. *Psychosomatics* 25:95-106.

Cantwell, D. P. (1975). *The Hyperactive Child: Diagnosis, Management and Current Research*. Jamaica, N.Y.: Spectrum Publications.

Dewald, P. A. (1983). Elements of change and care in psychoanalysis. *Archives of General Psychiatry* 40:89-95.

Eyre, S. L., Rounsaville, B. J., and Kleber, H. D. (1982). History of childhood hyperactivity in a clinic population of opiate addicts. *Journal of Nervous and Mental Disease* 170:522-529.

Feighner, J. P. (1983). Open label study of alprazolam in severely depressed inpatients. *Journal of Clinical Psychiatry* 44:332-334.

Feighner, J. P., Meredith, C. M., Stern, W. C., Hendrickson, G., and Miller, L. L. (1984). A double blind study of bupropion and placebo in depression. *American Journal of Psychiatry* 141:525-529.

Feinberg, I. (1983). Schizophrenia caused by a failure in programmed synaptic elimination in adolescents. *Journal of Psychiatric Research* 17:319-334.

Feinstein, S., and Miller, D. (1979). Psychoses of adolescence. In *The Basic Handbook of Child Psychiatry*, ed. J. Noshpitz. New York: Basic Books.

Ford, K., Hudgens, R., and Welner, H. (1978). Under-diagnosed psychiatric illness in adolescents: A prospective study and seven year follow up. *Archives of General Psychiatry* 35:279-288.

Gittleman-Klein, R., and Klein, D. F. (1976). Methylphenidate effects in learning disabilities' psychometric changes. *Archives of General Psychiatry* 33:655-664.

Gutheil, T. G. (1982). The psychology of psychopharmacology. *Bulletin of the Menninger Clinic* 46:321-330.

Hechtman, L., Weiss, G., Perlman, T., Hopkins, J., and Weiner, A. (1981). Hyperactives as young adults: Prospective ten-year follow-up. In *Psychosocial Aspects of Drug Treatment for Hyperactivity*, ed. K. D. Gadow and J. Loney. Boulder, Colo.: Westview Press.

Hunt, R. D., Mindexcai, R. B., and Cohen, D. J. (1985). Clonidine benefits children with attention deficit disorder and hyperactivity: Report of a double-blind placebo-crossover trial. *Journal of the American Academy of Child Psychiatry* 24:617-629.

Jacobson, E. (1938). *Progressive Relaxation*. Chicago: University of Chicago Press.

Karasu, T. B. (1982). Psychotherapy and pharmacotherapy: Toward an integrated model. *American Journal of Psychiatry* 139:1102-1113.

Klein, M. (1950). The technique of analysis in puberty. In *The Psychoanalysis of Children*, ed. J. Rivere. London: Hogarth Press.

Knesper, D., and Miller, D. (1976). Treatment plans for mental health care. *American Journal of Psychiatry* 133:65-80.

Levinson, D. J. (1978). *The Seasons of a Man's Life*. New York: Knopf.

Lipinski, J. F., Cohen, B. M., Frankenburg, F., Tohen, M., Waterneux, C., Alvesman, R., Jones, B., Harris, P. (1984). Open trial of s-adenosylmethionine for treatment of depression. *American Journal of Psychiatry* 141:448–450.

Mahler, M. S. (1965). On the significance of the normal separation-individuation phase. In *Drives, Affects and Behavior*, ed. M. Schur. New York: International Universities Press.

——. (1972). A study of the separation-individuation process and its possible application to borderline phenomena in a psychoanalytic situation. *The Psychoanalytic Study of the Child* 26:403–424.

Malan, D. (1963). *A Study of Brief Psychotherapy*. London: Tavistock.

Masterson, J. (1976). *Psychotherapy of the Borderline Adult: A Developmental Approach*. New York: Brunner/Mazel.

McGlashan, T. H. (1982). DSM III: Schizophrenia and individual psychotherapy. *Journal of Nervous and Mental Disease* 170:752–757.

Miller, D. (1959). The rehabilitation of chronic open ward neuropsychiatric patients. *Psychiatry* 17:347–358.

——. (1970). Parental responsibility for adolescent maturity. In *The Family and Its Future*, ed. K. Elliott. London: Churchill.

——. (1974). *Adolescence: Psychology, Psychopathology and Psychotherapy*. New York: Jason Aronson.

——. (1978a). Affective disorders in adolescence, mood disorders and the differential diagnosis of violent behavior. In *Mood Disorders: The World's Major Public Health Problem*, ed. F. Ayd. Baltimore: Ayd Publications.

——. (1978b). Early adolescence: Its psychology, psychopathology, and implications for therapy. *Adolescent Psychiatry* 6:434–447.

Perris, C. (1966). A study of bipolar and unipolar recurrent depressive psychosis. *Acta Psychiatrica Scandinavia*, supplement, 162:45–51.

Piaget, J., and Inhelder, B. (1958). *The Growth of Logical Thinking*. New York: Basic Books.

Ratey, J. J., Morrill, R., and Oxenberg, G. (1983). Use of propranolol for provoked and unprovoked episodes of rage. *American Journal of Psychiatry* 160:1356–1357.

Raubolt, R. R. (1983). Problem-focused group psychotherapy with adolescents. *American Journal of Orthopsychiatry* 53:157–165.

Serbang, J., and Gidynski, A. (1979). Relationship between cognitive defect, affect response, and community adjustment in chronic schizophrenia. *British Journal of Psychiatry* 134:602–608.

Szymanski, L. S. (1980). Psychiatric diagnosis of retarded persons. In

Emotional Disorders of Mentally Retarded Persons, ed. L. S. Szymanski and P. E. Tanquaray. Baltimore: University Park Press.

Teasdale, J. D., Fennell, M. H. V., Hibbert, G. A., and Aries, P. L. (1984). Cognitive therapy for major depressive disorder in primary care. *British Journal of Psychiatry* 144:400–407.

Winnicott, D. (1965). *Maturational Processes and the Facilitating Environment*. New York: International Universities Press.

Wolpe, J. (1958). *Psychotherapy by Reciprocal Inhibition*. Stanford, CA: Stanford University Press.

Work, H. H. (1982). Depression in childhood and adolescence. In *Psychiatry, Annual Review*, ed. L. Greenspan. Washington, D.C.: American Psychiatric Association Press.

6

Adolescent Violence and Predatory Behavior

INCIDENCE OF VIOLENCE

In the United States, males are more likely than females to be adjudicated as delinquent, to commit a violent act, and to be killed. Between 1959 and 1976, the rate of death from homicide for white males between the ages of fifteen and nineteen rose by 177 percent, from 27 to 75 for 100,000 of the population. At the same time the rate for blacks slightly declined, and so in 1976 it was 46.8. In the same period, the annual suicide rate among same-aged white males rose from 85 to 109 deaths per 100,000. The overall white population had a suicide rate of 11 per 100,000 (National Center for Health Statistics 1984). Although the actual number of young people known to be involved in suicide and homicide is 10,000—not a large percentage of the youth population—the figures are almost certainly seriously underestimated (Miller 1982).

The same national trend is evident in the delinquency figures. Between 1957 and 1974, the number of delinquent individuals between the ages of ten and seventeen who appeared before
juvenile courts rose from 19.1 to 37.5 per 100,000. However, in
the five years between 1967 and 1972, the frequency of self-
reported acts of delinquency in boys fell by 9 percent, and the
seriousness of these acts (larceny, assaults, and the like) fell by
14 percent. For girls during the same period, self-reported delinquency increased by 22 percent, but this increase was especially
due to an increase in marijuana and alcohol abuse. Although
these figures have recently declined somewhat, assaults on
teachers rose by 55 percent between 1970 and 1973, and the
number of confiscated weapons in a number of surveyed schools
rose by 54 percent (Wynne 1979).

In 1975, the rate of female juvenile arrests for serious violence in Philadelphia was 37 per 100,000; in males it was 296 per
100,000. Males surpass females in the incidence of homicidal acts
in a ratio of 9:1, for robbery 12:1, and for assaults 5:1. In the five
years between 1970 and 1975, the number of women arrested
for violence increased by 74 percent, despite the decline in self-
reporting figures, although society still expects females not to
behave violently. Furthermore, females committed for violent
crimes are generally dealt with less harshly than are males.

VIOLENCE AND AGGRESSION

In ethology, aggression and violence are synonymous, requiring
the intention to do harm or injury to a significant target and the
performance of a response sequence involving one or both of
these (Anderson and Lupo 1976). The intention may be not to
inflict irreparable damage but to inflict pain. Aggression in humans is used as a synonym for both violence and assertiveness.
The psychoanalytic concept of the aggressive drive does not
necessarily imply violence but is used mostly to imply assertiveness.

Violence, the use of force to damage persons or property, is described as a physical or emotional destructive act that occurs between people (Sodoff 1971). Likewise:

> Violence is destructive aggression. Dangerousness is an estimation of the probability of dangerous behavior, which usually refers to violent physical assault against another, or sometimes the self. It involves the use of physical strength directed against another person or an object, animate or inanimate. (Steadman 1976)

Property may symbolize the person whom an individual wishes to hurt or destroy, and property destruction may be a generalized temporary displacement of rageful action onto things rather than people. Violence directed at the self or others may result from a failure to maintain the psychological equilibrium necessary for emotional comfort (Menninger et al. 1963).

Violence may imply direct body-to-body contact, or it may be mediated through the use of stones, bullets, knives, and bombs. When homicide occurs, direct body-to-body contact probably implies a greater capacity to dehumanize the other person than when weapons are used. Those who do not observe actual violence but are exposed only to its representation by the media may have no real emotional awareness of how shocking the effect of a bullet or a knife is on the human body. Children of the street who may see actual homicides, however, rapidly accommodate themselves to these sights, and they are not less violent because they have observed real violence.

Three prerequisites for violent behavior are "perceptual precognition," finding a potential victim; "motivation," the wish to perform the act; and "execution," its performance.

Affective violence in humans typically occurs after a perceived stress and is associated with intensely rageful feelings. Predatory violence is goal directed, is much more consciously planned, and is associated with tension and anxiety rather than rage. The intent is to obtain revenge, goods, or, sometimes, excitement. The mood is different in quality and intensity from that involved in affective violence. Predatory violence may, however, produce a stress that then produces affective violence. The psychobiology of affective and predatory violence is different.

PREDATORY VIOLENCE OR
HUNTING BEHAVIOR

Techniques of destroying animals by means of hunting them are still taught. Children's play, even in cities, has atavistic remnants of such techniques. Children's group games still involve concepts of chase and capture, winning and losing, cops and robbers, and cowboys and Indians. The concept built into the game is that of ingroups and outgroups, leaders and followers. Of importance is who is picked to be included in the more-valued group and who is excluded from that group. In this sense, children's games ultimately define one type of adult behavior.

In all societies, the males' primary task is to master and control the environment. This originally was done by directly obtaining food by hunting wild animals, protecting domesticated herds from predators and hostile others, or acquiring land. Nowadays, in industrialized and agriculturally based societies, hunting has been abandoned as an important food-gathering technique, although it is still used for sports and fur trapping. Young males are typically taught to hunt by their fathers or older peers.

Hunting means acquiring, against the odds, supplies that may or may not be needed; it includes competitive excitement and the ability to plan, to be physically active, and to demonstrate one's prowess. It thus becomes a technique through which one may gain and reinforce a sense of self-worth. Even as a solitary activity, though hunting usually takes place in groups, its results are told and boasted about to others. The fishing story is perhaps as important a part of solitary fishing as is the actual fishing.

During early adolescence, a sense of masculine self-worth and identity is particularly reinforced by the competitive demonstration to peers of one's physical, sexual, and vocational ability (Miller 1969), a process that begins in childhood and continues throughout adult life.

In many Western societies, in those groups that do not prey on others, boys have generally been offered sublimations for hunting behavior, which almost always involve some degree of apparent dehumanization. Contact sports put individuals into distinctive uniforms, and the more violent is the sport, the less human will the antagonist appear. Perhaps because females cause society less of a problem of predatory violence, until recently they have been offered fewer sports-related sublimations, but in some parts of the West this is now changing.

Particularly in deprived individuals who may perceive themselves as entitled to goods, with little concern for either the possessions or the persons of others, hunting behavior continues, although it is now regarded as predatory violence directed against others. Because it is goal directed, predatory violence is based on the conscious concept that it is necessary for individual survival, satisfaction, and usually excitement.

Predatory violence is learned behavior and not a manifestation of a mood disorder. It is usually triggered by visual perception, although humans may plan it on the basis of internal imagery. For animals, predatory violence is the destruction of natural prey, usually for food. Many young animals are taught by their parents or the pack the techniques of predatory violence. Just as in humans, the play of animals also is preparation for these tasks. For most mammals, predatory violence is the destruction of another species; almost alone among mammals, humans hunt their own kind. A reasonable hypothesis is that humans can do this only by making others not human, so that those individuals who are the most dangerous can hunt and perhaps kill for gain their dehumanized victims. This type of violence is uncommon in adolescent girls. Outside very deprived institutional settings, such behavior is usually permitted for girls only when they are affiliated with boys' gangs.

Predatory violence is mediated by approach behavior (Grey 1972). A typical animal example is of cats stalking birds. Cholinergic mechanisms are typically involved. The cat's back is not arched; there is no vocalization; and the fur is not ruffled. Such behavior can be elicited from the experimental stimulation of the hunger-mediating areas in the lateral hypothalamus.

Only in wartime and for law enforcement agencies do democracies find predatory violence directed against others culturally acceptable (Barnard et al. 1965). In some societies, however, it remains acceptable in the pursuit of political and economic power. In wars the enemy is dehumanized by being called by nonhuman epithets. To make killing acceptable, people have to abandon empathy with their victim, and so the object of such violence is made nonhuman (Miller and Looney 1976).

VIOLENCE AS
ACCEPTABLE LEARNED BEHAVIOR

Learning is affective as well as cognitive and it also requires modeling behavior and identification. For predatory violence to be acceptable, it generally—although not always—must be present in and acceptable to both the nuclear family and significant individuals in the community.

Predatory violence may help some adolescents avoid the helplessness of experiencing overwhelming rage that is out of control; that is, it is more acceptable to act in what feels like a reasoned manner than to be emotionally swamped. Predatory violence is thus commonly used by individuals who also experience affective rage syndromes: they prove to themselves that they are in control. In a sense, they use violence to control violence.

The importance to adolescents of feeling in control of their own experiences is such that they may insist that they have control when they clearly do not:

> One 14-year-old youth in the middle of an argument with his parents impulsively tried to throw himself off a 15-floor balcony. The father prevented this only by grabbing at his son in the nick of time. But the boy insisted that this obviously impulsive attempt was within his control.

If parents strike their children as a means of punishment, then the acceptability of violence will be imprinted. This acceptability of violence is demonstrated in children playing with dolls who, by hitting their dolls, act out their own experience of being hit. Children who are brutally treated may similarly destroy their own toys in violent rages. And when their parents regard the children's play violence as acceptable and amusing, they further reinforce the idea that it is acceptable. Children commonly use the techniques taught by their parents:

A small, 15-year-old girl was hospitalized as a constant victim of violence, of being beaten up in the high school. Her response to stress, which had a biopsychological cause, was to become over-whelmed with affective rage, and then she slapped people. She had no judgment as to whom she would slap: it could well be a boy of six feet or more who replied in kind, another girl, or members of other ethnic groups. In her "integrated" high school, she was thus constantly assaulted.

When this girl's parents were angry, they always slapped her. The tension that had to be relieved was biologically pro-duced, and the patient's responsive technique was a learned response.

When overwhelmed, some parents may treat their infants as if they were not human (Miller and Looney 1974), a common side effect of inadequate bonding. The child is then seen as a frustrating object. Although the medium- and long-term effects of physical and sexual abuse are poorly understood (Newberger et al. 1983), child abusers themselves have usually been abused as children. To such individuals, the imprinting of the experience of abuse is significant, but to the developmentally damaged off-spring of abusing parents, a child's demands are felt as intoler-able.

VIOLENCE AND BOREDOM

Although the psychological changes associated with predatory violence are relatively few, the sense of excitement produced by planning such activity is a significant determinant in its appear-ance. For example, an idle, devalued adolescent—other things being equal—may act violently to relieve the internal tension produced by boredom.

Boredom is a symptom of a number of psychological difficul-ties, such as personality distortions, mood disorders, identity disturbances, and schizophrenia:

One boy who was always getting into fights with his peers justified his behavior because it helped him feel less bored. He was also asked if he ever passed his time by reading. "No, at times I sometimes watch television, but that's pretty dull. I guess my reading is too slow, and so I can't get into a book. Anyway, no one in my family reads."

Given the excitement of planning hunting behavior, and as the behavior itself often is a relief from internal boredom, it is particularly appealing. Nonviolent physical activity is an important way of dealing with boredom, and it is not unusual for adolescents to engage in antisocial and violent activities when such an outlet is closed:

In a low-cost housing development in England, the local youths would play soccer around the base of the buildings. The lower floors were occupied by elderly tenants who complained of the noise to the building manager, who stopped this physical activity. There was thereafter a statistically significant rise in local delinquent activity. (Miller 1969)

Contact sports may also provide a sublimation for both participant and spectator, although in sports such as ice hockey or football, violence among the participants is not unusual and is usually associated with rage rather than excitement.

The relationship between physical activity and the likelihood of violent behavior is clear in pubertal boys. If outlets for normal aggression are not provided, as they are not in many junior high schools—for example, free play at approximately two- or three-hour intervals—the likelihood of the children's fighting with one another seems to increase. The human need for play may also substitute for physical violence, particularly in early adolescence. I believe that in American high schools, in which there is no free break between classes, there seems to be a great deal more tension and nastiness, both physical and verbal, among early adolescents than in school systems in Europe, in which there are many more opportunities for play during the school day.

Watching television in order to avoid being bored is also regarded as a significant cause of violence among youth (Rubenstein 1983). Violent programs may produce violence in children because of parental reinforcement. If children see movies that contain violent action, they are likely to act out, noisily, being a character in the film. If their parents' response is to hit them to make them be quiet, then the adolescent's violence will only be reinforced.

ASSESSING DANGEROUSNESS

The location of the treatment of both suicidal and violent patients depends on an assessment of how controllable and likely these behavioral symptoms would be if the individual remained free in the community.

Violence has many causes, and its roots are found in social organizations, in biology, and in individual psychology. There is little or no direct relationship between psychiatric diagnosis, personality disorder, and dangerousness (Langevin et al. 1982). However, the interrelationship among biopsychosocial processes may lead to violent behavior as a response to actual or perceived stress.

The problem of treating and assessing either socially intolerable predatory violence or affective violence has been relatively neglected by mental health professionals. This diagnostic differentiation is not usually made either clinically or in research studies. Although it is thought that psychiatrists cannot accurately predict the likelihood of violent and homicidal behavior (Clement and Ervin 1972), probably because when they do predict dangerousness, they do not take into account either the relative likelihood of its occurring or its biopsychosocial causes.

The lack of socioeconomic privilege and the presence of implicit societal permission clearly influence the appearance of violence. Nowhere is this more apparent than in adolescents. Serious personality disturbances and/or biological vulnerability are necessary for the appearance of violence in the prepubertal child, but group violence is a common etiological issue in adolescence.

Social pathology is one of the main causes of adolescent group violence. Not all neighborhoods and cities have street gangs, but the responsibility for such disturbances is often placed only on these groups or, for more widespread violence, on "troublemakers." Sometimes society at large is blamed, for example, for race riots in the schools and the penal system. These are, however, specific determinants that lead to the appearance of a violent outburst, and these often can be clearly elucidated (Gault 1971, Zinn and Miller 1978).

If, as has been claimed by the American Psychiatric Association, the likelihood of violent behavior cannot be predicted, then its treatment becomes effectively impossible. Successful treatment, implying as it does that increasing responsibility should be given to the young as they mature, suggests the ability of professionals to assess the likelihood of violent behavior in the adolescents they treat.

The basic issue is that a given personality type, with certain biological vulnerabilities, is likely to respond in a predictable way to a perceived or real stress. The perception of stress, however, is partially determined by the amount of support that the healthy part of the personality is able to receive at any one time from the environment and the individuals in it. Thus, only for certain individuals can the absolute certainty of violence be predicted. Because behavior has many causes, the appearance of violence must depend on the relative weight of the biopsychosocial stress on and the support of the vulnerable individual at any one time.

For adolescents, there are three types of violent syndromes that may lead to homicide, and using these, one can predict their likelihood (Miller and Looney 1974).

Class I is very high risk violence and usually means both predatory violence and total dehumanization (Ottenburg 1968). The predatory violence is egosyntonic. Destruction is looked upon as inconsequential, and it will take place when the attacker's wishes are actually or potentially thwarted.

It has been hypothesized that besides a nurturing experience that includes emotional deprivation and/or incomprehensible and inconsistent parental violence—with the perceived collusion of the other parent—a particular type of genetic vulnerability is required. Generally there is no associated affect with the violence. The genetic difficulty may prevent the individual from developing a capacity for an affective response (Chang, Thompson, and Fisck 1982). This failure alone does not necessarily imply violence; rather, the child's perceived nurturing experience has to make the violence acceptable to the personality.

In humans, neither dopamine nor norepinephrine probably are increased in predatory violence. Thus there should be no increase in the central nervous concentration of these substances in this type of violence; if anything, their concentration should decrease. On the other hand, there should be an increase in central aminoacetylcholine. A basic genetic vulnerability is hypothesized, because not all children exposed to inconsistent parental brutality and severe emotional deprivation become violent and homicidal. Except for those generally vulnerable to schizophrenia and mood disorders and those who become borderline personalities, others seem to make an apparently satisfactory life adjustment, even though they may have profound emotional difficulties. Similarly, not all children who show the classical triad of fighting, temper tantrums, and school truancy necessarily become violent adolescents.

Class II is high-risk violence that involves partial, intermittent, pathological dehumanization and is associated with affective violence. Violence is acceptable to such an individual only when he or she perceives others as not human. But when the individual does not perceive this, he or she can contain the violent impulses or deflect them onto things rather than people. This type of violence occurs when the attacker is overwhelmed with affective rage. For example, the homicidal slaughter of helpless others takes place during episodes of dyscontrol, when they become the repository of the attacker's projected hatred. Class II violence appears as a response to a specific external provocation that stimulates an internal conflict and creates potentially intolerable psychic tension. In association with an affective storm, this leads to defensive splitting and projection onto a temporarily dehumanized other.

Class III is low-risk violence in which dehumanization is either total or partial. It is associated with an episodic dyscontrol syndrome that does not appear without environmental permission. This may be psychological when there is a group permission for violence, as, for example, in mass slaughter (Gault 1971), or mass suicide and slaughter, or when a group bands together in a violent attack on one person. The individual who actually kills has his or her conflicts reinforced by others, whose joint action gives permission to the killer:

> At the age of 11, James was seen by a psychiatrist who thought he might become an adult killer because of the intensity of rage he projected onto others. Five years later, at the age of 16, he was involved in an episode in which he and six others brutally molested and killed a girl of 17. He described with a near tenderness in his voice how he cut her throat after the boys had beaten her.

James's infancy and early childhood were characterized by violence. His father unpredictably beat him while his mother stood by helplessly. James saw himself as valueless: he had no code of ethics to help him modify his behavior, and he usually expressed his violence by means of destructive fantasies. He also had complex sexual conflicts and talked of how he would enjoy using women. On the one hand, he needed to perceive women as perfect, pure, and protective, and when they failed to meet this expectation, they became worthless objects to be condemned and eliminated. James related to authority males in a passive and submissive way, which seemed to give him gratification. As a rather small, unattractive, lonely youth with an intense need for acceptance, James found joining a gang immensely supportive. His later victim had the reputation of being a promiscuous girl who had been unfaithful to the gang's leader. The group then perceived the girl as a whore, and the excitement of kidnapping her to take her away to be punished allowed James to play out his fused sexual and violent feelings. He blandly described the gurgle as he cut the girl's throat and his feelings of warmth after the slaying, similar to feelings he had felt after sexual intercourse.

Thus, in low-risk violence, the murderer impulsively slaughters others onto whom is projected an unacceptable part of his or her own personality. This type of impulsive violence occurs only under circumstances in which the individual receives group support for the behavior. The individual may or may not feel rage at the moment of violence; the action may seem to be quite automatic. Permission is given for action either by others or by the presence of a weapon.

There is no direct relationship between emotional deprivation in infancy and childhood and the likelihood of a violent syndrome in the child or adolescent. Families to whom physical violence is not acceptable are not likely to produce a violent offspring.

PREDICTING DANGEROUSNESS IN CLINICAL PRACTICE

It becomes necessary if people are to be treated, against their stated wishes, in psychiatric hospitals, to predict when they might be dangerous to others. Despite changes in the mental health laws of the last decades, which generally require the prediction of dangerousness to others (Monahan et al. 1982), this remains a problem in psychiatry. Proof of potential danger is required, which is generally taken to mean that the patient has already displayed behavior that is dangerous to the self or others. This prediction of likelihood is also used in the model penal code to justify segregation in maximum security areas.

At any one time in the United States, some 50,000 individuals are predicted as being dangerous and so are detained in psychiatric hospitals. It is not unusual for psychiatrists to be asked to testify about them. The failure of a psychiatrist to report the danger of possible violence, as manifested by threats uttered in a therapeutic setting about a potential victim, is a cause for legal intervention (*Tarasoff* v. *Regents of the University of California* 1976).

A side effect of the Baxstrom study of the likelihood of violent behavior was the development of a Legal Dangerousness Scale (Steadman 1973). According to this study, a juvenile record of violence is not predictive of future violence in adults. A study of assault proneness in 4,000 male offenders with a mean age of nineteen showed that most of them had been misclassified: 28 individuals had been correctly classified, and 200 had been misclassified (Derschowitz 1974). Two-thirds of those individuals who were predicted by professionals to be dangerous and who then were released by the court against the professionals' advice had not committed a violent crime five years later (Kozol 1972).

Psychiatrists may overpredict violence because the syndromes of violence are not usually differentiated. Furthermore, psychiatrists have more direct legal and ethical responsibility than do other professionals. Psychiatrists are said to be worse predictors than are social workers, judges, or custodial officers (Derschowitz 1974). A study of discharged patients from New York facilities for the criminally insane (Steadman 1973) suggests a high rate of false prediction. However, even though these individuals' potential for violence was not realized upon their discharge, this does not prove that they were not dangerous when they were admitted to the hospital.

The therapeutic problem is that a decision must be made as to whether an individual that might be dangerous might respond violently to a perceived stress. Sometimes an initial violent act will resolve the individual's conflict, which may make it unlikely that he or she will repeat the act.

The chance of most violence's appearing is low, and most violent individuals are in Class III, the low-risk violent group, for which violence usually requires environmental permission. The prediction of future violence in those who have already been violent thus entails the following issues:

1. Is the violent behavior affective or predatory? The former is an excessive response to a perceived stress. The history of the violent behavior thus needs to be taken with care, as the causes that led to its appearance are highly significant.
2. Is violence acceptable to the individuals concerned?
3. Those adolescents who require societal permission to behave dangerously are more likely to do so if they receive explicit or implicit permission from their immediate social environment. Many with episodic dyscontrol syndromes become violent with what seems to be minimal external stress.
4. How pathological is the adolescent's capacity to dehumanize others? Is the dehumanization total or partial?

A clinical example demonstrates the use of the diagnostic technique:

Tom was a 16-year-old black youth who was referred by his mother to an adolescent clinic because of violent episodes at home in which, when frustrated, he beat his fists against the wall, broke furniture, and screamed and yelled. He had accidentally hit a family member when a piece of a chair had flown across the room, but this was clearly not a deliberate attack. This seemed to be a rather classic episodic dyscontrol syndrome.

Tom was unemployed, and he was asked during his clinical evaluation how he got money. Tom replied that he had two jobs: he worked intermittently for a chop shop, stealing cars to order. He earned about $200 per month from this job. He also occasionally mugged Hispanics—"never whites; the police get mad about that." He was careful with the weapon he carried, a knife, and indicated that he would not use it.

Tom's episodic dyscontrol episodes were precipitated by stress related to a struggle for autonomy from his mother; violence was not acceptable to his family. Tom had not been treated violently by his parents, and he did not attack people. Despite Tom's criminal behavior, it was concluded that he was not a high-risk dangerous individual of Classes I and II. Indeed, he was only marginally in Class III, even though mugging was an acceptable way of life for him.

Besides the clinical history, psychological tests are of some help in predicting violence. Some psychological tests given to inmates of correctional centers have been able to predict the possibility of violent behavior. Individuals who give explosive responses to color on the Rorschach cards tend to erupt in violent explosive behavior, and passive individuals usually respond to the blues and greens, not the reds (Cerney and Shevrin 1974). Such violence may be directed toward the self as well as toward others.

PREDATORY VIOLENCE AND ITS TREATMENT

The treatment of violence-prone children and adolescents requires three types of intervention:

1. A social system designed to reduce the likelihood of the

individual's experiencing intolerable stress, that is, a system that provides appropriate protection.

2. Psychological treatment to resolve personality difficulties and the developmental impasse created by the syndrome.

3. Biological treatment to deal with neuroendocrine and other disturbances that will respond to psychopharmacology.

A major problem for society is those individuals who are predatorily violent, coldly dehumanize, and do not have a capacity to trust others. If homicide is acceptable to such individuals, they are extremely dangerous. At the present time there is little or no satisfactory treatment for such individuals. They may be incarcerated for long periods of time or, in the United States and elsewhere, subjected to judicial homicide if they commit murder.

Adult bonding may be helpful in the treatment of such individuals. With symbiotic relationships similar to those in infant bonding (Bowlby 1969), it implies that all judgment has been abandoned. It usually occurs during the acute stress of life-threatening situations in which extreme helplessness and terror are inflicted. Safety is sought by psychological surrender to those inflicting the stress. The values of the enslavers are internalized. This was perhaps what happened when Patty Hearst was kidnapped. She was kept in a closet for two months, could determine the passage of time only by means of her menstrual cycle, and was a victim of the sexually predatory behavior of one of her captors. She then joined the Symbionese Liberation Army.

If a lower socioeconomic class youth is in a psychiatric treatment center in which the penalty for holding a girl's hand is to be placed in isolation and for hitting another person means strap restraints, this perhaps has the same irrationality to him as terrorist behavior has to its victims. Because these centers seemingly help some of those who do not usually make trusting relationships, it is theoretically possible that such an individual may, as it were, "bond" to the system's values. If this happens, providing that the system stands for socially acceptable values, a predatorily violent, untrusting individual may learn to function in a more socially acceptable way. On the other hand, an individual who makes trusting relationships and who has internalized society's positive values may find extremely traumatic prolonged exposure to highly aberrant social systems. This may then be highly destructive to his or her personality organization: some such process may be used in Soviet psychiatric prisons.

The capacity to behave in a predatorily violent way depends on the extent to which an individual pathologically dehumanizes, which is partly related to his or her capacity to sustain ambivalence. If hatred can destroy love, then people may be capable of infinite evil. The type, quality, and amount of violent behavior depends on the implicit and explicit acceptance of violence in the individual's current life situation. A potentially predatorily violent individual who is able to make emotionally meaningful interpersonal relationships is also able to abandon such behavior if the norms of the therapeutic social system consistently condemn its acceptability.

When prepubertal children are violent, the situation may be relieved by working with the patient's psychobiological difficulties and the nuclear family. Adolescents may withdraw their emotional involvement from a family system that previously provided long-term developmental support (Blos 1974). A violence-prone adolescent usually cannot be treated in the home environment, as the weight of psychobiological intervention cannot prevail against the pressure of a social system to be violent, which may exist in the larger community. Sometimes the family itself contributes to the violence, but the high cost of hospital treatment may preclude helping the patient. However, a premature discharge from such a setting may lead to a recurrence of the violence.

The emotional significance of the social system to which the adolescent belongs is almost as relevant to the control of antisocial behavior as is the significance of an emotionally meaningful relationship. In the larger society, a neighborhood in which violence seems to be the norm does not necessarily mean that every child will become violent. The strength of other attachments, with parents and with emotionally significant other adults, may protect the child, especially if all of them condemn violence.

"Street smarts," the ability to avoid trouble, is also the ability to survive in violent neighborhoods. These children have to seem unafraid and to be unwilling to make subtle behavioral challenges to the hunters of the street. They also have to suggest that they expect no trouble but can handle it if it comes:

One 17-year-old boy who went to work in a grocery store in a violent neighborhood was taught by the store manager how to walk in the street outside the store, how to walk by the group of youths who hung about outside, and what to do if they made jeering remarks. This was at least as important as how to relate to the customers in the store.

Adolescents with little sense of themselves can acquire from the environment the capacity both to be violent and to dehumanize. This can be seen in correctional centers, which are almost always dehumanizing institutions. A great deal of covert, if not overt, violence is the norm. Inmates are statistically likely to produce more violent crimes when they are discharged than before their admission (Miller 1969). Adolescents who have withdrawn significant dependent attachments from their parents are more likely than adults are to identify with the attitudes of other people and social systems. A correctional center often dehumanizes its inmates by failing to meet their developmental needs. The inmates may be exposed to other inmates' violence and threats, and they are not offered emotional relationships with nonviolent individuals. The consistent implicit values of such systems both dehumanize other persons and collude with any violence toward them. Those who are vulnerable will then internalize such violence as being acceptable.

Individuals who internalize violence toward others as acceptable will not necessarily show other signs of psychological immaturity. Whether or not they behave in a predatorily violent way depends on the ease, under stress, with which they dehumanize others and the extent to which they consider violence toward others as acceptable.

Society's response to violent behavior depends on its severity, and all attempts at treating the individual may be abandoned. So far, the return to capital punishment in the United States has not led to the judicial murder of adolescents, but this is perhaps only a matter of time.

REFERENCES

Anderson, D. C., and Lupo, V. J. (1976). Nonhuman aggressive behavior, trends and issues. In *Rage, Hate, and Other Forms of Violence*, ed. D. T. Madden, and J. R. Lion. Jamaica, NY: Spectrum Publications.

Barnard, A., Ottenburg, P., and Redl, F. (1965). *Dehumanization: A Composite Psychological Defense in Relationship to Modern War.* New York: Science and Behavior Books.

Blos, P. (1974). *The Young Adolescent.* New York: Free Press.

Bowlby, J. (1969). *Attachment and Loss,* vol. 1: *Attachment.* New York: Basic Books.

Cerney, M., and Shevrin, H. (1974). The relationship between color dominated responses on the Rorschach and explosive behavior in a hospital setting. *Bulletin of the Menninger Clinic* 38:443–455.

Chang, P., Thompson, T., and Fisck, R. O. (1982). Factors affecting attachment behavior between infants and mothers separated at birth. *Developmental and Behavioral Pediatrics* 3:96–99.

Clement, C. E., and Ervin, F. R. (1972). Historical data in the evaluation of violent subjects. *Archives of General Psychiatry* 22:621–624.

Derschowitz, A. (1974). Dangerousness as a criterion for confinement. *Journal of the American Academy of Psychiatry and the Law* 1:189.

Gault, W. B. (1971). Some remarks on slaughter. *American Journal of Psychiatry* 128:82–86.

Grey, J. S. (1972). The structure of emotions and the limbic system. In *Physiology, Emotions and Psychosomatic Illness. CIBA Symposium* 8:92–93.

Langevin, R., Paitich, D., Orchard, B., Hardy, I., and Russin, A. (1982). Diagnosis of killers seen for psychiatric assessment: controlled study. *Acta Psychiatrica Scandinavica* 66:216–228.

Kozol, H. (1972). The diagnosis and treatment of dangerousness. *Crime and Delinquency* 18:371.

Menninger, K. A., Mayman, M., and Pruyser, P. (1963). *The Vital Balance: The Life Process in Mental Health and Illness.* New York: Viking.

Miller, D. (1969). *The Age Between.* London: Hutchinson.

——. (1970). Parental responsibility for adolescent maturity. In *The Family and Its Future,* ed. K. Elliot. London: Churchill.

——. (1978). Affective disorders in adolescence: mood disorders and the differential diagnosis of violent behavior. In *Mood Disorders: The World's Major Public Health Problem,* ed. F. J. Ayd. Baltimore: Ayd Publications.

——. (1982). Adolescent Suicide. *Adolescent Psychiatry* 9:327–363.

Miller, D., and Looney, J. (1974). The prediction of adolescent homicide. *American Journal of Psychoanalysis* 34:187–198.

Monahan, J., Ruggicio, M., and Fredlander, H. D. (1982). Stone-Roth model of civil commitment and the California dangerousness standard: operational comparison. *Archives of General Psychiatry* 39:1267–1271.

Monthly Vital Statistics Report. (1984). 32:13. Hyattsville, MD: National Center for Health Statistics.

National Center for Health Statistics. (1978). Washington, D.C.

Newberger, E. H., Newberger, C. M., and Hampton, R. L. (1983). Child abuse: current theory base and future research needs. *Journal of the American Academy of Child Psychiatry* 22:262–268.

Ottenburg, P. (1968). Dehumanization in social planning and community psychiatry. *American Journal of Psychotherapy* 22.4:585–591.

Piaget, J., and Inhelder, B. (1958). *The Growth of Logical Thinking.* New York: Basic Books.

Rubenstein, E. A. (1983). Television and behavior: research conclusions of the 1982 NIMH report and their policy implications. American Psychologist 38:820–825.

Sodoff, R. J. (1976). Violence in families: an overview. *Bulletin of the American Academy of Psychiatry and Law* 4:292–296.

Steadman, H. J. (1976). Predicting dangerousness. In *Rage, Hate, and Other Forms of Violence,* ed. D. T. Madden and J. R. Lion. Jamaica, N.Y.: Spectrum Publications.

Tarasoff v. Regents of the University of California (1976). 17 Cal. 3d 425, 551, P.2d 334 (1976), Vacated 13 Cal. 3d 177, 529, p. 28, 552 (1974).

Wynne, E. A. (1979). Facts about the character of young Americans. *Character* 1:1.

Zinn, D., and Miller, D. (1978). Riots in adolescent inpatient units. *Journal of the National Association of Private Psychiatric Hospitals* 9:43–51.

7

Mood and Behavioral Disturbances

Mood disorders in adolescents show a variety of symptoms, some of which appear to be culture free. These include an inexplicable variation in affect between elation and experiences of boredom and emptiness, which may occur many times a day, or sometimes the episodes last longer; sleep difficulties due to intermittent wakefulness; a lack of appetite often until noon or later; and extreme morning irritability. All of these may be present in adolescents with mood disorders, irrespective of social class or ethnic group.

Inexplicable mood variations make individuals feel excessively helpless, and they then use a variety of techniques to try to overcome this feeling. These include drug abuse, antisocial behavior, self-starvation, and sometimes violence, which may lead to suicide, homicide, or "accidental" death, especially in automobile accidents.

Biopsychosocially determined behavior represents a way to

release tension. Its variations are almost solely determined by psychosocial issues. For example, in a society that equates thinness in women with beauty, women are more likely to self-starve themselves. A society that is preoccupied with and reinforces violence is likely to be visited by violent behavior, and in recent decades, adolescents have become more likely to die in accidents, be murdered, and kill themselves.

DEPRESSION

The label *depression* is used to describe a number of moods, including anaclitic depression, caused by emotional deprivation, and reactive depression and mourning, caused by the loss of a loved person. Other types of depression, with or without deprivation, are caused by genetic loading. The different affective illnesses carry such labels as schizo-affective disorder and bipolar and unipolar disease. In adolescents the situation may be further confused. Adolescence as a process already involves shifts of mood. As children mature, they go through a period of sadness associated with trying to master their developmental feelings of helplessness and hopelessness. Such feelings appear when parental support, which implies childlike dependence, is abandoned, and they are often referred to as *depression*. Anhedonia, the inability to enjoy life, is also common among adolescents. Although it has been considered symptomatic of depression, it also is present in other types of illness.

Depression has been described as a mood disturbance occurring in the absence of schizophrenia, drug abuse, alcoholism, organic brain disease, or personality disorders that has a sustained negative effect. But this definition of depression applies only to adults who are thought to have previously had a healthy personality.

Unipolar and bipolar illnesses are not easily diagnosed in children and adolescents, and in addition there can be biological shifts in the presence of preexisting personality difficulties. Adolescents cannot have mood disorders without some disturbance in their personality growth. Few early and middle adolescents show the apparent guilt typically associated with depressive types of mood disturbance seen in many adults.

Because of diagnostic confusion, and variations in personality development, the incidence of affective disorder during adolescence and later is unclear (Wing and Bobbington 1982). Some studies claim that 25 percent of patients suffer from clinical depression (Frommer 1968); others claim that it is 40 percent (Masterson 1970); and still others claim that depression is rare (Schacheter 1971). The language compounds the confusion: the word *depression* often is used loosely to define many moods, as is the term *adolescence*, which means different things to different people.

Depression probably has many genetic causes. From 20 to 37 percent of those who suffer from such mood disorders have relatives with similar difficulties, whereas only 7 percent of those who do not suffer from depression have relatives with these syndromes (Gershon, Hamovit, and Guroff 1982). Although formal statistics for adolescents are not available, clinical experience shows the same figures. Sex-linked dominance is seen in some families and straight heterogeneity in others.

It is probable, but not proven, that bipolar and unipolar illness are revealed in different ways in children and adolescents. Severe depression has been claimed to appear in at least 29 percent of elementary schoolchildren (Brumback and Stanton 1983). Children's and adolescents' mood disorders respond to the same medication as do adults' mood disorders: lithium carbonate and tricyclic and nontricyclic antidepressants.

In infants, the beginning of a manic-like mood disorder may be diagnosed by the presence of affective instability and a dysphoric reaction to early attempts at autonomy. This may include temper tantrums or, sometimes, hyperactivity. Such children may often enjoy acting. The infant's circadian rhythms do not modify to fit the family schedule and cause family tension, mainly because the parents do not get much sleep. The child who regularly gets up to play at 3:00 A.M. may cause havoc in the family, as sleepless parents become less competent and more irritable. It is thus quite common to discover that children who show borderline personality disturbances and who are unable to separate themselves from their parents in an emotionally meaningful way also suffer from an underlying mood disorder. A grandiose idealization of the self often persists into later childhood. As well, impulsiveness, bizarre eating problems, and disturbed sleeping habits continue.

In adolescence, genetically vulnerable children are likely to show excessive rebellion, negativism, overconfidence, and an insistence on well-being. Their self-esteem is exaggerated. Such youngsters' grandiose conceptions of their physical, mental, and moral powers infuriate adults, who see them as refusing to accept reality. Restless hyperactivity is the norm (Feinstein, Feldman-Rotman, and Woolsey 1984); these youngsters squander goodwill rather than money. There also may be an exaggeration of libidinal impulses with aggressive sexual behavior. Those who are psychosocially vulnerable may be excessively violent. In addition, a biologically based mood disorder may be seen in those who abuse drugs, who are labeled as delinquent (Alessi et al. 1984), or who show self-starvation syndromes. In both prepubertal children and adolescents, a borderline personality is a common concomitant of all types of mood disorders.

Biological markers, such as the presence of high urinary-free cortisol, high urinary MHPG (3-methoxy-4-hydroxyphenylglycol) levels (Rosenbaum and Rosenbaum 1983), and the failure to suppress cortisol excretion with dexamethasone (Carroll, Curtis, and Mendelo 1976), are not as reliable in adolescents as in adults. More than half of those adolescents diagnosed as genetically depressed with a unipolar type of illness will show, on clinical examination, normal results on the dexamethasone suppression test (DST) (Klee and Garfinkel 1984).

When the dexamethasone suppression test required collecting urine samples over a 24-hour period, it was particularly difficult to give to adolescents, as they would do everything from failing to collect the specimen to arranging for their friends to offer a specimen instead. But the discovery that the test is just as accurate with blood samples alone makes it now easier to use. Individuals with a dysthymic disorder (depressive neurosis) or with a bipolar illness show a normal response to dexamethasone. But normal suppression in adults, as in adolescents, does not necessarily exclude the diagnosis of endomorphic depression.

Like older adults, children show significant differences in sleep architecture attributable specifically to major depression

(Puig-Antich, Goetz, and Hanlon 1982), and two-thirds of severely depressed prepubertal children report intermittently waking up during the night.

DEPRIVATION SYNDROMES

Deprivation syndromes follow the loss of a developmentally significant object, often before the adolescent has developed the capacity for adequate psychological reconstitution, or if the environment does not provide enough emotional support to enable recovery. The severity of such a characterological distortion depends on the age when loss occurs, on the individual's genetic vulnerability, and on the environment's emotional support to relieve the stress.

Early adolescents' initial response to acute or chronic traumatic loss is almost always denial, which helps them avoid its implications, an important internal coping mechanism. This denial implies omnipotence, as it suggests that "this cannot be happening to me." Traumatic loss reinforces the helplessness of early adolescence. Adolescents avoid psychological disintegration by trying to control both themselves and their environment. Their techniques include manipulating their experiences so that there will be a new loss and persecution. The actions designed to relieve this tension will reproduce the experience of loss, but this time it is not now inflicted from outside the self. The individual may again master the situation, even though the results may be negative. For example, those who lose a parent tend to arrange their lives so that they will lose significant others, or the children of divorce themselves become divorcing adults.

Behavioral responses are most likely to begin in early and middle adolescence, although at this time children may not yet realize the irrevocability of their loss. Some may not understand the true meaning of death, because along with feeling omnipotent, they have not yet developed an adult sense of time. As mentioned earlier, others see death as an experience from which they can return alive.

When adolescents have gone through secondary separation-individuation, they can have an adult feeling of loss. Thus if children do not reach late psychosocial adolescence, because of psychological trauma, they will not be able to have an adult mourning experience.

Mourning implies an emotional recognition of loss, and many adolescents with little or no sense that a loss is permanent can make only a pseudoreconstitution. Often, the youngsters appear to be making a good adjustment, but as adults, they are often unable to involve themselves in an emotionally meaningful way with people and things outside themselves. They exist rather than live. Unable to mourn satisfactorily, adolescents may be left with unresolved feelings of anger and guilt. For those who easily dehumanize and who accept violence, such behavior becomes a way of relieving the ensuing tension. Anger is dissipated in a violent expression of feeling, and guilt is dealt with either by remorse for what has been done or, more usually, by external punishment:

> Charles, age 14, was in a juvenile correctional center for repeated muggings in which he attacked his victims with a switchblade knife. In the center, he provoked bigger and older boys to beat him up. He was in a series of accidents, in one of which, part of a brick wall he was helping to build fell on him.
>
> When he was 11, Charles's father had died after having had cancer for two years. Charles had witnessed his suffering and became violent after the death. His therapy consisted of helping him to mourn, by talking with the staff about his father, whenever the opportunity arose. This led to a cessation of the behavior. Its potential remained, however, as the idea of violence was acceptable to him, and he retained the capacity to dehumanize under stress.

MAJOR DEPRESSION

A major depression may be either continuous or intermittent and is biological in origin. Some young people always react to stress with potentially painful depression, in addition to the more usual fight-flight behavior that involves tension and anxiety, rage and denial. Some attempt to cope with this by means of various withdrawal techniques; others, by excessive conformity; and still others, by aggressive and violent antisocial responses. The essential disturbance is in the neuroendocrine regulation of affect. Depression probably is a failure of the normal brain inhibitory influences on the hypothalamic-pituitary-adrenal (HPA) system. This failure of inhibition suggests that there is an abnormal system drive on the HPA axis that originates in the limbic system—the hypocampus, amygdala, thalamus, and midbrain. A functional connection between emotion and hypothalamic-pituitary-adrenal (HPA) activity can thus be related to these autonomic sites.

Some types of central HPA regulation, such as circadian rhythmicity, respond clinically to stress stimuli, but this has not been experimentally confirmed. The critical period for circadian HPA organization is from 11:00 P.M. until midnight. Some depressed patients have a defective HPA mechanism, which includes an increase in cortisol secretion, particularly an increased release of cortisol at night.

The HPA system not only reacts to psychological stress, but it also responds to medical and surgical illnesses, acute infections, myocardial infarctions, uncontrolled diabetes, and severe malnutrition and weight loss. Defective HPA regulation may be present in anorexia nervosa, although that change is probably due to malnutrition. An adolescent whose presenting symptom is self-starvation may show a false positive biological marker for depression.

According to clinical studies, some individuals with a defective HPA regulatory mechanism appear to be intermittently hypersensitive to stress. Often, from very early infancy onward, because of an abnormal endocrine discharge that becomes excessive under stress, these children experience undue psychic pain. They are therefore driven to try to avoid the stress or to reduce it. Thus, they maneuver themselves in their world with their prime motivation being to reduce psychological pain. Their biological goal is to produce the cortisol and ACTH inhibition that will make them neuroendocrinologically more stable. An optimal experience of internal tension allows for personality growth and development. But children and adolescents with this type of mood disorder will sacrifice significant aspects of their personality development in order to avoid psychic pain:

Joe was brought by his parents for treatment when he was 16 because for a year he had not been able to do any schoolwork. He missed classes, did not do his homework, and caused his parents considerable anxiety. But Joe was quite unconcerned and said that he could always make a living by being a gigolo. His severe depression became evident in a family diagnostic session when he wept as his parents described his failure to become autonomous. He had always been good and had never been troublesome, either as a 2-year-old or at puberty. When his parents said that they thought he was really very sad was when he began to weep. Psychological tests showed a serious depression with many hints of suicidal intent. He failed to show cortisol suppression on the dexamethasone suppression test.

Depressive syndromes with biological causes, as opposed to those associated with psychosocial deprivation, can be understood as a genetically induced aberrant reaction to stress. The individual learns to avoid stress in two ways. In one, children may conform so well to the environment's demands that their stress is never perceived; thus a very good child from a consistently loving and constructive environment may appear healthy but cannot cope with developmental stress.

This often describes the youngsters who attempt suicide in grades 11 or 12. They do so because the social demands for autonomy, leaving school, and going to college cause stress, and depression follows:

Bob made three serious suicidal attempts from the age of 15 to 17, and he was hospitalized three times for brief periods. At one time he was believed to be biologically vulnerable and given inadequate doses of imipramine because his psychiatrist did not believe it would work. Bob overdosed on the drug in one of his attempts. Until the age of 15, he had been highly conformist and very bright and was never a trouble to anyone.

Bob's DST was negative, but he had a history of poor sleep over many years and a lack of appetite in the morning. He was given imipramine in therapeutic doses, and his depression remitted. The issue then became for him as an adolescent to develop genuine emotional involvements outside his family.

Another response occurs when the environment's explicit and implicit demands are inconsistent, a situation that the highly vulnerable, potentially depressed adolescent may not be able to tolerate. Environmental consistency is obtained by obeying the implicit communication of the system and the individuals in it. The adolescent learns to predict the system's responses and can transform into a real experience the confusing sense of environmental persecution, which reinforces the helplessness felt by those who are depressed. That is, instead of the persecution's being perceived in fantasy, it occurs in fact.

Sometimes a type of monosymptomatic behavior appears with episodes of depression. Adolescents may experience inexplicable variations in their ability to do schoolwork; for several months they may be unable to pay attention and then for weeks and months, their functioning improves, only to have the inattention return:

> Tony, age 17, sought help in an adolescent treatment center because of anxiety associated with school failure, suicidal ideation, threats to quit school, and drug abuse. Since the eighth grade, for two to three months each year, he had found it difficult to concentrate on his schoolwork. Because he was bright, when his ability to concentrate returned, he passed each grade. Until grade ten he satisfied the requirements satisfactorily, if not brilliantly. But as a junior, the pressure of work increased, and Tony found it increasingly difficult to catch up. His despair over this led to increasing drug abuse, and when he found himself unable to stop, he sought help.

> Inquiry about Tony's experiences during his episodes of inability to work revealed that he had no appetite until 1:00 P.M., was excessively irritable (his own words) in the morning, and would awake intermittently throughout the night. The parents revealed that a paternal cousin was an alcoholic and that a great aunt was reputed to have killed herself.

Tony was diagnosed as suffering from a unipolar type of depressive illness. On therapeutic doses of imipramine his mood lightened. Therapy was directed toward correcting the developmental impasse that had occurred as a result of both his mood disorder and a three-year history of marijuana abuse. Tony was a hospital inpatient for five weeks, in a partial hospital program for two months, and then was seen in supportive outpatient psychotherapy for three months. One year after he was first seen, he was drug free, had graduated from grade 12, and was bound for college.

Adolescents with episodic major depression may sometimes also show intermittent violence:

> Peter, age 14 and the offspring of a family that regularly used alcohol, was hospitalized because he would have impulsive rage attacks in school in which he would attack others with minimum provocation. The school was in a neighborhood in which violence was rare. The boy's attacks had begun when he was quite small but had become more serious as he became pubertal and grew very tall: he was six feet, four inches.
>
> The school's initial response to Peter's attacks was to refer him to a school social worker. To everyone's pleasure and surprise, his attacks then settled down and did not appear again. But some months later, the attacks started once again. This time the school staff became angry and referred him to a psychotherapist outside the school, and the same process occurred. Finally, after a third episode of violent attacks on other youngsters, Peter was hospitalized.
>
> Peter was using a lot of marijuana, which he said was a way of helping him feel calm and cool. Once he was in the hospital, the symptoms all appeared to settle down, and he appeared to be quite competent, a pleasant young boy of 14. After some two to three weeks in the hospital, quite impulsively and with minimal provocation, he began to attack others. On one occasion, for example, while playing table tennis, he missed a shot, threw the paddle at the nurse with whom he was playing, and split open her head.

Peter was treated with imipramine, the basic biological cause being thought to be a depressive illness. He required therapy for his character disturbance, but at a five-year follow-up, he had had no further episodes of violence.

Peter had a family history of alcoholism: his grandfather was reported to have died as an alcoholic, and a paternal aunt had been in a psychiatric hospital for unknown reasons.

When a behaviorally disturbed adolescent has a history of extreme conformity and suddenly begins to behave problematically, the genetic neuroendocrinology of depression should always be considered. When an adolescent has a monosymptomatic difficulty that may or may not be violent, such problems may initially appear intermittently. There may be periods in which a youngster appears to behave satisfactorily, then suddenly behaves very antisocially, and then is normal again. Such young people often have a family history of unipolar and bipolar depression, alcoholism, or psychosomatic illness. Psychological tests may show evidence of depression, as do those of some adolescents who suffer from episodic dyscontrol syndromes. Typically, the tests may also show evidence of deprivation with a consequent inability on the part of the boy or girl to become satisfactorily adolescent and develop a firm sense of autonomy.

For most adolescents with mood disorders, failure, disruption, and rejection have been, from an early age, recurring experiences. When their behavior is violent or antisocial, it leads to intrafamilial and intraeducational rejection. In social agencies they go through a cycle of acceptance and rejection. Their expected pattern of life is movement. Disturbances of time and place, which are common for many adolescents in our society, become for them a merry-go-round of time-place distortion, often with the unconscious and unwilling collusion of those whose goal is to be helpful.

These individuals' characterological disturbance is that they neither develop a conscious wish to change nor feel any ability to establish a warm and trusting relationship with persons whose goal is to be helpful. They thus create the self-fulfilling prophecy that adults in authority are useless and not to be trusted.

Adolescents with mood disorders that are similar to adults' major depressive illnesses appear to respond to tricyclic antidepressants, such as imipramine, and the nontricyclics. If their dexamethasone suppression test is positive and their cortisole secretion is not impaired, this is a clear indication to give imipramine. But if the test is negative and if the clinical history suggests a major depression, antidepressants should be tried.

Imipramine has been used for many syndromes and has tended to produce variable results. When imipramine is given to prepubertal children, there is no latency of action, as there is in postpubertal adolescents and adults. But in puberty, according to clinical observations, this latency is sometimes present. The mechanisms involved in this are unclear. Children develop a tolerance to imipramine in 8 to 12 weeks, but there is no evidence of this in adolescents. Despite the insistence of some that there is no therapeutic window for this drug, if a patient is drug resistant and if the diagnosis is incontrovertible, then a serum level of imipramine and desipramine should be taken.

The usual dosage of imipramine in children is 25 mg three times a day; in adolescents the usual therapeutic dose is 100 to 150 mg daily. Imipramine-resistant adults have been reported to take up to 1,000 mg daily. For adults, a high percentage of imipramine is protein bound, although this appears to be less true for children. Serum levels of imipramine are measured in nanograms; a therapeutic response is usual at 200 nanograms per milliliter. The long-acting capsule of imipramine seems not to produce a therapeutic level of imipramine and desipramine in adolescents.

For adolescents, the optimal dose of imipramine appears to be 3.5 mg per kilogram of body weight. If desipramine rather than imipramine is used, 40 percent of patients may have blood levels that are too high for a therapeutic response.

Just as with adults, adolescents may become toxic if given more than 5 mg per kilogram of body weight and will show electroencephalograph changes. These are reversible with propranol in the rare event of an overdosage. In this situation the imipramine should be removed from the stomach, and activated charcoal should be given for 24 hours, with supportive measures for the cardiovascular and respiratory system, which should be monitored.

When imipramine is given successfully, it seems at the present time that it can be withdrawn after one year's treatment with little likelihood of relapse. The long-term effects are not yet known.

Along with treating the mood disorder, the consequent characterological problems must be resolved. In particular, environmental controls and therapy, using nonpersecutory identification models, must always be provided to clarify reality.

The successful treatment of violent adolescents was described by one patient in the following way: "I feel myself getting angry; the anger rises up inside of me, but somehow I do not want to lose control. I find it easier to take control of my feelings rather than to allow them to take control of me and to explode."

ATTENTION DEFICIT DISORDERS

What used to be called hyperkinesis or minimal brain dysfunction has now been relabeled attention deficit disorder with or without motor hyperactivity (DSM III 1980). These two symptom complexes may represent differing phenomena with differing core attention deficits (Lahey et al. 1985), but the neuromaturational deficit appears to be in the frontal part of the brain when the disorder is primary. It may be present with learning problems and may have a mood disorder as one of its causes. In adolescents, drug abuse and other types of brain insult, especially schizophrenia, may be associated with the syndrome as either a cause or an effect. It may appear in children as early as the age of three (Safer and Allen 1976). It is an important cause of many types of disturbed behavior and is consistently underdiagnosed and often inadequately treated.

The essential features of attention deficit disorders are developmentally inappropriate inattention and hyperactivity. Many adolescents seen with behavioral difficulties, especially those with delinquent and violent syndromes, show both of these symptoms, which often precede the report of antisocial or violent behavior. An attention deficit disorder is characterized by impulsivity, inattention, and hyperactivity. The disorder may persist into adolescence (Lever and Lever 1977) and adulthood (Amado and Lustman 1982). Because attention difficulties reinforce an inner experience of helplessness and are likely to lead to a distortion of the environmental response, the child will try to master them after puberty—when the family can no longer contain his or her anxiety—by means of either a regressive withdrawal from school or more aggressive and antisocial behavior (Menkes et al. 1967).

With or without hyperactivity, attention deficit disorders are difficult to diagnose. The most seriously affected children are usually boys, who show a poor attention span, impulsiveness, excitability, and hyperactivity. By the time they reach adolescence, these children commonly refuse to go to school and appear to have abandoned any attempt to learn in school. This syndrome is diagnosed more often in the United States than elsewhere (Sprague 1979). Neuroendocrine abnormalities have also been reported that are similar to these found in those with bipolar illness, episodic rage, and marked mood variations. It may be, however, that the biology of attention deficit disorders is multidetermined and that the type responding to lithium, although the symptom is the same, is a syndrome different from that responding to pemoline or clonidine (Hunt et al. 1985). Serotonin, norepinephrine, and dopamine all have been proposed as significant causes (Wender 1971), and urinary MHPG excretion was found to be much lower in hyperactive boys than in the controls (Sheken, Dehermenjian, and Chapel 1979).

In a careful study, the number of children diagnosed as suffering from an attention deficit syndrome with hyperactivity was found to increase between the ages of 5 and 7 (Chapel et al. 1982), but as new social and educational demands are made at this age, this is to be expected.

Some young people with mood disorders are unable to pay attention in school. Like those with attention deficit disorders, with or without a learning disability, they may attempt to gain control over their situation by refusing to try; they can thus fantasize that they could work if they made the attempt. Refusing to go to school and disruptive classroom behavior are thus common in adolescents with both mood and attention deficit disorders. A boy of 15 described his experience when he was found, at age thirteen, to have a learning disability in mathematics: "Dr. R. tested me and told me I was learning disabled in math; I just refused to do it then. I have not done it since."

Young people who are labeled as difficult and antisocial may incorporate this into their self-concept and thus develop a false identity.

Some affectively violent adolescents have attention deficit disorders that do not appear to be related to mood disorders:

Pamela was brought to the inpatient unit of an adolescent treatment center at the age of 13. Although very bright, she had never been able to concentrate in school and had consistently underachieved. When seen, she was enraged with both parents, was inordinately greedy and self-centered, and was obsessed with the idea that anything she wanted she ought to have. She had been drug abusing and promiscuous. Her preferred sexual activity for two years had been fellatio.

Pamela did not respond well to specific and nonspecific psychosocial interventions. Lithium carbonate made no difference and so was discontinued. In class she could not pay attention, although there was no evidence of a learning disability. She was then given pemoline (Cylert) in therapeutic doses, and the results were dramatic.

When seen at a school staff meeting three months later, before returning to high school, Pamela seemed to her teachers to be "perfectly healthy." This was not completely accurate, but she returned to school and was asymptomatic.

On the other hand, some young people may have disorders in which violence appears that may have multidetermined, biological causes:

Bill was referred by the public school system for psychiatric assessment and treatment from a residential treatment center because for three years he had been violently disruptive and constantly fighting. He repeatedly absconded, taking other children with him. Bill was a liar and stole money from his parents and radios from automobiles. He also abused alcohol, marijuana, and LSD. He could not pay attention in the classroom.

A big 15-year-old, Bill was surly, resentful, and threatening, attempting a variety of naive manipulations of others. His mother was depressed and receiving antidepressants, and there were others in the family history who had had mood disorders.

Bill was thought to be suffering from both an affective disorder and a serious characterological distortion. After being "dried out" from marijuana, he was given lithium carbonate. This greatly reduced his intense nastiness which occurred along with a marked daily mood disturbance. He usually fluctuated between mild elation and sour misery many times a day. These mood shifts were not related to any apparent stress.

While he was taking the lithium, Bill began to show significant maturation in the classroom. He was now an amiable boy who did nothing. He never completely abandoned his marijuana abuse, smuggling it into the hospital whenever possible. He could not accept that the drug was of no value to him, which was thought to explain his lack of motivation in school.

Bill said that he did not wish to go to school and would leave at 16. Then, because of his relationship with his therapist, he began to try to do schoolwork, but he then complained that he could not concentrate. Pemoline in therapeutic doses along with the lithium carbonate led to a dramatic improvement in Bill's school performance.

When Bill returned to high school, however, the improvement lasted for only a few weeks, and he again began to miss classes, fail his schoolwork, and get into fights. He had returned to polydrug abuse. Although his lithium level remained therapeutic, it was clear that this biological intervention was no longer helpful.

Pemoline has been thought to be less effective than methylphenidate (Gilman, Goodman, and Gilman 1980), but this appears not to be true for postpubertal adolescents. However, pemoline does not seem useful in attention deficit disorders with associated learning difficulties, until the learning difficulties have been resolved, as it cannot change the defensive reactions of young people who have decided not to work because they cannot tolerate the feeling that they are unable to do so.

In a correctional center for boys, there was a statistically significant number who had been incarcerated for serious crimes (violence and repeated criminal behavior) and who showed serious neuropsychological dysfunction, as measured by the Luria-Nebraska battery (Brickman, McManus, Grapentine, and Nessi

1984). A heterogeneous group of children with various emotional and behavioral problems are likely to show one or more areas of specific learning disability (Silver 1980). Some will show hyperactivity or distractibility, and many will show developmentally retarded personality functioning and secondary emotional problems.

Differences in developmental history, neurological maturity, familial and social variables (Satterfield, Cantwell, and Satterfield 1979), and different neuroendocrinological syndromes may produce different subtypes of attention deficit disorder, but as we have seen, the psychosocial variables clearly influence how the syndromes will be presented.

AFFECTIVE VIOLENCE

Not all adolescents who show serious behavioral disturbances can yet be shown to have significant biological impairment. Most, however, are not adequately diagnosed. Multiple biological disturbances with cognitive incompetence, along with personality disorders, are hypothesized to be present in all disorders of behavior.

For adolescents, the term *affective violence* includes violent behavior that may occur as a symptom of unipolar and bipolar illness as well as that due to other causes such as schizophrenia, epilepsy, drug abuse, and attention deficit disorders with hyperactivity. Thus, affective violence has multidetermined biopsychosocial causes.

Affective violence can be a response to a real or threatened attack or to the infliction of a painful stimulus. It is almost certainly hormonally responsive. It appears to use pathways widely distributed in the spinal cord, hypothalamus, and ventral midbrain. The neurotransmitters involved almost certainly include norepinephrine (NE), dopamine (DA), indole 5 hydroxytriptamine (5HT serotonin), and aminoacetylcholine. These appear to be responsible for certain independent actions in the different types of violence (Reis 1974).

Schizophrenic syndromes, which may or may not include

violent behavior, are imperfectly defined; they encompass patients with different etiologies, divergent pathogenesis and they have various treatment requirements and heterogeneous outcomes (Carpenter 1976, p. 173). Both dopamine and monamine oxidase are also elevated in the brains of individuals who suffer from such syndromes (Melzer 1976). The best-known dopamine pathway is from the cell bodies in the substantia nigra to the corpus striatum, the caudate nucleus, and the putamen. This pathway is related to Parkinsonism, whose symptoms are alleviated by L-dopa, the precursor of dopamine. Dopamine is a precursor of norepinephrine, into which it is transformed by dopamine hydroxylase. In mice, the release of norepinephrine in the central nervous system facilitates and initiates affective violence. Drugs that are precursors of norepinephrine, including the amphetamines, also increase the frequency of fighting behavior in mice.

A similar relationship may well be present in humans, but the evidence for this is indirect. Although there is no clear demonstration that dopamine and norepinephrine are associated with affective violence, a number of amphetamine abusers show a relationship between their intake and homicidal behavior (Ellinwood 1971). Furthermore, an amphetamine psychosis is probably the best current drug model of schizophrenia (Snyder 1976).

Knowing that such disorders have biological origins therefore calls into question some well-known psychosocial treatment techniques. Violent adolescents in psychiatric hospitals may be isolated in "quiet rooms" or "time out rooms," sometimes restrained to bed frames by their ankles and wrists. Some professionals justify this as a therapeutic maneuver (Garrison 1984). The penal system also often uses isolation cells.

The use of apomorphine, an artificial precursor of dopamine, increases fighting behavior in rats. Rats' dopamine will increase when they are isolated and in pain, and afterwards they will exhibit fighting behavior. The biology of the rat's central nervous system is in many ways similar to a human's. One hypothesis is that isolation may encourage violent behavior in individuals whose behavior is related to an increase in central nervosa system dopamine. There are clearly some patients who become more disturbed with such techniques.

Apart from this issue, these methods of control, which almost always include violent responses from the staff, carry implicit messages about acceptable behavior. That is, the staff's response may contradict the explicit message that violence is unacceptable. Furthermore, such techniques do not respect the individuals' personal integrity.

Violence and sexual behavior have been shown to be related to each other, particularly in connection with maleness. In the pubertal male, plasma testosterone is inhibited by anxiety. In rhesus monkeys, the concentration of testosterone in the plasma is related to dominance. However, prepubertal children are also capable of affective violence, and there is no evidence that excessive amounts of androgen are related to their violence.

The biology of violence in humans is thus not yet clear, but there are obvious biochemical relationships among mania, schizophrenic syndromes, and affective violence, just as there are similarities in their clinical pictures. Because imipramine increases norepinephrine transmission, not surprisingly, those types of violent behavior that are not related to unipolar or bipolar illness may be encouraged by tricyclic antidepressants and monoamine oxidase inhibitors. This has been seen in experiments with mice. For adolescents who use violence to relieve the tension of a major depression, this violence may be relieved by tricyclic antidepressants. But if the violence is not so related, such drugs may make the individual more violent.

Lithium carbonate has an antiaggressive effect on humans, which is probably caused by an enhancement of 5HT serotonin. For violent children, lithium carbonate eliminates a substantial number of unprovoked violent outbursts (Siassi 1982).

Lithium was used first to control prisoners with a pattern of a rapid recurrent violent response to provocation. Lithium given to these individuals was said to improve their behavior (Sheard 1975), although there was no clear distinction made between predatory and affective violence. The predatory violence that affectively violent adolescents may use to gain a sense of mastery over their own violent outbursts is not directly affected by lithium carbonate.

The response to lithium carbonate in therapeutic doses is satisfactory in adolescents in whom affective violence is a symptom of bipolar and episodic dyscontrol syndromes. It is also valuable in those vulnerable individuals with marked daily affective lability. Some adolescents do not appear to respond until the serum lithium is at the top level of therapeutic safety, 1.8 mg per milliliter, although others respond at a level of 0.8 mg.

Affective violence is always pathological in humans. Psychologically, it manifests an acute or chronic ego failure and a third order of dyscontrol (Menninger, Mayman, and Pruyser 1956). The psychological goal of affective violence may be understood as an attempt to avert more catastrophic psychological disintegration. It indicates a weakening of personality functions and minimal success in the individual's efforts to control and restrain dangerous impulses. In subsequent externally directed attacks, it signifies a denial of reality.

AFFECTIVE VIOLENCE AND STRESS

An adolescent who uses affective violence may respond to perceived stress with destructive behavior that ultimately is beyond his or her control. He or she will repeat this rage response whenever the stress is experienced. Sometimes the stress may be quite subtle, for example, a stimulus that may cause an implicit conflict, like anxiety about invasion of the body space. Sometimes stress can occur with any type of frustration. If only psychosocial treatment is available, modifying the perception of the stress and changing somewhat the individual's personality may reduce the frequency of rage outbursts:

> A 17-year-old boy had been in treatment for three years for destructive outbursts of anger in which he would break furniture and slam his fist into walls. He understood a good deal about the situations that made him angry. In particular, the episodes occurred whenever he felt that his mother was being intrusive and that he was torn between a wish to be close to her and a wish to be distant from her. With psychotherapy alone, the frequency of the attacks had considerably diminished, but when they occurred, their quality was unchanged. But the attacks ceased altogether when lithium carbonate was given.

Apart from psychiatric treatment, the frequency of violent episodes may sometimes slow spontaneously. For example, developmental shift may occur with personality development so that a conflict then may no longer be so stressful. Or sometimes a violent act will change the perception of stress, or the familiarity associated with the repetition of a stressful situation may make it less tension producing.

EPISODIC DYSCONTROL SYNDROMES

Intermittent outbursts of affective violence may be grouped together as episodic dyscontrol syndromes, which are always related to a defined perception of stress. They have been traditionally associated with temporal lobe epilepsy. Such episodes may be accompanied by a disturbance of ongoing sensory experiences, that is, illusions with hallucinations. Auditory hallucinations, in particular, are often felt as painful. It has been argued that the violence associated with EEG changes in the brain's temporal lobe—focal spikes, sharp waves, or electrographic seizure activity over the area—is associated with the reaction to the individual's seizure by people in the environment (Daly 1975), who attempt to restrain him or her. The violence, however, may be preceded by a premonitory sense of mounting tension and a sense of helplessness and depression.

In another type of episodic dyscontrol, the violence may occur without apparent warning, and the stress is evident only retrospectively. The attack may last for minutes to hours. Observers may perceive the violent individual as being in touch with reality, but after the event, he or she may have little or no knowledge as to what happened and may be remorseful when told what has occurred. In this type of organic episode, biting, gouging, and spitting are common, and abuse may be verbal as well as physical (Mark and Ervin 1970). Such violence may be related to organic changes in the limbic system, especially in the posterior hypothalamus. Amygdalotomy is said to abolish the rage of such a dyscontrol syndrome (Hitchcock, Latinen, and Vernerk 1972).

In still another type of episodic dyscontrol, the stress is obvious to outside observers, but the individual's response is excessive. For those to whom such violence is acceptable and who dehumanize, this may lead to homicide.

Episodic dyscontrol may start as an uncontrollable experience that the individual cannot remember. As the episode progresses, however, the memory of it may return, and by the end of it, the individual may be aware that he or she has committed a wrongful act. The individual then tries to hide the episode. Because many persons accused of homicide or serious assault will deny that they had either control or recall of the episode, the situation may be both medically and legally confusing. However, the individual who suffers from true episodic dyscontrol is both dangerous and unpredictable and has no control over its occurrences. Realizing this makes the genuine sufferer extremely anxious, as he or she feels as intolerable the helplessness of being out of control.

Episodic dyscontrol may occur with no electroencephalographic evidence of brain dysfunction. It is then apparently similar to the affective violence seen in mammals, other than humans, following a clear threat. Sometimes in adolescents the relationship of these violent attacks to stress may not become apparent until after psychotherapeutic and diagnostic studies have been made:

Jane was a 14-year-old girl whose life behavior was dominated by hostile outbursts, consisting of verbal and physical threats and abuse and physical attacks on others. These episodes were intense and were incited by provocation that was always apparent after the event, for example, adults' failure to respond to her wishes with what she felt was appropriate speed. The attacks could occur at any time, and Jane was not aware of what precipitated them. Her behavior was apparently uncontrollable.

Jane would kick, bite, and scratch. She was a big girl and so this terrified her peers, who withdrew from her. Outpatient therapy and different kinds of special schooling over the years had no effect. The attacks had begun when Jane started school at the age of 5 or 6. Finally Jane was hospitalized. She denied the significance of the attacks and felt that hospitalization was unnecessary.

With ongoing therapeutic intervention, Jane gained some awareness of her problem and began to understand her rage attacks as well as the kinds of situations that precipitated them. She also began to recognize the relationship between her past experiences and the current situations that provoked her rage. With this increasing synthesis in her personality functioning, Jane began to seek out and attempt to utilize external controls. The frequency of attacks diminished somewhat, but when they did occur, they were violent as ever. The underlying identifiable common denominators usually were feelings of disappointment, perceptions of being unloved and insignificant, and a sense of being unjustly treated.

Jane explained that when she started to become angry, there always seemed to be a possibility that a chance intervention—which she found to be supportive—could assuage her anger. But more often than not, she would lose control. She then had some vague feelings that violence had occurred but could not give any details about it. In the hospital such episodes would require two to four staff members to contain her and "talk her down" so that she could regain control of herself. This process would usually last about an hour before she would recover. When she was finally treated with lithium carbonate, shortly after its introduction, the attacks ceased.

The episodic dyscontrol syndrome does not necessarily involve extreme physical violence. For instance, those to whom such behavior is unacceptable and who come from families that do not behave violently do not act in this way.

> Jennifer, age 16, had had a history of intermittent episodes of rage for as long as her parents could recall. By the time she reached puberty, she would become overwhelmed with fury. Sometimes she would try to cope with this by running away from home; on other occasions, she would get into verbal fights with her brother, age 10. She was finally hospitalized because she began to use marijuana in an attempt to control her rage. The family did not use physical violence to discipline their children. After Jennifer dried out, she would become angry whenever she felt rejected and would pour out a string of verbal abuse, however inappropriate the social situation. She did not show any physical violence.

At one time, Jennifer had been diagnosed as suffering from a juvenile manic-depressive illness. Her outbursts of rage did not seem to be cyclical, and she did not have any noticeable affective fluctuation during the day. Her outbursts would last about 20 to 30 minutes. Her tendency toward loud abuse seemed to be related to her family's style, as they were not a quiet, verbally controlled family. In addition to the dyscontrol episodes, Jennifer was also suffering from a hystrionic personality disorder.

Sometimes such episodes are associated with inner-directed as well as outer-directed violence:

> Katherine was a 13-year-old girl with a history of epilepsy, petit mal and grand mal, which had been present since the age of two. From the age of six, she had had episodes in which, from time to time, she would become enraged, kick adults in an uncontrolled manner, and destroy furniture. During these episodes, she would bang her head so violently against a wall that others became concerned that she would hurt herself. After puberty, these attacks had increased in frequency. The episodes were not related to epileptic seizures but were apparently related to situations in which she was frustrated and could not get her own way. They had not responded to a ketogenic diet, Dilantin, and Mysoline. These had helped control the epileptic seizures but in no way had controlled the outbursts of rage.

Katherine was admitted to an adolescent treatment center because she had made a homicidal attack on her sister, attacking her during a rage episode with a carving knife. The episodes ceased when she was given lithium, as well as her other medication. When somewhat impulsively, Katherine's mother stopped giving her the lithium, the episodes returned. Thus, when such violent dyscontrol appears in those who suffer from grand mal epilepsy, a recommendation for lithium carbonate should always be considered:

> Jack was a 13-year-old boy who suffered from grand mal epilepsy which was reasonably well controlled with phenobarbital and Dilantin (phenytoin). Following the attacks, Jack would bang his head against the floor or wall, and it became almost impossible to

control this behavior, which was clearly self-damaging. When lithium carbonate in a therapeutic dose was added to Jack's medications, the behavior ceased.

The frustration of some individuals who suffer from these syndromes is clear to observers and does not require subtle psychological techniques to be elicited:

Jonathan, adopted at one week of age, was now a 15-year-old boy who was always said to have done "just as he pleased." He was reported to have been a bully with other children and was often physically abusive to his younger siblings. The second child had been adopted when Jonathan was eighteen months old.

Jonathan had been in therapy since he was eight, and he had been treated for excessive rage outbursts. Thorough neurological investigation at that time revealed no evident organic etiology. His rage outbursts occurred whenever he was frustrated and his wishes were not granted. But they would not occur in the presence of individuals whom he perceived as being able to control him. When he reached adolescence, he used large quantities of marijuana to relieve his tension, and he also handled his rage by running away from home. On several occasions, he violently attacked his peers. His rage was always clearly related to frustration, for example, when he wanted $50 and was given only $45.

Jonathan's anger was clearly explosive, and although others could understand the cause of his irritation, the intensity of the affect was totally inappropriate.

Jonathan was hospitalized after a family fight over the use of the bathroom. He thought his mother was giving preference to his younger sister, and so he attempted to strangle his mother, because she jeered at him, "All right, kill me then." He did not remember the episode. One week after being admitted to the hospital, he asked a nurse for a light for his cigarette, and when asked to wait because she was busy, he became enraged and impulsively reached across and attempted to strangle her.

Cases similar to this have been reported in the literature, especially concerning issues of homicidal behavior (Satten, Menninger, Rosen, and Hayman 1960, Miller and Looney 1974).

Episodic dyscontrol may also be associated with suicidal behavior:

> Ed, age 14, was brought by his parents for treatment because in the middle of their criticism of his poor grades, he impulsively ran to the balcony of their 28th-floor apartment and began to climb over it in order to jump. Only quick action by his father saved his life; his father wrestled him to the ground and reported that his son had seemed "quite out of it for about two minutes." The boy had had a long history of what was perceived as excessive rage attacks when he was frustrated.

Unusually for a boy of his age, Ed wanted help. He did not feel, and never had felt, consciously suicidal, but he was aware that his lack of control during the attack made him both helpless and unable to predict a possible recurrence.

Despite the many clinical examples of episodic dyscontrol, some professionals still deny its existence as a separate syndrome, and it is not named in the third edition of the *Diagnostic and Statistical Manual of Disease* (1980). Nevertheless, episodic dyscontrol is frequently apparent to clinicians who see violent adolescents. It may occur as a concomitant of trauma, minimal brain dysfunction, tumor, infections, hypoglycemia, and cerebral vascular disease. It may also be present in association with some types of schizoaffective disorder, in paranoid schizophrenia, and following drug ingestion, particularly of amphetamines.

REFERENCES

Alessi, N., McManus, M., Grapentine, L., and Brickman, A. (1984). The characterizations of depressive disorders in serious juvenile offenders. *Journal of Affective Disorders* 6:9–17.

Amado, H., and Lustman, P. J. (1982). Attention deficit disorders persisting into adulthood. *Comprehensive Psychiatry* 12:200–214.

Brickman, A. S., McManus, M., Grapentine, L., and Alessi, N. (1984). Neuropsychological assessment of seriously delinquent adolescents. *Journal of the American Academy of Child Psychiatry* 23:453–458.

Brumback, R. A., and Stanton, R. D. (1983). Learning disability and childhood depression. *American Journal of Orthopsychiatry* 53:269–281.

Carpenter, W. T. (1976). Current diagnostic concepts in schizophrenia. *American Journal of Psychiatry* 133:172–175.

Carroll, B. J., Curtis, G. C., and Mendalo, J. (1976). Neuroendocrine regulation in depression. *Archives of General Psychiatry* 33:1039–1044.

Chapel, J. L., Robins, A. J., McGee, R. O., Williams, S. M., and Silva, P. A. (1982). A follow-up of inattentive and/or hyperactive children from birth to seven years of age. *Journal of Operational Psychiatry* 13:17–25.

Daly, D. D. (1975). Ictal clinical manifestations of complex partial seizures. *Advances in Neurology* 11:57–83.

Diagnostic and Statistical Manual of Mental Disorders III (1980). Washington, D.C.: American Psychiatric Association.

Ellinwood, E. H. (1971). Assault and homicide associated with amphetamine abuse. *American Journal of Psychiatry* 127:90–95.

Feinstein, S. C., Feldman-Rotman, S., and Woolsey, A. B. (1984). Diagnostic aspects of manic depressive illness in children and adolescents. In *Pathways of Human Development: Normal Growth in Infancy, Childhood and Adolescence*, ed. M. Shafii and S. Shafii, pp. 96–103. New York: Thieme-Stratton.

Frommer, E. A. (1968). Depressive illness in childhood. In *Recent Developments in Affective Disorders*, ed. Coppen, A. and Walk, A. *British Journal of Psychiatry* 2:117. (Special issue—Kent, England: Headley Bros.)

Garrison, W. T. (1984). Aggressive behavior, seclusion, and physical restraint in an important child population. *Journal of the American Academy of Child Psychiatry* 23:448–452.

Gershon, E. S., Hamovit, J., and Guroff, J. J. (1982). Family study of schizoaffective, bipolar I, bipolar II, unipolar and normal control probands. *Archives of General Psychiatry* 39:1157–1167.

Gilman, A. G., Goodman, L. S., and Gilman, A. (1980). *The Pharmacological Basis of Therapeutics*. 6th ed. New York: Macmillan.

Hitchcock, E., Latinen, L., and Vernerk, L. (1972). *Psychosurgery*. Springfield, IL: Thomas.

Hunt, R. D., Minderaa, R. B., and Cohen, D. J. (1985). Clonidine benefits children with attention deficit disorder. *Journal of the American Academy of Child Psychiatry* 24:617–629.

Klee, S. H., and Garfinkel, B. D. (1984). Identification of depression in children and adolescents: the role of the dexamethasone suppression test. *Journal of the American Academy of Child Psychiatry* 23:410–415.

Knesper, D., and Miller, D. (1976). Treatment plans for mental health care. *American Journal of Psychoanalysis* 133:45–50.

Lahey, B. B., Schaughency, B. S., Fraine, C. L., and Strauss, C. C. (1985). Teacher rating of attention problems in children experimentally classified as exhibiting attention deficit disorder with and without hyperactivity. *Journal of the American Academy of Child Psychiatry* 24:613–616.

Lever, R. J., and Lever, M. P. (1977). Response of adolescents with minimal brain dysfunction to methylphenidate. *Journal of Learning Disabilities* 10:223–228.

Mark, V. H., and Ervin, F. R. (1970). *Violence and the Prison.* New York: Harper & Row.

Masterson, J. (1970). Depression in adolescent character disorder. *Journal of the American Psychopathological Association* 59:242–257.

Melzer, H. (1976). Serum creatinine phosphokinase in schizophrenia. *American Journal of Psychiatry* 133:192–197.

Menkes, M., Dawe, J., and Menkes, J. A. (1967). A twenty-five year follow-up of the hyperkinetic child with minimal brain dysfunction. *Pediatric* 39:393–399.

Menninger, K. A., Mayman, M., and Pruyser, P. (1963). *The Vital Balance. The Life Process in Mental Health and Illness.* New York: Viking.

Miller, D., and Looney, J. (1974). The prediction of adolescent homicide. *American Journal of Psychoanalysis* 34:187–198.

Puig-Antich, J., Goetz, R., and Hanlon, C. (1982). Sleep architecture and rapid eye movement. Sleep measures in prepubertal children with major depression: controlled study. *Archives of General Psychiatry* 39:932–939.

Rosenbaum, A. H., and Rosenbaum, M. (1983). Toward a biochemical clarification of depressive disorders, vii: urinary free cortisol and urinary MHPG in depressions. *American Journal of Psychiatry* 140:314–318.

Safer, D., and Allen, R. P. (1976). *Hyperactive Children: Diagnosis and Management.* Baltimore: University Park Press.

Satten, J., Menninger, K. A., Rosen, I., and Hayman, M. (1960). Murder without apparent motive: a study in personality disintegration. *American Journal of Psychiatry* 117:48–53.

Satterfield, J. H., Cantwell, D. P., and Satterfield, B. T. (1979). Multimodality treatment: a one-year follow-up of hyperactive boys. *Archives of General Psychiatry* 36:965–974.

Schacheter, M. (1971). Étude des depressions et des episodes depressifs chez l'adolescent. *Acta Ped-Psychiatrica* 38:191–207.

Sheard, M. (1975). Lithium in the treatment of aggression. *Journal of Nervous and Mental Disease* 160:108–118.

Sheken, W. O., Dehermenjian, H., and Chapel, J. L. (1979). Urinary

MHPG excretion in minimal brain dysfunction and its modification by d-amphetamines. *American Journal of Psychiatry* 136:667–671.

Siassi, I. (1982). Lithium treatment of impulsive behavior in children. *Journal of Clinical Psychiatry* 43:482–484.

Silver, L. (1980). The minimal brain dysfunction syndrome. In *The Basic Handbook of Child Psychiatry*, ed. J. Noshpitz. New York: Basic Books.

Snyder, S. (1976). The dopamine hypothesis of schizophrenia: focus on the dopamine receptor. *American Journal of Psychiatry* 133:197–205.

Sprague, R. L. (1979). Hyperactivity in children. In *The Prevalence of Hyperactivity*, ed. R. L. Tortes. Baltimore: University Park Press.

Wender, O. (1971). *Minimal Brain Dysfunction in Children*. New York: Wiley Intersource.

Wing, J. K., and Bobbington, P. (1982). Epidemiology of depressive disorders in the community. *Journal of Affective Disorders* 4:331–345.

8

Adolescent Suicide

INCIDENCE OF SUICIDE

Many young people who are particularly vulnerable to stress depend for a sense of worth on being valued by others. The internal world of many such individuals often appears void of conscious fantasy. They may thus depend for psychological stimulation on external forces, mainly music, drugs of abuse, loveless sexuality, and antisocial behavior. In a society that implicitly (and sometimes explicitly) devalues living, a destructive attack on the self or an internalized image of others becomes common. Between 1970 and 1982, the annual suicide rate per 100,000 adolescents between the ages of 15 and 24 increased from 8.8 to 12.5 percent (National Center for Health Statistics 1984). During the same period, the overall white male suicide rate increased by 11 percent. In 1980, suicide was the second most common cause of death for white males aged 18 to 24 (*Vital Statistics in the United States 1960–1980*). Suicide is the third most common cause of death in adolescents aged 15 to 19, greater than leukemia and appendicitis (Weisman 1974). For those aged 10 to 14, suicide causes as many deaths as do appendicitis and diabetes. Excluding automobile accidents, each year there are probably 10,000 violent deaths among white males aged 15 to 19; the rate for black youth is higher.

There are probably five times as many suicides as are actually reported, and ten times as many suicidal attempts as completed acts. These conclusions reflect the judgment of thousands of local health authorities and coroners. Many adolescent suicides are thought wrongly by authorities to be accidental deaths, and so there are really no reliable statistics (Petzel and Cline 1978). Young people generally do not leave a farewell note, and accidental death is a more acceptable idea than suicide, both to the parents and society.

The incidence of suicide varies from country to country, except among adult women (Stack 1983), a variation not necessarily related to religion. Roman Catholic Austria, which is a highly industrialized country, has almost the highest suicide rate in Europe, but Roman Catholic Ireland, which has much less industry, has the lowest rate.

The differing incidence among social classes and national groups suggests that social determinants must be significant. Although there are no formal statistics relating suicide to social class, its increase among adolescents seems, clinically, to be among middle-class adolescents. It is improbable that the basic biological vulnerability changes from country to country, but it may well be that mood disorders are precipitated by differing kinds of social stress.

Young people who are apt to attempt suicide often have a long history of social and psychological problems, including a failure to make satisfactory interpersonal relationships and a pervasive feeling of emptiness. Antisocial behavior, particularly of a monosymptomatic type, and drug abuse, including drug dealing, are common in those who are suicidal.

SOCIAL DETERMINANTS

In the United States, minority groups such as blacks, Hispanics, and Jews are particularly vulnerable to suicide. These victims of society's prejudices may unconsciously identify with society's devaluation of them, and many incorporate a sense of inferiority into their self belief.

Recent changes in society have made adolescence into an excessively complicated developmental period. Because of divorce, there has been a massive disintegration of the nuclear family which makes it less effective as a buffer against stress. Family relationships, therefore, far from being developmentally supportive in the adolescent age period, can become a source of increasing tension. Parenting divorce is almost as common as marital divorce, which in any case almost invariably puts an end to shared parenting. This means little reality against which the adolescent can resolve conflicts about sexual and personal identity. There has also been a breakdown of the extended family, and consistent social ties have disintegrated because of vertical and horizontal social mobility. The absence of significant extraparental adults and the presence of tenuous peer relationships also make it more difficult for adolescents to model themselves on their parents. Finally, the easy availability of regressive drugs of abuse has made it difficult for many young people to become meaningfully involved with others and to learn to tolerate frustration which is essential to mature psychological development.

Again, the attitudes of the larger society appear contemptuous of human life. The almost casual discussion in the press about nuclear war, the attitude that megadeath is acceptable, and the possible destruction of all life on this planet are not lost on those adolescents interested in current events. The media constantly report homicides, suicides, and other violent deaths, thus creating a seeming casualness about the importance of being alive. These ideas of the implicit acceptability of violent death are easily internalized by the young.

Along with this is the powerful feeling that human beings are not responsible for one another. In the cities of the United States, adolescents are constantly exposed to the sight of old and young derelicts who are clearly treated as not human. The basically selfish attitude that pervades the social system enables adolescents not to consider the feelings of others.

It is thus easier for young people to argue that individuals are entitled to do whatever they wish with their lives, even if this includes disposing of oneself. They accept predatory violence as it pertains to themselves. Those who suffer from mood disorders that involve low self-esteem and psychological pain then become particularly vulnerable to suicide if they believe that it is acceptable behavior.

Society's abandonment of its mourning rituals means that ways to deal with the guilt commonly associated with the death of a parent, friend, or peer are not generally available. In particular, there are few techniques to help young people deal with the self-inflicted death of a peer:

> Because they could not marry, a boy of 16 and a girl of 15 threw themselves off the roof of a building in a suicide pact. The staff of an adolescent treatment center noticed that the next day, the children all were extremely quiet and depressed. When the unit psychiatrist made his morning rounds, he discovered that a 15-year-old female patient, a friend of the dead girl, had cut out and pinned to her dress the paragraph of the local newspaper that described the death.

This patient reported that six months before, the dead girl had attempted suicide and no one had done anything. In a long session, she talked of how bad she felt, how she might have done something but had not. Arrangements were made for her to call on the dead girls' parents and to go to the funeral. The staff talked with the children about death, the false belief of some suicidal young people that death was not permanent, and how guilty, helpless, and hurt suicide made others feel. About half of the children raised this issue in their psychotherapy in the following week.

This group's feelings were not unique to a patient population but belong with the experiences of all adolescents exposed to a suicide. Adolescents in high schools need an experience of group mourning in order to deal with their conflicts and distress regarding the suicide of a peer. The ritual of a general assembly in schools, which helps give a sense of corporate identity to the students, may have disappeared from the large public high school. Thus the opportunity for involved young people to deal communally with their feelings is not easily available. The immediate friends of the dead youngster should attend the funeral and the wake if there is one, and they should call on the parents of the suicide victim. Preferably, a member of the school staff should help all parents understand what the children are likely to be feeling. The children need an opportunity, in groups or as individuals, to discuss the death.

If these helping devices are not made available, one suicide in a high school is likely to be followed by a cluster of attempts, if not deaths, as adolescents are particularly susceptible to group contagion.

The parents of children who attempt suicide may unwittingly reinforce the likelihood of its recurrence. If an adolescent commits or attempts suicide, the responses aroused in the parents and in all those emotionally involved with the youngster include anxiety and guilt. If an attempt is not successful, the environmental response is similar to that seen in close relatives and professionals involved with a dying patient: the initial anxiety and guilt is often followed by denial, rage, depression, fear, and, finally, acceptance. Denial sometimes makes the parents seem unconsciously to wish to destroy their child—for example, when, because of intense denial, parents remove their youngster from treatment against medical advice.

A 17-year-old boy attempted suicide in the last weeks of high school, by overdosing with a mixture of alcohol and his mother's Valium pills. A diagnostic assessment in an adolescent treatment center showed that the patient was a self-centered, immature youth whose reaction to frustration was to avoid it or to become enraged. He had smoked marijuana regularly for three years. He boasted, in the hospital, that he could get his mother to take him out of this "rowdy place." His attitude was that suicide was a perfectly acceptable solution if he wished to use it.

The parents had scheduled a ten-day vacation, and the center made no effort to stop them, and so they left shortly after their son was admitted. On the parents' return to the city, they took their son home against medical advice. The risk of another attempt was explained to them in the patient's presence. The mother wept and said she could not believe her son "would do such a thing."

Later, it was thought that the center's not objecting to the parents' vacation had effectively reinforced their denial and had also ignored their unconscious rage. Sometimes denial prevents parents from using their common sense. The suicidal children of physicians not uncommonly use drug samples left lying around. It is not unusual for such adolescents to make more than one such suicidal attempt if the samples continue to be available. In nonphysician families, medications that have been prescribed for one family member may be used by a suicidal offspring and, if left in a medicine cabinet, may continue to be available.

Sometimes families collect guns or have available a loaded firearm in the house. It is not at all unusual for this to be the weapon that a suicidal adolescent uses. The implicit message of owning a gun is, at best, that one is entitled to kill others in order to protect oneself, an idea that is not too difficult to apply to oneself. At worst, the message is that lethal violence is of great interest to the parents, an interest that a self-destructive hostile adolescent may be only too willing to satisfy. When adolescents in treatment begin to say, prematurely, that they have recovered, their parents' earlier denial of their suicidal intent makes it more likely that they will believe their youngsters and remove them from treatment.

PSYCHOLOGICAL DETERMINANTS

At one time, it was possible to divide adolescence into three separate, if overlapping, stages (Miller 1974). Early adolescence, lasting approximately three years and including puberty, was associated, in all cultures, with a high degree of internal turbulence. Middle adolescence, lasting two to three years, was the time of consolidating one's identity and conforming to adult norms (Offer 1973). Late adolescence was the period of coping and the time during which adolescents tested, experimented with, and enlarged their new sense of self.

Nowadays, except for those young people who do not abuse drugs, who have an intact family, who have valued extrafamilial relationships, and who have a broad educational experience that includes cognitive, creative, and imaginative stimulation, adolescence in these terms hardly exists and, indeed, may no longer be the norm in some parts of Western society. Many young people have difficulty developing an autonomous sense of self and, instead, have become, in a psychological sense, other-directed adults (Riesman 1950). A feeling of one's own self-worth has come to depend almost entirely on the approval of others, often perceived as an amorphous "they," and autonomy is hardly present. Furthermore, the span of today's adolescence has become so elongated that many chronologically young adults are still as much prisoners of the present as early adolescents would be in a more traditional developmental mode. The blurring and lengthening of the phases of adolescent development means that many young people now inappropriately maintain an early adolescent attitude through their chronological early adulthood: a conviction of their own omnipotence and immortality. Besides conflicts about omnipotence and helplessness, these young adults have an inadequate sense of time and still seek inappropriate environmental mastery. It is also inconceivable that an individual can be emotionally aware of a suicidal intent without being able to understand affectively the concept of death.

It is astonishingly easy to feel worthless and devalued if one does not have a firm sense of self-love, which is different from self-preoccupation. Furthermore, the feeling of omnipotence without a firm sense of time means that some adolescents find it difficult, if not impossible, to envisage death as a permanent state. So they may attempt suicide in order to discover what the experience is like. They may want to seek the experience of death without dying, and they also may wish to frighten others. Paradoxically, a failed attempt in such young people may reinforce their sense of omnipotence and their conviction of the ease of the act and of the probability of their survival.

A genuine suicidal intention requires an accurate concept of death. A concrete thinker perceives death as a deliberate going away, and even this awareness may depend on having lost an important object, person, or thing.

Adolescents who cannot think abstractly are not really able to understand the permanence of death; they see everything in the present and do not understand the past or the future. Early and middle adolescents often are not able to mourn an irrevocable loss. They thus deny the concept of death, and so when a loved individual does die, adolescents may feel that the person they have lost is still alive inside themselves, like an internal ghost. Indeed, they may use these ghosts to soothe themselves; for example, they may talk to a loved internal figure as a child might talk to a teddy bear. When asked, many young people report that they frequently think of dead friends, parents, and grandparents, and on further inquiry, many will say that they think of such loved people especially when they are under stress:

> A 14-year-old girl had lost her loved grandmother when she was eight. She often thought of her, particularly when something bothered her. Finally, when she was fourteen, her parents divorced, and she then attempted suicide by shooting herself. She said, "It was so horrible at home that I decided I wanted to be with grandmother; I thought I would join her."

To this child, her relative was both dead and alive; thus, her own death would allow her to be with someone who loved her.

When adolescents deal with loss by internalizing the image of the dead loved one, this can also create realistic emotional deprivation. Because they are involved with an intrapsychic ghost, they may emotionally withdraw from real people and become more isolated, deprived, and empty. Their experience of stress is then even more likely to create a wish to join the lost loved one.

If adolescents were not able during infancy to develop a sense of trust, they are less likely to be able to develop a capacity to handle mixed feelings, or ambivalence, in an age-appropriate way. And if they cannot develop ambivalence without constant external support, they are likely to remain dependent on an archaic superego. Thus they constantly need to seek from external sources freedom from unbearable guilt (Freud 1917, Fenichel 1954, Menninger 1931). If these sources are mainly in fantasy and are not real, it requires very little environmental stress for such individuals to become overwhelmed with despair. If, for example, the mother is either loved or hated—usually before ambivalence becomes possible—hatred is felt as unbearable. This tension is resolved by becoming symbiotic with mother. This occurs not out of love but out of hatred, the fusion is with the attacking object (Zilborg 1936). Finally, adolescents with no sure sense of themselves are extraordinarily vulnerable to separation (Boyer and Giovacchini 1967), and so suicide may be a defense against this experience. Furthermore, if to relieve internal tension they become chronic users of marijuana, the depression produced by this drug may make them even more vulnerable.

The thought of suicide, however, may protect the individual from actually carrying it out:

A 16-year-old girl had a two-year history of uncontrollable intrusive thoughts, which were either sexual or self-destructive. They included visual hallucinations of throwing herself out the window. Throughout this time, however, she felt sure that she would not actually kill herself.

Outpatient psychotherapy having failed, she was referred to an adolescent treatment center. She was placed in their special care unit and diagnosed as suffering from a schizophrenic reaction. She was given haloperidol, 2 mg twice a day. The intrusive thoughts disappeared, but for the following weeks she became acutely suicidal.

Alternately, the thought of suicide may precede the act:

A 16-year-old boy was admitted to an adolescent treatment center with a history of repeated self-mutilation in which he had attempted to stab himself. Under stress, he became acutely delusional and heard a voice telling him to kill himself. This was a precursor to the suicidal behavior. He also used threats of killing himself as a way to get his parents to grant his impossible wishes to get married.

Adequate medication with phenothiazines ended these hallucinatory episodes, but it did not stop his threats of self-mutilation.

If the individual accepts the idea of suicide or self-mutilation, then a relatively transient wish to damage or destroy the self, which may occur in an acute experience of helplessness and hopelessness, may be carried out. To some extent, all suicidal adolescents dehumanize themselves. Those who make repeated attempts often discover how easy self-destruction seems to be, and this reinforces their contempt for their own bodies and personalities. Thus, the self-dehumanization becomes greater. In this respect, suicidal and homicidal behavior are similar. For example, the serial killer's behavior may be reinforced by its success, and the same may be true of those who attempt suicide.

BIOLOGICAL DETERMINANTS

When individuals under stress are genetically vulnerable to depression (Miller 1978), they may avoid intrapsychic pain by seeking and conforming to the environment's consistency. If a well-adjusted nuclear family has issued consistent explicit and implicit messages, such young people may appear quite healthy. The unavoidable stress is the ultimate societal psychosocial demand for autonomy and separation, which appears toward the end of high school. Sometimes these young people enter college and commit suicide during their first year. Others may last until graduation.

In addition to their psychological immaturity, some adolescents and young adults who abuse drugs and alcohol may also have a genetic neuroendocrine vulnerability. Thus they may impulsively commit suicide when they are intoxicated, particularly if their genetic sensitivity has not been recognized:

> An 18-year-old boy killed himself while he was intoxicated. This was his third attempt, and on this occasion he succeeded. He had been hospitalized in the early 1970s at the age of 16, with a history of marijuana and alcohol abuse for three years. Psychosocial treatment was the only modality used. At that time, the relationship between the boy's alcohol abuse and suicidal behavior was thought to be only a psychological problem. The alcohol was regarded only as inhibiting his controls. The possibility that a genetic vulnerability was being stimulated by alcohol ingestion was not seriously considered at that time.

It is, of course, impossible to know whether the sophisticated use of antidepressants would have made a difference for this patient, but a retrospective look at the case material indicated that it might have. The intoxicated suicidal adolescent may be destroying a bad introject, because alcohol or drugs may weaken superego controls. On the other hand, alcohol or drugs may affect the brain biochemistry of the genetically vulnerable.

Unipolar and bipolar illnesses are still commonly misdiagnosed in children and adolescents because of their atypical presentation. The same is true for schizophrenia. Adolescents who suffer from the episodic dyscontrol syndromes are vulnerable to suicide because of the helplessness that the syndrome engenders. So, adolescents who suffer from epilepsy may be vulnerable to suicide (Gunn 1973), particularly those who suffer from temporal lobe epilepsy. Those who do not develop a capacity for predatory violence as a defense against affective rage are also more likely to be suicidal risks.

All adolescents' depression is associated with behavioral disorders (Masterson 1970). These may include passive compliance or focal anger directed toward the possessions of individuals who come to represent an externalization of the image of unloving parents. Mood disorders, pregnancy, menstruation, and physical illness all are significant to the etiology of suicidal behavior.

TYPES OF SUICIDAL BEHAVIOR

Intentional Suicide

Suicidal behavior can be classified in a variety of ways which, when the attempt fails, are guidelines to the appropriate intervention.

Intentional suicide must be acceptable to those individuals who commit it. They must consciously believe that they are entitled to destroy their own body if they so wish; implicit in this attitude is that they are not responsible for their own or others' well-being. Although such suicidal individuals do commit a violent act against a person, the self, they do not necessarily accept the destruction of others.

Intentional suicidal behavior is often preceded by warnings of the self-destructive wish. These may appear deliberate to others, although that may not be the adolescent's conscious intention. Often, the warnings are subtle and commonly seem to take place only when the idea of suicide is or has recently been in the youngster's mind. For example:

> A 16-year-old girl, who had been hospitalized for a mood disorder associated with many self-mutilating gestures, said to a group of her friends, as she pointed to a 12-story building, "I will jump off the roof of that building one day." When she was seen, as an emergency, by her psychiatrist, she said, "I say things like that when I feel wild; I was only joking." But on further inquiry, she recalled that earlier in the day she had felt miserable and uncared for, and she had thought that if she were dead, people would be sorry.

If such warnings are ignored, this may well reinforce the likelihood of the act's occurring. Thus, all suicidal threats should be taken seriously, and skilled intervention should be sought. All suicide attempts are an indication for hospitalization (Hawton 1982). The transient expression of a feeling such as "I wish I were dead" is not the same as "I'm going to kill myself."

The warning of an intent to commit suicide may be deliberate and have the conscious goal of trying to find out whether anyone cares; it may also be manipulative so as to try to force others to meet the adolescent's wishes. Often those who have failed at suicide will report after the event that they told a friend or parent who did not attempt to stop them ". . . so they didn't mind if I did it." Sometimes, the would-be suicide's attempt to find out whether life will be preserved is much less conscious, as when ignored efforts at communication reinforce the likelihood of the act's occurring. The warning of a suicide intent may also be conveyed casually:

> A 17-year-old boy committed suicide in a hospital chapel, by placing a plastic bag over his face. He had been a patient on an adolescent medical ward and was about to be discharged to outpatient psychiatric care. It had been concluded that his physical symptoms did not have an organic basis. He had appeared comfortable and accepting of this idea; thus his death was then even more shocking.

One reaction to such a death by the involved survivors, particularly those in the helping professions, is to wonder whether the suicide could have been avoided. Nowhere is this more evident than in a hospital when a patient commits suicide:

> The only possible indication of intent took place on the previous day. He was out for a walk with a young female patient, and in the midst of a rather long philosophical discussion, he mentioned, apparently in passing, that individuals should have control of their own destinies, including their own lives.

The intentional suicide that is associated with a cognitive conscious decision to kill the self is one type of predatory violence (Grey 1972) directed against the self rather than others. There need not necessarily be evidence that the aggression is directed against a bad introject (Zilborg 1937), although some young people will say that they see themselves as being so like a certain person whom they consider bad, that they are not entitled to live.

The suicidal decision may be kept secret by an individual who has shown no previous evidence of intent. This may happen when an apparently well adjusted adolescent, who never gave trouble to anyone—not parents, teachers, or peers—at the age of 17 or so, apparently inexplicably, commits suicide. Such young people often do not have an apparent history of psychiatric illness.

Two types of individuals are involved in such cases. Some, retrospectively, have been withdrawn, isolated people who have not made a significant emotional investment outside themselves; they are individuals with acquaintances but no true friends. Because conformity is highly valued in the United States, particularly in its educational system, these youngsters are not perceived as having problems. But when seen after a failed attempt, these adolescents are diagnosed as highly schizoid individuals. Sometimes their suicidal attempt is either a despairing rejection of profound feelings of emptiness; sometimes they may be overtly schizophrenic and the attempt represents their obedience to delusional ideas. Some such individuals have been severely depressed for years because of either emotional deprivation or neuroendocrine vulnerability. Some have been apparently symptom free and so fall into the category of being genetically vulnerable and conforming to the life-style of a healthy family.

In order to understand these adolescents, one should study those who have failed in their suicidal attempt. Many who attempt suicide in the last year of high school seem highly vulnerable to an inability to deal with emotional separation. At this point they become acutely depressed and attempt suicide.

Individuals who are intentionally suicidal (or homicidal) may sometimes be trying to destroy a bad self. In suicide, this can be understood in the following way: the development of a sense of self requires the capacity to introject and then incorporate the perceived image of emotionally significant individuals and the interaction with them (Miller 1974). A "bad" introject develops when adolescents perceive themselves as being treated with overt cruelty by their parents or the environment in which they are placed. One way that children and adolescents deal with this stress is to identify with the behavior either overtly or covertly (Miller and Looney 1976). When they become homicidal, such adolescents may project the bad internalized self onto dehumanized others. When they become suicidal, although they may make such a projection, they also internalize the bad object. In this process they destroy their own sense of being alive, and in destroying the bad internal self, they then destroy themselves. Sometimes the adolescent kills the individual onto whom he or she projects this badness and then kills himself or herself. In this way, both the introject and the projection are destroyed.

Adolescents may also intentionally attempt to commit suicide when they have experienced acute emotional deprivation. If, as is usual, the unloving individuals are the parents, the child assumes, considering the parents to be all-powerful, that their behavior is justified—that they have withdrawn their love because the child is so bad. As one 16-year-old boy, who had been brutally beaten by his father, confessed:

> "I am a very bad person. My father was right to strap me; I deserved it."

On the other hand, such children may be furious with the depriving figures who, they then feel, deserve to be punished.

This may be associated with the wish to kill oneself in order to take revenge on them. Self-destruction is the ultimate punishment that adolescents can inflict on others, even if they know that such individuals care for them but yet feel that they do not.

Sometimes adolescents may deliberately kill themselves in a narcissistic rage. The idea of hurting others is irrelevant to them, for at an emotional level, others do not exist. This rage is associated with the acute feeling that one is not receiving what one deserves:

> An adolescent girl of 13 in a psychiatric hospital was enraged with her physician because he would not give her a weekend pass. But this was not communicated to the unit staff, who later took her out for a walk. Suddenly she attempted to dash in front of an automobile and was stopped only because the staff member was quick enough. The girl explained, "I was just mad, and so that seemed the best way out."

Another type of intentional adolescent suicide is associated with public self-immolation. Altruism and self-sacrifice are common in many adolescents. At one level these may be understood as an ascetic psychological defense against infantile greed and dependence. But in some highly indulged or deprived adolescents who are also excessively greedy, this is a tenuous reaction formation. Such individuals are particularly vulnerable to group contagion.

Chronic contagious group pressure for self-destruction is transmitted by the media. Reports in the late 1960s of monks in Saigon burning themselves to death produced imitators in Prague and then in the West. Such a suicide appears designed to save the world, to convey to the world an awareness of its deficiencies, or to protest against its perceived badness. Sometimes it is an isolated act, and the motive is unclear. Such self-immolation is acutely distressing to the relatives of these adolescents, as often the act is unexpected. Self-immolation may occur with individuals or with very small groups of two to three people.

Individuals who intentionally try to commit suicide may suffer from neuroendocrine vulnerability, schizophrenia, unipolar and bipolar illness, or a serious character disturbance. These character disturbances include borderline syndromes and pathological primary narcissism. Those who suffer from chronic disabling and often painful physical illnesses also may attempt suicide. Such a suicide may be attributed to an unwillingness to burden others and a refusal to tolerate the slow destruction of one's sense of self. This is commonly seen in accident victims:

> A paraplegic 17-year-old boy, the victim of a gunshot wound sustained in a gang fight, was in a psychiatric unit for severe depression. When he was refused permission to leave, he set fire to the blankets on the gurney to which he was strapped, having obtained matches from his mother, who had just visited him.

The intentional suicidal act generally requires an identification with a societal attitude that devalues the significance of human life. This may exist along with either an altruistic or a revenge leitmotiv, which, paradoxically, may also exist together. Furthermore, the presence of biological vulnerability does not lessen the significance of the psychosocial etiology; that is, not all those who experience mood disorders destroy themselves, however great their psychological pain.

Group Suicide

Group suicide and homicide have a long history, particularly among persecuted minority groups, such as the Israelites of Masada and the Jews of York in the thirteenth century. More recently, the followers of the Reverend Jim Jones in Guyana committed mass suicide and homicide. This group's perception of external hostility was seen by the outside world as unjustified, but apparently the group disagreed. Such group destruction can be understood by considering the psychology of those individuals who join cults. Adolescents who have no real sense of an autonomous self can gain other-directed support by joining cults and are thus particularly vulnerable to their techniques of indoctrination. If a charismatic cult leader can convince a group in acute stress that self-destruction is better than being destroyed from the outside, group suicide (and intragroup homicide) will become a preferred solution.

The psychosocial causes of mass suicide are similar to those of mass homicide (Gault 1971), and its determinants appear to be as follows:

1. Self-destruction is an acceptable concept.
2. The enemy is everywhere.
3. The responsibility for the act is shared.
4. The pressure to act out self-destructively is reinforced by a charismatic leader who shares the group's conflicts.
5. The leader reinforces in the group the concept that life is irrelevant, and dehumanization of the self is then reinforced as the group feels dehumanized by others.

The similarity of mass suicidal behavior to the group slaughter of others is remarkable.

Marginally Intentional Suicide

Marginally intentional suicide is usually a chronic behavior and is typically seen in those individuals who severely neglect themselves, for example, those who are suffering from anorexia nervosa or those who are accident prone. Adolescents who are repeatedly involved in one-car accidents, motorcyclists who do not use protective clothing, and adolescents who drive when intoxicated on alcohol, marijuana, or other drugs all are engaged in marginally intentional suicidal behavior.

Drug and alcohol abusers are particularly vulnerable to marginally intentional suicide. This group includes the middle-class youth who drives when intoxicated and the ghetto youngster, normally streetwise, who "deliberately" exposes himself on the turf of hostile gangs. The chronic heroin abuser, who knows that the heroin's cut may vary yet continues to use it, is also marginally suicidal. These adolescents seem to be engaging in a type of Russian roulette; their attitude seems to be that if the gun's chamber is loaded, then they deserve to die. Conversely, such behavior is also death defying. Thus it is not then surprising that on clinical examination, these individuals often appear excessively omnipotent and excessively self-referent and that repeated attempts reinforce their own sense of omnipotence (Peterson, Awad, and Kendler 1973). They seek a "supermastery" to deal with their own helplessness, as they often suffer consciously from a pervasive sense of low self-esteem. Their death-defying behavior seems designed to make them feel better about themselves.

The "Russian roulette" concept may also be externalized, in that marginally intentional suicidal behavior may be directed toward deciding how valuable others perceive the individual to be. Such persons may attempt suicide apparently with the belief that if they are found, they should be saved but that if they are not, then their death is justified. For example, they may take a lethal dose of sedatives just before their parents are due to return home. Sometimes the omnipotence is striking:

> A 16-year-old boy had a two-and-a-half-year history of undiagnosed major depression. He had twice been in psychotherapy, but to no avail. At the beginning of the school vacation when no one was home, the boy went into the garage and turned on the automobile's engine. His attitude was that if he could talk himself out of suicide before he became unconscious, he would turn off the engine, but that if he became insensible first, then so be it. He did not die, nor did he tell his parents.

Sometimes such adolescents use telephone help services, but when having threatened self-destruction, they refuse to give their names or location; they may be waiting to see whether they will be rejected. If the person at the service should hang up, this will confirm their belief that no one cares.

Accidental Suicide

It is quite common for adolescents to attempt suicide and then change their mind and seek assistance. But sometimes, the assistance does not arrive in time, and they die "accidentally." This type of behavior should not be dismissed as "attention getting";

rather, self-destruction as a plea for help represents profound despair about oneself and a disregard for the integrity of one's own body. Self-mutilation is a common technique. Fortunately, wrist and arm cutting rarely hits arteries. More often, tendons and nerves are severed, and the risk is of some degree of crippling.

Some social systems reinforce adolescents' self-mutilating behavior. For example, bodily mutilation in psychiatric hospitals and correctional settings is always an institutional symptom. Self-mutilation may also be highly eroticized. It, too, is apparently designed to project helplessness and rage onto the environment and at the same time force the environment to return negative attention. Typical behavior includes making suicidal threats; cutting one's wrists, arms, abdomen, or thighs; or putting one's hands through glass.

Although this behavior is rarely suicidal, it may lead to accidental suicide. Vulnerable individuals who are able to continue this type of behavior gain environmental permission; that is, if such behavior is not stopped, such individuals may believe that it is acceptable. Intentional suicide may also follow because the adolescent has concluded that the outside world is uncaring. In a statistically significant number of cases, suicidal gestures are followed by suicide (Patel 1974).

Some adolescents, particularly those who are drug toxic or schizophrenic, have no conscious intention to commit suicide. They appear to do so because of a wish to reconcile or fuse the disintegrated feeling of being aware of different parts of the self, an experience that is sometimes a consequence of psychosis. This has been seen in twin studies (Resnick 1972), but it can also occur in those schizophrenic adolescents who perceive themselves as having living introjects. They perceive others as occupying their personalities or bodies, often symbolized by a feeling of being possessed by the devil. Some deaths also can be associated with a symbolic self-castration with a desire to engage in a fantasized experience (Miller 1984). For example, adolescents who tie themselves up and put ropes around their necks in order to reinforce masturbatory excitement may accidentally hang themselves.

ACCIDENTAL DEATH

Accidental death may sometimes be thought to be accidental suicide, usually in regard to those adolescent males who are unaware of their own physical limitations. Most urban adolescents are no longer tested against natural forces; there is no bodily aging in adolescence; and there is also very little emotional awareness of physical fragility. In the United States, contact sports that enhance an awareness of physical vulnerability are the preserve of the few. A false sense of personal power is given to adolescents who are allowed to drive automobiles at the age of sixteen, when they may find it difficult to place the boundaries of the automobile in space. At this age many boys are still growing and have not yet developed a final sense of their own body image. In addition, they still have poor reality testing regarding their own relative impotence and are thus highly vulnerable.

Many athletic boys, brought up in cities and adequately protected by their parents, have little or no actual awareness of their own physical limitations. They have been well protected from natural hazards and so may have no sense of necessary physical constraints. Death due to poor judgment of their physical ability is particularly likely to occur in adolescents who are skating, swimming, or sailing. Such young people are like small boys climbing too-large trees. Expert mountain climbers who are killed when climbing alone are marginally intentional, not accidental, suicides. Often such marginally intentional suicides are thought to be accidental deaths; but mountaineers well know that they should not climb alone.

EVALUATING SUICIDAL POTENTIAL
IN CLINICAL PRACTICE

The initial interview with adolescents helps indicate the likelihood of self-destructive behavior. Even if the adolescent has made a positively felt relationship with the interviewer, he or she is unlikely to bring up any ideas of suicide, unless there is acute distress. Even then, the subject may appear only if the interviewer asks about thoughts of, or previous attempts at, killing oneself.

In evaluating the likelihood of suicide, the interviewer should assess the presence of the social, biological, and psychological determinants of such behavior and gauge the acceptability to the adolescent of self-destruction.

Treatability is assessed primarily on the basis of the adolescent's capacity to make a meaningful emotional relationship with a therapist so that the problem behavior can be contained, the type of frustration that produces the problem behavior, and its severity. With behavior that is dangerous to the self or others, there is no room for symptomatic maneuverability; the behavior must be stopped.

Deciding where treatment should take place depends on whether the adolescent is able to commit himself or herself to the point that he or she will not attempt suicide without giving the therapist a chance to intervene. A clinician cannot function with the persistent anxiety that a boy or girl in treatment is likely to attempt suicide. If such an assurance cannot be obtained, inpatient treatment is always necessary. Adolescents are almost always honest about this. If they are unable to agree not to kill themselves without first contacting the therapist and offering a chance for appropriate intervention, they will make this clear.

A history of parental suicide makes adolescents particularly vulnerable (Maxmen and Tucker 1973). The explicit and implicit message of this act is that such behavior is acceptable. Mourning in children and adolescents for lost parents is almost always incomplete, but in parental suicide it seems almost impossible. The child who loses a parent of the same sex may have to attempt to replace that parent with the one who survives, but the preoccupation of this parent with the loss makes him or her even less emotionally available. After parental suicide, if the remaining parent remarries, it represents another loss to the child. The surviving parent has then made what the child may feel to be a further abandonment. A suicidal attempt often reveals a history of significantly perceived parental rejection.

Besides parental suicide, other types of parental conflict are common in the etiology of adolescent suicide. Parents may be significantly overinvolved with their youngster and may be highly intrusive; they may depersonalize their child by being overpermissive or overrestrictive; or they may angrily wish their child dead.

Patients who think seriously of suicide generally have a plan, but there is no evidence that direct questioning about this puts it into operation. It is important to check whether such patients have the means to kill themselves. If they are known to have these and they are not withdrawn, this will put the clinician in a position of colluding with the patient's intention.

A common pervasive feeling before attempting suicide is that of extreme helplessness and a frantic need to act. It appears to the patient that the only effective way of changing the situation is self-destruction. Sometimes this helplessness is related to an overpowering feeling of rage.

Fifteen-year-old Karen had been in therapy twice a week because she "could not get along" with her parents. She never told her therapist of her frequent thoughts of suicide. She was rejected by her boyfriend because he was told that she was promiscuous. In a fit of despair and rage, she impulsively swallowed 100 acetaminophen tablets. She was near death in intensive care for the next two days.

Many patients faced with overwhelming despair may repeatedly attempt suicide and ultimately they may be successful.

In conclusion, then, the diagnostic clues to potentially suicidal behavior are as follows:

1. Upon inquiry, the patient will reveal that he or she has thought of suicide and generally accepts the concept of killing oneself. The reasons for abstaining from suicidal attempts are unsatisfactory: "I am afraid I will fail" or "I don't want to damage myself." Either a neuroendocrine or a deprivation depression is present. The act is associated with guilt, anger, and thoughts of revenge; depression may be felt as an emptiness.

2. There is a history of previous attempts, often associated with episodic dyscontrol as a stress response.

3. There may be a history of previous treatment and its failure. Sometimes the failed treatment may be of a physical illness; thus, adolescents who are fearful of a recurrence of a serious illness, such as carcinoma, may attempt suicide. For example, a 15-year-old boy thought he had a secondary malignancy of a bone carcinoma in his arm and attempted to shoot himself. Suicide is also a serious risk for adolescents in dialysis, and often they may refuse further treatment in order to accomplish this goal.

4. There may be unresolved problems with separation and bereavement. Death causes guilt in surviving children. Those who feel acutely guilty may attempt to kill themselves, which is also related to the fantasy wish of joining the loved one. Particularly at risk are the offspring of parents who committed suicide themselves. It is as though the suicide has sent a powerful message as to the acceptability of this act.

5. The patient may tell relatives that he or she is thinking of suicide although the patient will not indicate this to the physician. If this is not reported, the relatives' inaction will be taken as permission.

6. There may be a history of repeated accidents, especially in automobiles.

7. The basic personality structure prior to the attack is significant. Many who previously had a highly organized compulsive personality, when faced with overwhelming despair, are likely to attempt to kill themselves.

TREATING SUICIDAL PATIENTS

If a suicidal crisis is a reaction to an overwhelming stress, emergency protection will be needed. If divorce or death is the precipitant, besides its effect on the adolescent, the surrounding social system will become less supportive.

Sometimes a suicidal crisis or the possibility of violence represents an internal decompensation, the equivalent of a fourth-order reaction (Menninger 1931). The reality stress may not then be so apparent to others, as it may be more related to the patient's internal perception.

Institutional care, in a setting in which both protection and an etiological diagnosis can be offered, becomes necessary when control in an outpatient setting is impossible. This will partly depend on the strength of the relationship that is made with a potential therapist and whether continuity of care can be offered. A further issue is whether others in the patient's world are willing and able to offer the necessary support and assistance. The likelihood of a suicidal attempt depends not just on the patient's psychobiological state but also on the tensions in the social environment, that is, whether or not it implicitly permits violent or suicidal behavior.

Some adolescents have no emotionally significant people in their lives. When such individuals are also drug dealers, inevitably as exploiters, they alienate others. When the adolescent perceives family and friends as hostile and disinterested, individual survival then may seem irrelevant. Such persons may become highly suicidal, and even in a psychiatric hospital, they remain acute suicidal risks. When such adolescents are in the hospital, their parents should be advised of the appropriate suicidal precautions and should be informed that it is impossible to guarantee their child's survival; absolute protection involves such a high degree of external control that this would make therapy impossible. This issue of informed consent is crucial, especially as it is effectively not possible to protect a patient who is determined to kill himself or herself.

When suicidal precautions in a hospital setting respect the patient's dignity, they reduce the likelihood of self-destructive acts. Unfortunately, some hospitals' suicidal precautions seem to strip the patient of every modicum of self-worth. If every object of value is removed from the patient, this implicitly will devalue him or her as a person. Furthermore, some suicidal precautions imply that there is an expectation that the patient will attempt self-destruction, and this only reinforces the likelihood of the act.

An essential attitude by the therapeutic staff who look after potentially suicidal individuals is an expectation that they will survive, that life is worth living, and that human dignity will be respected. Suicidal precautions in programs that provide adequate specific and nonspecific care need not be as stringent as those in units that are emotionally depriving; if self-destruction and violence are neither expected nor condoned, their appearance is considerably less likely. Even the hospital's design is relevant: some buildings make it easy for a patient to hurt himself or herself, but others offer both safety and comfort. With adequate numbers of well-trained staff, suicide in hospitals should be extremely rare.

If a suicidal individual is also suffering from mood disorders, medication will be necessary, although most antidepressant drugs will not have an immediate effect. There are a number of problems. When the patient is living at home, it may be infantilizing to have the parents give the medication to the youngster; but on the other hand, if the youngster gives himself or herself the medication, it may be used to attempt suicide. There is also the problem that for those who abuse drugs, especially alcohol and marijuana, the medication may not work. If the therapeutic level of a drug fluctuates, there is always the possibility that when it does begin to take effect, the patient will become more actively self-destructive. This is a problem similar to that when medication is started. The parents should be told about these problems as well as about the possible side effects of treatment. The parents should also be warned that as with adults, the period of initial recovery from depression is when the patient is most vulnerable.

When their personality controls disintegrate, adolescents' behavior may be greatly influenced by their phenomenological experience. In some psychiatric settings, for example, seriously disturbed adolescents very rarely mutilate themselves, but in others, this behavior is an epidemic problem:

> In a treatment center that had been in existence for five years, in which cutting had never previously occurred, a boy was admitted who used this behavior apparently to prove to other youngsters

how "macho" he was. In the center, all the children had comfortable rooms in which there were many objects that they could use to mutilate themselves.

When this boy cut himself, the staff bandaged his arms, removed the offending instrument, and dealt with the problem in the boy's individual treatment. But the behavior rapidly spread through the unit, among both boys and girls. Within weeks, about one-third of the patients had cut themselves.

This system's behavioral controls were based on a number of assumptions. The first was that disturbed adolescents would conform to consistent explicit and implicit social demands and that the more disturbed the youngster was, the more likely it was that he or she would conform. In other words, disturbed youths were particularly susceptible to what was "done" and "not done" in social organizations. This program therefore had had consistently few contradictory behavioral implications. The fact that violent behavior directed toward the self continued in this way led us to believe that in some subtle way we had to have colluded with the patients:

Apologizing for failing to look after them properly, the program chief then told the children in a group meeting that when the cutting occurred, it would mean that everything potentially or actually sharp would be removed from the patient's immediate environment until the wounds healed. This meant that a youngster could have a stereo receiver but no records, a soft crayon but no pencil, and could go to a ball game but had to eat under supervision using a paper plate and a nonbreakable plastic spoon.

With this consistency of approach, the self-mutilation ceased and did not reappear for another 18 months. When it did, what had become known as "sharp precautions" were reinstated, and it then disappeared again. There was no discussion of self-mutilation during the year and a half. It was as if the symptom did not exist, even though there were many adolescents in the program who might have been vulnerable to this type of behavior.

The mortality rate for all age groups has significantly declined since 1950, except the death rate for violent death: the suicide rate for those aged 15 to 24 years has steadily increased since 1976. In 1979, violent death accounted for 75 percent of all adolescent deaths: the most common cause of death among young whites was automobile accidents; among young blacks it was homicide. Proper diagnosis and treatment of those at risk are essential, but of all age groups, children and adolescents fortunately still have the lowest suicide rate in the population.

REFERENCES

Boyer, L. B., and Giovacchini, P. L. (1967). *Psychoanalytic Treatment of Schizophrenic and Characterological Disorders.* New York: Jason Aronson.

Fenichel, O. (1954). *The Psychoanalytic Theory of Neurosis.* New York: W. W. Norton.

Freud, S. (1917). Mourning and melancholia. *Standard Edition* 14:237–258.

Gault, W. B. (1971). Some remarks on slaughter. *American Journal of Psychiatry* 128:82–86.

Glover, E. (1955). *The Technique of Psychoanalysis.* New York: International Universities Press.

Grey, J. S. (1972). The structure of emotions and the limbic system. *Physiology, Emotions and Psychosomatic Illness: Ciba Symposium* 8:92–93.

Gunn, J. (1973). Affective and suicidal symptoms in epileptics. *Psychological Medicine* 3:108–114.

Hawton, K. (1982). Attempted suicide in children and adolescents. *Journal of Child Psychology and Psychiatry* 23:497–503.

Masterson, J. (1970). Depression in adolescent character disorders. *Proceedings of American Psychological Association* 59:242–257.

Maxmen, J. S., and Tucker, G. J. (1973). No exit: the persistently suicidal patient. *Comprehensive Psychiatry* 14:71–79.

Menninger, K. A. (1931). Psychoanalytic aspects of suicide. *Archives of Neurology and Psychiatry* 35:270–291.

Miller, D. (1974). *Adolescence: Its Psychology, Psychopathology, and Psychotherapy.* New York: Jason Aronson.

———. (1978). Affective disorders in adolescence: Mood disorders and the differential diagnosis of violent behavior. In *Depression: The World's Major Public Health Problem*, ed. F. J. Ayd. Baltimore: Ayd Publications.

———. (1978). Early adolescence: its psychology, psychopathology and implications for therapy. *Adolescent Psychiatry* 6:434–447.

———. (1983). *The Age Between: Adolescents and Therapy.* New York: Jason Aronson.

Miller, D., and Looney, J. (1976). Determinants of homicide in adolescents. *Adolescent Psychiatry* 4:231–252.

National Center for Health Statistics. (1984). *Monthly Vital Statistics Report* 32:13.

Offer, D. (1973). *The Psychological World of the Teenager: A Study of Normal Adolescent Boys.* New York: Basic Books.

Patel, N. S. (1974). A study of suicide. *Medicine, Science and Law* 14:129–136.

Peterson, A. M., Awad, G. A., and Kendler, A. C. (1973). Epidemiological differences between white and nonwhite suicide attempts. *American Journal of Psychiatry* 130:1071–1076.

Petzel, S. V., and Cline, D. W. (1978). Adolescent suicide: epidemiological and biological aspects. *Adolescent Psychiatry* 6:239–266.

Piaget, J., and Inhelder, B. (1969). *The Psychology of the Child.* New York: Basic Books.

Resnick, H. L. P. (1972). Eroticized repetitive hanging: a form of self-destructive behavior. *American Journal of Psychiatry* 26:4–21.

Riesman, D. (1950). *The Lonely Crowd.* New Haven, CT: Yale University Press.

Stack, S. (1983). The effect of religious commitment on suicide: a cross-national study. *Journal of Health and Social Behavior* 9:362–374.

U.S. Department of Health, Education and Welfare. (1976). Provisional statistics. *Annual Summary for the United States* 24:13.

Vital Statistics in the United States. (1960–1980). *Mortality Rate Part B.*

Weissman, M. M. (1974). The epidemiology of suicide attempts. *Archives of General Psychiatry* 30:737–746.

Zilborg, G. (1936). Differential diagnostic types of suicide. *Archives of Neurology and Psychiatry* 35:270–291.

———. (1937). Considerations of suicide with particular reference to the young. *American Journal of Orthopsychiatry* 7:15–31.

9

Adolescent Substance Abuse

Drugs of abuse fall into three categories: sedatives, stimulants, and hallucinogens. Most are used initially for the special sensations of a perceptual and emotional "high." Sedatives include alcohol, cough medications that may be used because of their alcohol content, minor tranquilizers, Librium, Valium, barbiturates, methaqualone, and over-the-counter hypnotics. Although they actually have a sedative effect, morphine derivatives, including heroin, are used mostly for their stimulant effect. Generally, drugs that induce drowsiness carry the slang name of *downers* and are often used for deliberate or "accidental" suicide attempts (Miller 1983).

The stimulant drugs include cocaine, the amphetamines and their derivatives (speed), and solvents that are sniffed and are used especially by early adolescents (Masterton 1979).

The hallucinogens include marijuana, LSD (lysergic acid diethylamide), and PCP (phencyclidine). A mixture of these, often with strychnine and a variety of amphetamines added, are sometimes sold as mescaline, THC, and, more recently, *ecstasy*. A

fantasy among adolescents is that the active principle of marijuana has been isolated and made available for street use. Middle-
class adolescents, in particular, often believe that natural substances are safe. Mescaline and peyote (Mexican cactus buttons)
are thought to be available, but actually they are hardly ever
accessible. All hallucinogens induce toxic states that poorly mimic
naturally occurring mental disorders (Lipton 1970).

Social class still determines, to some extent, the drug used.
Solvent sniffing and the abuse of amphetamine-like drugs
(speed) are more usual in lower-socioeconomic-class groups. Cocaine is common nowadays among the affluent, including delinquent gang members, but it is rarely used by early adolescents.

Individual users have been formally classified by the National Commission on Marijuana and Drug Abuse (1972). Experimental users are defined as those who use a drug once a month
or less. This definition may fit adults, but it does not describe
experimental adolescent users who generally try a drug two or
three times and then stop. Intermittent users are defined as
those who use a drug from two to ten times monthly; moderate,
eleven times monthly to daily; and heavy, from several times
daily to chronic intoxication. These definitions are of little value
clinically and indicate nothing as to outcome.

The use of illicit drugs represents the end stage of a sequence
that commonly starts with cigarettes and liquor, both of
which generally are socially acceptable to adults (Kandel 1982).
The frequency of use is not so significant as the frequency of
intoxication. The need to become intoxicated should always be
regarded as an indication of adolescent disturbance, although
this need may be both acute and transient.

There is confusion as to when substance use is substance
abuse, as society seems to regard adults'—and sometimes adolescents'—recreational use of alcohol and cigarettes as acceptable.
At one time, the use of coffee and tea was diagnostically classified
with drugs such as marijuana, even though "under certain circumstances" they were regarded as "normal and appropriate"
(DSM II, 1976).

Both the incidence of drug abuse and the type of drug used
vary. According to the National Institute on Drug Abuse (1984),
5.5 percent of 17,000 high school students used marijuana daily,
a decline from 10.7 percent in 1978. Some have suggested that if

this decline is representative of the total high school population, it may mean that adolescents finally are recognizing the hazards of using drugs. However, there is no clinical evidence of such a decline, and twice-weekly marijuana abuse creates chronic toxicity.

Clinical observation indicates a variation in the use of LSD. At one time, its use may be frequently reported; then for two or three years, there is a decline; and then there is another increase. It is as if adolescents do not retain their realization of LSD's dangers.

There is now a widespread adolescent fantasy that cocaine is a safe drug, and its use among adolescents is increasing: twice as many late adolescents reported trying cocaine in 1983 (17 percent) than in 1975. Young people have the additional excitement of buying a drug that is distributed quite differently from marijuana, is expensive to procure, and puts the user on the fringes of the dangerous underworld.

Drugs are used by some adolescents who, in a variety of ways, need to reinforce their sense of omnipotence. Others, who are struggling with issues of self-destruction, play a type of Russian roulette with drugs. They may recognize the dangers intellectually but take the drugs on the basis of two conflicting assumptions: one is the omnipotent feeling of personal inviolability, and the other is the despairing attitude that taking risks is unimportant.

Early adolescent sniffers of paint thinner may be aware that its inhalation causes brain damage, but because they both are prisoners of the present and do not consciously experience this, it is an irrelevant realization. Adolescent heroin users, similarly, may know of the danger inherent in buying the drug on the street because of the variation in its purity and thus its potency. When there are a number of heroin dealers in any one community, one of them becomes known for selling the drug that is cut with the fewest contaminants. This dealer then tends to collect most of the customers and then cuts the heroin with more and more contaminants. The heroin users then change dealers, and it is at this point that accidental death is likely to occur.

All drug abuse is dangerous, and any use of self-prescribed, mood-changing drugs by adolescents should be a cause for concern. Such drugs directly affect the nervous system and may indirectly affect behavior. For example, alcohol is a major cause of automobile accidents. Because some states still allow adolescents under the age of 21 to buy liquor, despite the evidence that raising the drinking age significantly reduces automobile injuries, it became necessary in 1984 for the federal government to threaten to withdraw such states' highway funds if by 1987 they had not raised their drinking age. By 1986 only four states failed to do this.

Involvement with drugs is one way in which adolescents manifest an emotional development that is being impaired by acute or chronic biopsychosocial stress. In turn, the drugs further impede the adolescents' psychological development. It is thus in this context that the effects of different drugs and alcohol can be considered.

All mood-changing drugs, even if used briefly, produce idiosyncratic effects in some adolescents, and their chronic use always interferes with personality development. Nevertheless, the amount of drug abused, its type, the frequency of abuse, and the period of adolescence in which the drug is abused all influence the therapeutic and preventive response.

Clearly, the easy availability of alcohol and tobacco is produced by adult collusion. In large cities, there is no real effort not to sell adolescents cigarettes, and alcohol seems equally easy to obtain. Further, the decriminalization of the possession of small quantities of marijuana effectively reinforces its use. Marijuana may be distributed by high school students, but there seems to be no significant attempt to prevent this and drug dealing by older peers becomes an important issue in early adolescent drug abuse. That is, early adolescents use older peers as identification models, and so they are particularly apt to mimic the older adolescents' behavior.

DRUG EXPERIMENTATION

Drug experimentation is best defined as the use of one drug—usually not more than four or five times—to seek an intoxicant effect and to gain a sense of mastery over the experience. Experimentation in early adolescence is typically with tobacco, beer, wine, hard liquor, and marijuana (Kandel and Faust 1975). Generally, adults tolerate early adolescents' experimentation, but the youngster needs to feel that experimental drug and alcohol abuse are unacceptable. Otherwise adolescents probably will interpret an adult's failure to respond negatively to drug experimentation as permission to continue using it.

From a developmental standpoint, early and middle adolescence are times for social experimentation: it is as though young people, as they begin to try to establish autonomous mastery of the world outside the family, experiment with life in both a positive and a negative way. They explore the world at large, test their physical prowess, and experiment with their sexuality, first with themselves and then with others. Initially, adolescents' striving for autonomy may be revealed in rebellious behavior, which is apparent in some of their secret games. Privacy is sought through behavior that mimics that of adults: sometimes a solitary activity, a retreat to the world of fantasy, the experience of masturbation. At times they seek other adolescents, with whom they may use a private language; often they talk about sex. Early adolescents experiment with drugs partly to demonstrate that they now have achieved adult status. Young people unconsciously identify with the conflictual behavior of the older generation. Given the drugs' availability and use by older adolescents and adults, the young adolescent's experimentation with them need not be regarded as indicating a profound personality disturbance or a developmental impasse.

Although a drug experience may seem to be gratifying, its side effects may not. Alcohol may be found to have an unpleasant taste, but young people's need to join in adult or peer-related activities may persuade them to drink anyway. Thus the taste of hard liquor is commonly disguised with soft drinks or fruit juice, and a taste for beer generally has to be acquired. If the adolescent becomes drunk, the hangover is decidedly unpleasant.

When marijuana is first smoked, its taste may be thought of as particularly harsh and unpleasant, and furthermore, it has to be used two or three times before a high can be obtained. This makes it particularly appealing as an experimental drug, as it is almost as if it has a built-in initiation rite: an initial unpleasantness and the need for persistence in order to join the group's special experience.

The immediate psychological effects of drug toxicity make it relatively unusual for most experimenters to become regular users. Like the physical changes of puberty, intoxication produces both pleasure and a feeling of helplessness, and any activity that primarily reinforces the latter is likely to be abandoned.

Furthermore, nicotine and alcohol may also be abandoned because of their hangover effect. In some, marijuana does not produce such unpleasant aftereffects, but others may complain of sleepiness and disinterest. Because intoxication is felt to be uncontrollable, if its aftereffects are not felt to be excessively uncomfortable, adolescents tend to try it more than once. This is because adolescents need to reassure themselves about their capacity to master the experience.

Experimentation with drugs peaks during two age periods, between the years of 12 and 13 and then at the beginning of middle adolescence, usually at age 15 to 16. Late adolescents and young adults, however, may nowadays begin their drug experimentation with cocaine (Kandel 1983). Most early adolescents experiment with the drugs that their parents use, and those from disrupted families commonly add drugs used by older peers. Early adolescent experimentation thus not only imitates adults' regressive drug taking but also the drug abuse of older peers. In those early adolescents in whom the struggle for autonomy is intense, their experimentation usually has a defiant quality, and they may become even more rebellious and destructive. The probability of their experimenting with more dangerous drugs such as LSD, chemical sedatives, or cocaine then becomes more likely. Those who are even more vulnerable probably will move to regular drug abuse.

Middle adolescents who tried cigarettes and alcohol in early adolescence and did not become regular users may try again. Thus those who become regular users of cigarettes may now become highly dependent on them. Middle adolescents who wish to identify with their perception of adult behavior and, less consciously, wish to try out their new feeling that they have control of the self may now try the intoxicant effect of alcohol or marijuana. Early adolescents who become dependent on tobacco are more likely in middle adolescence to experiment with other drugs, and those who in early adolescence became regular users of marijuana are now more likely to try other drugs of abuse.

The drugs with which middle and late adolescents experiment seem less related to the drugs that adults use and more to the drugs that their peer group accepts: psychedelic drugs, sedatives, cocaine, and, more rarely among middle-class groups, heroin. Middle adolescents rarely experiment with marijuana unless they have already tried tobacco and alcohol. One sixteen-year-old boy reported his introduction to marijuana:

> "I was 13 and known as a 'straight kid.' Our neighbors were older guys who smoked pot. At first, I said no, but they finally persuaded me. I liked it, and the next day I smoked it again. By the end of the week, I smoked every day, and within three weeks, I was smoking five or six times daily. I had not even smoked cigarettes before that, but I do now."

FREQUENCY OF DRUG ABUSE

Drug abuse may be intermittent or regular. A differentiation on the basis of frequency, therefore, is of clinical value only if the use is so infrequent that it can be ascribed to a combination of moderate stress and easy availability. Regular weekend use should be regarded as indicative of psychological problems. It suggests, at best, the inability to engage in social interaction and initial heterosexual involvement without an artificial boost.

Progressive drug use is a move from one drug to another, generally from softer to harder drugs, from cigarettes to alcohol, to marijuana, to hallucinogens, to stimulants and sedatives, and, finally, to cocaine and heroin. It is impossible to become a regular user of any one of these drugs without becoming drug dependent. The emotional dependence on the high of marijuana can be as intense as a dependence on cigarettes. The fact that a drug is not physiologically addictive does not make it any easier to give it up. Like adults, adolescents who are dependent on these drugs often have a fantasy of self-control and insist that they would be able to give them up if they so wished.

DRUG ABUSERS' PERSONALITY CONFLICTS

Adolescents who are struggling to gain a sense of separate and individual self normally experience some degree of depression, if only because they are mourning the loss of their childhood dependence. For those whose personal vulnerability makes this process unduly difficult, adolescence is commonly filled with pervasive depression, anxiety, or emptiness. This is particularly desolating when the adolescent's fantasy life is impaired or fantasies are perceived as particularly distressing. The most common technique of dealing with this is by playing loud music and by listening to lyrics that express both conflict and solution.

The more disturbed the youngster is, the more that violence in lyrics and their delivery will appeal. Currently the punk rock singers and their followers seem to be mainly such young people. In any event, in both Britain and the United States, punk rockers, with their dedication to a special type of music and eccentric forms of dress, give confused youths a sense of identity.

Adolescents who become delinquent, academic underachievers, or sexually promiscuous are more likely to abuse drugs than is the adolescent population at large (Shearn and Fitzgibbons 1972). These are adolescents with low self-esteem, problems of identity and sexual conflicts. They seek relief from intolerable psychological tension and often suffer from mood disorders. In psychiatric inpatient facilities, drug abuse—described as the unprescribed use of one or more psychotoxic drugs, including alcohol, more than 40 times a year (Kling and Vizivi 1977)—was present in 76 percent of the population for marijuana and to 57 percent for other hallucinogens.

The drug used modifies the adolescent's perception of the world and interferes to a greater or lesser degree with the satisfactory treatment of the causes of the drug abuse. Regular and progressive drug abuse is nowadays likely for those who do not develop a capacity to make trusting relationships without constant external reinforcement. Toxic relationships do not demand genuine warmth: alcohol supplies a fake feeling of camaraderie, and marijuana produces a preoccupation with experiences rather than emotionally meaningful relationships.

Besides the experience of the high, drug users feel that they are sharing a common experience with others, including the effect of the drugs and discussions about them. One 16-year-old boy who had not only given up drugs and alcohol but who was also now trying to make up for lost academic time, described his new experience as follows:

> "I went to see John; he was my best friend, or I thought he was. He was stoned, and all he could talk about was drugs. He is so boring. . . . I don't think we ever really were friends. I'm working in school now, but Dad doesn't believe it. It's not easy after all this time. . . . I'm really scared of leaving home. . . . I don't know whether I can do that. . . ."

Drug abuse has added a new solution for those who lack a sense of inner security. Yet another solution is to join cults. Once involved with them, adolescents, like those on drugs, are unable to develop a sense of inner freedom. Membership in youth gangs, which in the large cities of the United States may span the ages from seven or eight to the mid-20s, offers a sense of self to uncertain young people, who may or may not abuse drugs. Even the gangs' names have meaning: the Unknowns, the Gaylords, the Kings.

Sometimes adolescents use drugs to facilitate identification with their parents:

> One 14-year-old boy had an alcoholic father who had begun drinking himself when he was 17; he was now in his mid-50s. The father made no effort to give up alcohol, stated he liked it, and could not imagine being without it. His son had exactly the same attitude toward marijuana. The father had been hospitalized several times because of organic difficulties precipitated by alcohol, but this did not help him stop. The son had "flashbacks" with marijuana, originally caused by his use of hallucinogens. These were psychologically painful to him but, likewise, did not motivate him to stop.

Some adolescents, especially those who have had a damaging infantile experience, may need physical activity, both to relieve tension and to maintain a sense of being alive and human.

Sometimes, therefore, such young people engage in violent gang activity; some are active in more or less violent contact sports; and some are comfortable only when they are away from people, often in active contact with nature. Physical immobilization may, in these individuals, lead to acute withdrawal from reality; for example, when some athletes are physically immobilized by fractures, they may become excessively withdrawn. One boy took drugs only while at home in the city. When he was in the country, he was always drug free:

> Donald, aged 16, was hospitalized because of his inability to stop using marijuana, which he was taking five or six times daily. He was unable to work in school and was hyperirritable. He was unreliable and unable to respect others' feelings. He did not keep himself clean, did not come to meals, stole the family car, and abused his small sister both physically and verbally. For the previous few years, his uncle had taken him camping for approximately six weeks in the Rocky Mountains. Donald reported that when he was climbing, hiking, and camping, he had no wish to "smoke." He remarked, "It's the only time I feel anything. As soon as I get home, everything bores me. Then I start smoking pot again."

Those young people who abuse drugs and who also suffer from personality disorders may become pubertal but do not develop a sense of adult autonomy. When they become adolescent, they appear as shallow, self-referent individuals with little or no capacity for empathy. They experience inner emptiness. When they abuse drugs during puberty, the drugs may become eroticized in the same way as alcohol. Indeed, such young people may then relate to drugs in the same way that normal adolescents relate to sexual feelings: their craving for drugs is similar to that of healthy adolescents for sex.

DRUG ABUSE AND MOOD DISORDERS

Adolescent drug abusers who self-medicate and who crave drugs only when a mood disorder is uncontrolled are the least difficult to treat. Those who abuse drugs mainly to deal with the feeling of emptiness associated with personality disorders or to establish a sense of self by becoming "freaks" are more difficult. If they abuse drugs long enough, a time period that varies among individuals, organic brain syndromes will follow. Such adolescents seem to lack social judgment and are usually unable to link their behavior with its consequences. Other adolescents refer to these brain-damaged young people as having "fried their brains" or as being "burn outs."

Adolescents' experience of psychological pain may be actual or potential. Young people go to great lengths to avoid psychological tension but may not be consciously aware that they are doing so. The most common reason for using drugs is to avoid the depressive affect associated with emotional deprivation, mood disorders, or both. All depressive illnesses, whatever their causes, lead to feelings of deprivation, but not all deprivation leads to depression. Deprivation may also produce anxiety and, depending on when it occurs, more or less severe disorders of character formation. Drug abuse may relieve psychological pain, in a variety of ways. Usually it does this through a combination of "feeling good" when high and not caring very much about oneself or others. Sometimes, abusing drugs is felt as a substitute for feeling loved. The drug is used like a small child's teddy bear, blanket, or doll for which the child reaches in moments of tension.

Emotional survival is not possible if one feels totally isolated from mothering. One boy described the experience of using a hallucinogen (LSD) as follows:

"I feel as if I am in a room manufactured by the government and given to all its citizens, which will take care of all my survival functions: eating, air, living. It will prevent me from hurting myself, and it can even hold my hand. In the room I have nothing to worry about. Everything is done for me; I have no fear. It is great."

Adolescents who suffer from mood fluctuations, that is, intermittent conscious feelings of emptiness, boredom, and sadness, often have an intense need for both the emotional support of people and the support of things. Using drugs may temporarily fill these needs. Drug abuse, however, commonly creates a sense of inner confusion; and it may then create or reinforce many of the symptoms occurring in those who suffer from mood disorders. Some drugs lower the energy level and make the user excessively sleepy. Others cause an aberrant food intake: the appetite stimulation of marijuana may produce the bingeing that precedes bulimia, and the appetite suppression of cocaine may mimic anorexia nervosa.

Apathy, loss of energy, loss of appetite, and sleep disturbance: all of these culture-free symptoms of mood disorders may also appear as a result of some types of drug abuse. Marijuana is used as a defense against depression, but it may also produce or reinforce depression. In either case, an accurate diagnosis is impossible unless the central nervous system can be cleared of the toxic breakdown products produced by the abused drugs:

> Mary, a 16-year-old girl, had a one-year history of mixed drug abuse: marijuana, alcohol, Quaaludes, and cocaine. She was defiant, would disappear from home for hours at a time, and was extraordinarily nasty to her parents. They found themselves unable to cope with their daughter, whom they saw as a self-centered, drug-abusing virago.

> Mary refused to try to stop abusing drugs: "All my friends do it, why shouldn't I?" and was admitted to an adolescent treatment unit. Without drugs she was even nastier. Other peoples' feelings were irrelevant to her; if she was frustrated, she would scream with rage, throw furniture, and sulk for long periods of time. It was clear that beneath this nastiness, she was miserable. She would agree that this feeling was present, even though she always ascribed the cause to the badness of others.

Based on the clinical history of poor sleep, lack of appetite, and irritability, a diagnosis of a major depression was made. Mary was treated with imipramine in therapeutic doses, individual and family therapy, and special schooling. She showed steady improvement.

Mood-disordered adolescents who respond to tricyclic antidepressants generally need to take them for about a year before they can be withdrawn without the risk of the symptoms' recurring:

After three months of medication, Mary developed infectious mononucleosis. Her enlarged liver meant that imipramine could not be given for about four weeks. Two weeks after stopping the medication, Mary began to pressure her parents to allow her to see her old drug-taking friends again. She began to ask for an increase in the frequency of family therapy because "my mother is such a bitch." "Jokingly," she asked to be readmitted to the hospital. Two weeks after the imipramine was reinstituted, she once again became calmer and more pleasant.

In depression caused by deprivation, common in adolescents, they sometimes abuse drugs to test whether they are loved. Drug paraphernalia (pipes, bongs, rolling papers, and incense) are left lying around in the bedrooms of middle-class children for their parents to see. Those parents who do nothing are thought not to care and are seen as giving permission. Similarly perceived are those parents who accept statements that are clearly untrue or those who fail to notice the flushed face and the false bonhomie of their stoned offspring.

SEXUAL ANXIETY AND DRUGS

Drugs may be used as a substitute for sexual intercourse or to allay anxiety about sexual incompetence, to facilitate masturbation, or to resolve conflicts about sexual identity.

The domain of promiscuous sexuality is fertilized with alcohol and marijuana, although cocaine and pills also may be present. Drugs are often used to facilitate loveless sex and sometimes are used as additional stimulants to orgasm. The idea seems to be that if there is no significant emotional relationship, the excitement of orgasm should be artificially enhanced.

Alcohol has long been known as simultaneously a facilitator and an inhibitor of sexual activity. Shakespeare has the porter in *Macbeth* describe this situation to Macduff, who asks, "What three things does drink especially provoke?"

Marry sir, nose painting, sleep and urine. Lechery, sir it both provokes and unprovokes, it provokes the desire but it takes away the performance. (Act 2, sc 3, lines 30–34)

Boys who have engaged in homosexual behavior may attempt to rationalize it by reasoning that they were high at the time and that they really did not know what they were doing:

> One boy of 16 reported that he had been "seduced" by a boy of his own age. "I slept over at Peter's house, and we smoked a joint together before going to bed. I had no idea that he was gay, but when I was stoned, he began to touch my cock. I thought, 'what the hell,' and we went on from there."

When asked later if he had known that his friend was homosexual, the boy indicated that he had thought of the possibility.

In regard to heterosexual behavior, both sexes know that if a girl is high, she is less likely to object to having sex:

> One boy reported establishing a friendship with a girl who refused to have intercourse with him. "I deliberately got her stoned and had her smoke two joints; she stopped saying no, and I fucked her three times."

Conversely, drugs may also be used to reduce the desire for heterosexual behavior. Many individuals report that if they are stoned, they become indifferent to sex. Males who are reluctant to engage in heterosexual activity can justify this because some drugs are known as inhibitors. Likewise, females who are unable to establish relationships with boys may substitute drug abuse:

> Karen was an extremely beautiful girl of 17 who was fearful of male sexual advances. Her parents had a dreadful relationship, and Karen blamed her father for this, calling him an "asshole." When she was ten, a man who was probably in his late 30s engaged in sexual play with her. He intimidated her by threatening to tell her parents, and this went on for a number of months. In puberty, she became extremely obese and came to treatment at the age of 16 because she was depressed. She lost weight, but before being able to risk relating to males, she would become stoned with her girl friends every weekend. When she went to "jock" parties at which many boys showed an interest in her, she always rejected their advances.

Some adolescent boys are not just inhibited about making emotionally meaningful relationships; they are also reluctant to have intercourse, as this degree of physical intimacy seems to create profound anxiety. When lower-socioeconomic-class males suffer in this way, they have the additional problem that masturbation is culturally forbidden to them and is considered infantile and homosexual. This may be one reason that amphetamine derivatives, or "speed," are more often used by lower-socioeconomic groups.

Boys who take large doses of amphetamines and their derivatives on the weekends—a typical time for establishing sexual relationships—become impotent while "speeding."

In small doses, the amphetamines are said to enhance a boy's capacity to maintain a penile erection, but in larger doses, no erection is possible. Thus boys with anxieties about emotional and physical intimacy can use the chemical impotence produced by amphetamines taken in large doses in order to save face with their peers and to avoid the tension they might experience because of sexual incompetence or disinterest (Miller 1974). Sometimes these young people will say that they use drugs and therefore do not need sex:

> One boy said, "If I take speed on Friday or Saturday, then I cannot get a 'hard on.' On Monday my cock can get hard again, and that feels great too."

The use of amphetamines as a substitute for intercourse is not just a prerogative of boys but may also be used in this way by girls:

> Irma was a 16-year-old girl who was diagnosed as suffering from a histrionic personality disorder with many exhibitionistic features. She had been a polydrug abuser from the age of fourteen. She was also sexually promiscuous. But when she contracted syphilis, she took seriously an injunction not to have promiscuous sex.

> Irma began to inject amphetamine derivatives, saying that the feelings she got with the injection were exactly like the feelings she got with having intercourse.

Irma was hospitalized for a brief period but did not perceive this as at all helpful and absconded. She went to live with a boy who would punish her when she angered him, by refusing to have intercourse. Whenever he did this, she would go and buy some speed and take it by mouth.

Promiscuous women may use heroin with loveless sex, as they feel less inhibited when "done up" with the drug. Men may use heroin to produce very prolonged erections that prevent ejaculation, which may make them seem particularly potent to their sexual partners.

In the homosexual community, amyl nitrite capsules often used to be inhaled during sexual activity, as this was felt both to enhance orgasm and to make anal intercourse more satisfactory for both partners. But the change in the legal scheduling of this drug, which made it effectively unavailable, led to the use of butyl nitrite derivatives. These are widely used by the homosexually promiscuous and not uncommonly by heterosexuals. One of them, *Rush*, is the name taken by a highly successful rock group.

Among the hallucinogens, LSD is sometimes described as making sexual intercourse especially erotic, although it appears more often to be associated with masturbatory activity. Some hallucinogens obliterate erotic experiences.

Many adolescents believe that sedatives, particularly methaqualone (Quaaludes) enhance erotic experiences. When they are known to be distributed at parties, adolescents are convinced that sexual activity will be more available. Sedatives are not thought to improve sexual performance but, rather, to increase sexual willingness.

Thus there are many reasons besides availability that make drug abuse likely, and so it is prognostically and diagnostically helpful to be able to recognize those adolescents who probably will become drug abusers. In addition to those young people who are biologically vulnerable, adolescents who abuse drugs and show other types of antisocial problem behavior may have a variety of psychosocial problems.

Those adolescents who have good self-esteem, who are

from a two-parent, stable family, who have a network of stable peer and extraparental adult relationships, and who do not accept the use of drugs will be less vulnerable to pressure to move from any transient drug experimentation with tobacco or alcohol to the abuse of other drugs.

Adolescents with impaired parental attachments, especially those from conflict-ridden, single-parent families, are more vulnerable. Even with concurrent significant emotional attachments to extraparental adults and emotionally satisfying peer group involvement, these young people are likely to show a symptomatic response to stress, which makes them more likely to become involved with drugs. However, depending on the strength of extraparental attachments and the involvement with significant social systems such as church, clubs, smaller schools, and peer groups who do not accept drug abuse, their vulnerability may be assuaged. In cities where there is strong local ethnocentricity, especially with strong church involvement—Roman Catholic families in the Polish areas of Chicago, for example—adolescents are less likely to abuse drugs other than alcohol. Families who use alcohol or who automatically handle tension with prescription and nonprescription drugs are more likely to produce children who abuse drugs or alcohol.

Some adolescents have good parental attachments but little or no emotional involvement with significant extraparental adults. They therefore may become emotionally overinvolved with their peers and so are open to the group's whims. Early adolescents who suffer this type of developmental deprivation are more likely than others to show evidence of psychological disturbance and to abuse drugs.

A more vulnerable group includes those adolescents whose capacity to make trusting relationships is impaired because of early nurturing deficits. These may be caused by biological vulnerability, emotional immaturity associated with psychological disturbance in one or both parents, and fragmented parental attachments. Even when extraparental adults and peers are available, the inability to trust makes it difficult to form emotionally satisfying relationships. If significant adults are not available, the tenuous peer group involvement of which those adolescents are

capable will make them even more susceptible to using drugs
regularly. For these adolescents, drugs fill up the void produced
by the absence of meaningful emotional relationships. They then
are highly likely to become progressive drug users and, often,
drug dealers.

Besides any underlying biopsychosocial vulnerability, those
who continue to abuse drugs impair the development of their
personality and show diminished social effectiveness as young
adults, even though the causal sequence is not completely clear
(Kandel 1984).

REFERENCES

Diagnostic and Statistical Manual of Mental Disorders II. (1976). Washington,
    D.C.: American Psychiatric Association.
Kandel, D. B. (1982). Adolescent drug abuse. *Journal of the American
    Academy of Child Psychiatry* 20:573–577.
——. (1983). Epidemiologic and psychosocial perspectives on adoles-
    cent drug abuse. *Journal of the American Academy of Child Psychiatry*
    21:348–353.
——. (1984). Marijuana use in young adulthood. *Archives of General
    Psychiatry* 41:200–209.
Kandel, D. B., and Faust, R. (1975). Sequence and stages in patterns of
    adolescent drug abuse. *Archives of General Psychiatry* 35:923–932.
Kling, V., and Vizivi, H. (1977). Characteristics of drug abusers in an
    adolescent inpatient facility. *Diseases of the Nervous System,* 8:275–
    279.
Lipton, M. (1970). The relevance of chemically induced psychoses to
    schizophrenia. In *Psychomimetic Drugs,* ed. D. H. Efron. New York:
    Raven Press.
Masterton, G. (1979). The management of solvent abuse. *Journal of
    Adolescence* 2:65.
Miller, D. (1974). *Adolescence: Psychology, Psychopathology, and Psychotherapy.*
    New York: Jason Aronson.
——. (1980). Treatment of the seriously disturbed adolescent. *Adoles-
    cent Psychiatry* 8:469–482.
——. (1983). Adolescent suicide: etiology and treatment. *Adolescent
    Psychiatry* 9:327–343.

ADOLESCENT SUBSTANCE ABUSE215

National Commission on Marijuana and Drug Abuse. (1972). *Marijuana: A Signal of Misunderstanding*. Washington D.C.: U.S. Government Printing Office.
National Institute on Drug Abuse. (1984). Use of Licit and Illicit Drugs by American High School Students 1975-1984. Rockville, MD.
Shearn, C. R., and Fitzgibbons, D. J. (1972). Patterns of drug use in a population of youthful psychiatric patients. *American Journal of Psychiatry* 128:1381-1386.

10

Treating Adolescent Substance Abusers

MARIJUANA

Humans have ingested the flowering tops of hemp since 2700 B.C. Marijuana (grass, pot) is a dilute form of a series of extremely powerful chemical substances, the tetrahydrocannabinols. Hashish is the resin obtained from the hemp plant and can be described as a cesspool of organic compounds.

In 1975, 18.2 percent of males under the age of eighteen admitted using marijuana before the tenth grade. In 1977, a survey of the graduating class of that year showed that the figure had reached 30.6 percent (Wynne 1979). By 1980, it appeared that the level of drug use had stabilized, but at the highest level in U.S. history (Johnson et al. 1982). The hypothesis that this was caused by the greater number of young people in the population has not been borne out statistically (Shapiro and Wynne 1981). Preventing drug abuse would mean radical changes in society, and because this is not likely, adequate treatment becomes crucial.

Theophil Gautier, a friend of Baudelaire, wrote in 1860 that "I perceived the hashish I had eaten in the form of an emerald scintillating with a million points of fire . . . my eyelashes elongated . . . like threads of gold on ivory spindles" (DeRopp 1957). Such visions are likely to make the drug enormously appealing to rootless adolescents. Such are the individuals who live in a world in which no one seems to care, in which there is stability of neither place nor person, and in which time speeds by and everything is finished quickly—from fast foods to fast travel to television with its "spots." Western society has, in recent decades, abruptly moved people from stable communities, in which "Where do you come from?" said a great deal about who one was, to a society of high mobility, in which a sense of place is no longer related to a sense of personal self. The feeling produced by marijuana, of being "in place," with a slowing of a sense of time, thus has to be attractive.

The conscious awareness of the marijuana high lasts usually about 20 minutes and not more than one to two hours. Users easily become euphoric and are aware for about two to four hours that they are stoned.

Typically, the high associated with marijuana is preceded by a period of anxiety that lasts for about ten to thirty minutes. Often the user is hyperalert and hypersuspicious during this period and while coming down from the intoxicated period. The drug produces a general feeling of pleasure and increased excitement, even though to the outside observer the user may appear unduly passive. Users have a distorted sense of time and space.

All biopsychosocial determinants are significant in the etiology of marijuana abuse. Those adolescents with mood disorders in which rapid inexplicable changes of mood occur with no apparent external cause will be attracted to marijuana. The depression, "vegging out," that is common after the high of marijuana, gives these young people an acceptable sense of personal control over their depressed mood. Such individuals are often unable to keep in touch with their own fantasy life. Excessive auditory stimulation is one way of filling this emptiness, and marijuana enhances the enjoyment of music and noise.

The deprivation caused by the absence of significant extra-parental adults or by the loss of one who has become important is commonly found as a precursor to abuse. As adolescents move psychologically from the family nexus, they need a significant other adult as a developmental model who can help them mature psychologically (Miller 1974). When these relationships, by de-sign, are very brief, they may sometimes have a significant im-pact on the young, but their loss is not traumatic. For example, when the Reverend Jesse Jackson, as part of his Operation Push, talks to audiences of high school students, he uses his charis-matic style to attempt to influence their way of life. The model is actually that of a religious conversion experience. The message may be internalized, and so the speaker's apparent disinterest is not seen thereafter as developmentally painful. The same pro-cess applies to celebrated former addicts who talk to school audiences. On the other hand, if a youngster slowly develops a relationship with a schoolteacher and, for what seem to the adolescent to be arbitrary reasons based on social system deci-sions, loses that relationship, such a loss may be painful. The youngster then will protect himself or herself from further pain by refusing to make relationships in the future. Often, he or she will lose interest in learning and may deal with the absence of significant adult developmental models by identifying with the drug culture.

The deprivation of an extrafamilial developmental network is a common experience for postpubertal early adolescents when their family moves in the fall of the year. This is because the structure of junior high school makes it almost impossible to establish stable peer group or adult relationships unless one has a special talent in sports or music. Furthermore, in the winter time in colder climates, there is no culture of the street. In addition, parents who have just moved are often themselves over-anxious. The adolescent with minimal emotional support, then, can easily become involved in peer-related drug activities because this group always appears ready to take in a newcomer.

The amount of time that adolescents spend each day with the drug and its procurement is an important therapeutic issue. If adolescents spend up to eight hours daily involved with drugs —two to four hours being toxic, two hours discussing the drug, and two hours obtaining it—its absence certainly will leave a void in their lives. Because they usually have given up their interests for the drug involvement, they must be helped to use their newly available time meaningfully.

Regular abusers of marijuana mix with one another, the common bond being the drug. When a youngster gives up the drug, a change of friends seems inevitable, and for those who are not outgoing, this becomes inordinately difficult:

> Mike, aged 17, was a senior who, after his second hospitalization, finally gave up marijuana. He described a visit to a friend: "I couldn't wait to see Karl after I got out, but it was awful. We had nothing to talk about. He's only into pot and doesn't seem interested in anything else."

As with all other drugs, the price of marijuana varies according to its supply and demand. In order to maintain their habit, adolescents may sell the drug and sometimes spend most of their allowance or earnings on buying it. Although marijuana cigarettes are passed around freely among users, the adolescent who smokes regularly and denies that he or she buys the drug is almost certainly not being honest.

Some adolescents report that getting high is more fun than being high. The ritual of feeling part of a group of peers behaving in ways of which authorities disapprove is felt as particularly enjoyable. Indeed, in the late 1960s, marijuana was the drug of the student revolt.

Although people have been using marijuana for approximately 4,000 years, little is known with scientific certainty about the psychological and physiological price that individuals pay for using it. Any abuse leads to the impairment not just of current effective functioning but also of psychological maturation. Continued abuse produces a chronic brain syndrome and, in some, permanent organic deficits. Both psychological tests and biological assessments are distorted by the abuse of marijuana. Electroencephalograms given to youngsters who have recently taken marijuana are likely to show a number of abnormalities, including rapid beta waves (Brill 1969). The effects of chronic smoking on the cardiovascular and respiratory systems are still unknown, although there are suggestions that the drug is as carcinogenic as is tobacco.

Although the experimental evidence for this is inconclusive (Stefanis, Boulougonis, and Liakus 1976), in clinical practice, many middle-class adults in their twenties who have smoked marijuana daily since their teens are found to be bland individuals. They often appear to have very little motivation to involve themselves productively with the real world, though this does not mean that every chronic marijuana user loses his or her motivation.

In a medical students' mental health service, many late adolescents and young adults who smoked marijuana showed an impairment of short-term memory. On this service, the most common cause of academic underachievement was the abuse of marijuana:

> Students who were not doing well in school would be offered the opportunity to be seen in a medical student mental health service, which was free and confidential.

> These students would often, after a day's work, "smoke a joint" before going to sleep. When it was suggested that this might reduce their learning efficiency and they desisted, their grades went up.

Similarly, bright high school students in grades 11 and 12 report that they do not use marijuana during the week, as they see the drug as interfering with their ability to function on academic tests. But all this does not necessarily prove that a decline in academic achievement can be ascribed to the use of marijuana, although it seems probable.

There is no question that marijuana produces tolerance in experimental animals (McMillan et al. 1970). Likewise, patients admit that when they use the drug regularly, they do not get as high as they do with its intermittent use. In double-blind experiments in which they do not know whether or not the cigarette will give them a high, such users find it very difficult to distinguish active from inactive cigarettes.

It takes approximately seven days to clear from the brain the last residue of alpha 9 THC (Lumberger et al. 1970), one of the breakdown products of marijuana, whose half-life is seventeen hours. Thus it is then difficult to regard casually even the occasional use of marijuana. It has been alleged that a chronic daily use of marijuana does not lead to an inability to involve oneself in a meaningful way with others and does not produce a lack of initiative (Schwartz et al. 1977), but that is not the usual clinical observation. Although there is no hard evidence that this may just be the individual's personality, clinical observation of adolescents unable or unwilling to abstain from taking marijuana indicates an increasing inability to make constructive decisions (Kandel 1982). Furthermore, if it has not been used for an excessively long time, abstention from marijuana for several months commonly leads to a better academic performance and more self-assertion. After having dried out over a period of time, many adolescents state that they give and receive more from human relationships.

Many adolescents have the fantasy that sex will be more exciting if one has intercourse when stoned or when having used amyl or butyl nitrate. But those sexually active adolescents who dry out commonly report an improvement in their sexual experiences. One boy remarked:

"I had always had sex while I was using the drug, not that I had to be stoned. Now that I am not, both my girl friend and I enjoy it so much more."

The depersonalization that is present in the chronic user makes marijuana attractive to those who are in conflict about intimacy and who have not developed a basic sense of trust.

The apparent blandness seen in marijuana abusers often covers a paranoid anxiety. Furthermore, many young people who suffer from unpredictable anxiety attacks use marijuana to attempt to gain some mastery over the experience; thus they make the cause of the anxiety explicable, even though the symptoms of the anxiety may make them feel worse. At one time, adolescents reported that they did not enjoy the taste of marijuana, but this comment has not been heard for many years. When asked, a number of adolescents answered that they find the taste pleasant.

Adolescents whose parents are marijuana abusers are now being seen in clinical practice. Such parents may even buy marijuana for their children: one father insisted that his son use only that marijuana that he (the father) bought for him because it would not be contaminated. The children of marijuana abusers may accept marijuana abuse or may try other drugs, especially cocaine. Others may defend themselves by joining very rigid religions:

> A 15-year-old boy had stolen his father's marijuana when he was 13 and given it away in junior high school. At the age of fourteen, he had become an Orthodox Jew. Because his family did not use kosher foods, he found it impossible to live with them. However, he identified with his father's law breaking, and, protected by his Orthodox dress, he became a successful shoplifter.

The distinct sweet smell of marijuana is noticeable in the clothing of regular users, but it is perfectly possible for an adolescent to be high without its being apparent to the observer. A flushed face and injected conjunctiva are rarely seen in those who use the drug regularly, although in the intermittent user, particularly early adolescents, these are usually apparent. When an adolescent is intoxicated, it is usually obvious to the individuals who know the youngster well, particularly if they talk with him or her for any length of time and the possibility of marijuana use is borne in mind. Over effusive speech is common, and to the observer the user may seem more distant. Hyperirritability also is not unusual as a user moves from the euphoric state to mild depression. Chronic users may be less obvious to others, as their bland, rather affectless, approach to life may become their expected personality.

The effect of marijuana partially depends on the user's expectations. When "good weed" is said to be available, many young people will say that their high is better than with their usual supply. A solitary adolescent may report a pleasant calming effect, but in a group the effect may be modified by the group experience. Marijuana is often used as a tranquilizer by youths who are easily angered and by those who suffer from schizophrenic syndromes. Some adolescents report having violent fantasies while they are intoxicated:

> In a correctional center, a sixteen-year-old youth returned from a weekend visit and reported to one of the staff that he had been involved in a knife fight and had killed another boy. His story was convincing, and inquiries were made in the district in which he reported the incident as having occurred. But no such crime had taken place, and the hospitals had not admitted anyone with stab wounds.

It is interesting that the word *hashish* has as its root the word *assassin*, and it used to be thought that marijuana could precipitate violence. In the Middle East in the eleventh century, hashish was a drug of protest. Hasan Sabah trained his disciples to terrorize the establishment of Persia and Egypt with sudden and effective assassinations: hashish was given as the reward, but it did not initiate the behavior (Miller 1974).

Because one side effect of the regular use of marijuana is sometimes hyperirritability, those who are prone to violence may become more easily enraged when using the drug:

> A 17-year-old boy who was smoking three or four joints daily became furious with his father when the latter refused to give him the family car. The situation came to a head when the parents refused to pick him up from his job in a local supermarket and insisted that he could easily walk the six blocks back to his house. The boy got home, called his father "an asshole," and they had a physical fight. The next day, having been awake most of the night in a rage, the boy again smoked. He called his mother and announced that he had a knife and would kill his father when he came home. He was so irrationally enraged that the mother called the local adolescent clinic's emergency number. The police called at the house and found the youth incoherent and toxic.

A lack of educational motivation or job initiative is common in the regular user, and a number of such young people have been misdiagnosed as suffering from learning disabilities. This error may be made when a regular user of marijuana takes psychological tests and the psychologist is not aware that the patient is high. The test results, however, will change about six months after the individual has dried out.

Like all drugs, there are idiosyncratic responses to marijuana: some adolescents who have used chemical hallucinogens such as LSD get "flashbacks" when they smoke "grass," and some hallucinate on marijuana from time to time, even without such a history. Although chronic use usually leads to a drop in academic performance, some adolescents are regular users and still receive high grades in school and college. Thus it is easy for families that regard academic or social competence as of prime importance to believe that marijuana use can sometimes be inconsequential. One fifteen-year-old who had used marijuana daily since he was ten said of his older brother:

> "My parents don't mind his smoking pot because he gets A's and B's in school. They sent me to the hospital because I don't do well. They say it's because of pot, but I don't believe them."

For such young people, marijuana is probably an efficient tranquilizer. Indeed, it is reasonable to hypothesize—and there is clinical evidence for this—that without marijuana, these adolescents' psychological disturbances might interfere with their academic productivity.

The principal side effects of regular chronic marijuana abuse are short-term memory impairment, a feeling of noninvolvement, emotional blandness, a general disinterest in others and the world at large, and the possibility of flashbacks. The longer the abuse has continued, the more likely that there will be short-term memory impairment, although the individual adapts to this and rarely complains. But even though marijuana impairs short-term memory and causes depersonalization, some psychotherapists continue to see individuals who are regular users of marijuana. It may be that in outpatient practice, task-oriented groups help adolescents try to give up their drug abuse (Weisberg 1979), but this has not been proven.

Chronic marijuana use produces a significant, subtle, all-pervasive depression. This depression may have been so insidious when it began that only when thoroughly dried out—which for the chronic user takes approximately four weeks—do adolescents realize its extent. Although marijuana has been thought not to produce physical addiction, in clinical practice it is clear that at the point when the last toxic products of marijuana are leaving the nervous system, the adolescent is likely to begin using it again.

Being depersonalizing, marijuana does not require intense attachments to individuals. Marijuana is therefore appealing to internally lonely and isolated individuals. Distrustful individuals can obtain gratification without the emotionally threatening demand for emotional involvement. For those middle and late adolescents for whom apparent heterosexual activity is really only a masturbatory relationship, sexual activity with a stoned partner may be especially desirable:

> A big, handsome 15-year-old boy, adopted at four weeks of age, could establish only distant relationships with others. He explained, "I have never trusted anyone in my whole life, and I don't expect I ever will." He liked nothing better than to give a girl a joint or two and then to have intercourse. He was asked whether he would not prefer sex with someone who was more involved with him. He replied that he didn't want that, "I just want them to do what I want. . . . I like to imagine having a girl tied up, and then I can fuck her till she comes. Sometimes I like to do that even if she does not want me to, and then I don't care how she feels. It's much easier to do that if she is stoned. . . . She will screw like a rabbit."

Marijuana Abuse and Its Treatment

If marijuana abuse is noticed early and then controlled, it is more likely to disappear:

> One 14-year-old was brought to a psychiatrist because of his daily marijuana abuse of approximately three months' duration. He defiantly stated that he was not prepared to stop; his parents expressed helplessness in the face of this defiance. But in a family conference, it was clear that they really did wish him to stop. The following recommendations were made to them: because their

son was not honest with them about his activities outside the house, clearly he should not be allowed to go out without them. Because he smoked on the way to and from school, obviously he would have to be taken by his parents and collected by them, and they would have to take him to the school office. Finally, because he might be given marijuana going to and from classes, special arrangements for an interclass escort would be needed.

The parents followed all these recommendations. Six weeks later the boy said, "I have never been so hassled in my life, no joint is worth it. . . . I will never smoke again."

Two years later he was still dry.

Given the causes of drug abuse, treatment programs devised only for symptomatic relief are less likely to be successful with adolescents than with adults. There are many reasons for this. Adolescents who have not yet developed a sense of self cannot genuinely admit that they have a problem. Therapeutic systems such as peer counseling and positive peer cultures may encourage adolescents to talk about their problems and the consequences, but these concepts are generally not internalized. Programs that deal primarily with symptoms and address only relationship difficulties are unlikely to be successful with those who are abusing drugs as a type of self-medication or as an attempt at self-realization.

Drug abusers are both distrustful and not to be trusted. Drug abuse in chronological middle and late adolescence leads to the persistence of early adolescent attitudes: a disregard for the future consequences of behavior, an omnipotent conception of oneself, a sense of persecution from the adult world, and a disregard for immediate responsibilities.

Successful outpatient intervention is possible only if the adolescent is ready to stop using marijuana. Because the individual must be dry before a relationship that might control drug use is possible, the initial abstention depends on the demands of reality, along with the parents' feelings and behavior and their relationship with their child. Nonetheless, parents and therapists sometimes remain casual about marijuana abuse. When a previous therapist has not commented about drug use, he or she has missed the chance to reinforce the patient's or the parents' perception of the value of an intervention that insists that marijuana not be used:

> Joe was a 17-year-old boy who had been in twice-weekly psychotherapy for excessive rage attacks for two and a half years. These occurred under a known stress, when he broke furniture, put his fists through walls, and used socially inappropriate language, all of which were highly aberrant for his social group. These attacks had been going on since childhood.

> In diagnostic consultation for a second opinion, Joe revealed that at one time in his therapy, he was smoking five times daily and that he now smoked three times weekly.
> "Did you tell your therapist?"
> "No, he never asked. If he had, I would have told him."
> "Were you ever dry during that time?"
> "Yes, for two months about eighteen months ago."
> "Did that make any difference in your temper?"
> "Yes, I was much less irritable."

Because in his initial outpatient contact Joe was toxic, having smoked marijuana the evening before, the parents were told that the diagnostic assessment could not be begun for about three weeks and that their son could tell them the reason for this if he wished. He admitted, "It's because I smoke pot two or three times daily, and he wants me to dry out." The parents replied, "We didn't think you smoked as much as that."

This interaction demonstrates some initial treatment issues: honesty, the ability to make a relationship, the parents' ability to help their child stop smoking marijuana, and the necessity for family support. An adolescent's refusal to stop smoking marijuana makes an adequate diagnosis impossible in such circumstances, and so a diagnostic assessment in a hospital is necessary. Recommendations made without determining a problem's causes are unlikely to succeed.

The adolescent is asked to abstain from using marijuana during the initial diagnostic phase. The clinician who makes the assessment should be able to be the patient's therapist if the adolescent and the parents so choose. It is our practice to make clear that some therapists do not insist on abstention but that we believe that the adolescent's drug use must be stopped. We believe that psychotherapy is impossible if the adolescent continues to abuse marijuana. Regular urine testing for cannabis alkaloids in those adolescents whose honesty is doubtful is a prerequisite for successful outpatient treatment.

Issues regarding confidentiality should be explained to both the parents and the patient. The parents should be told that drug use will not be reported to them but that if marijuana or other drug use continues, the outpatient intervention will be stopped. The parents should also be told that if they become concerned about their child, they should feel free to contact the therapist. The idea of the therapist's isolating himself or herself from the parents applies to strict psychoanalytic techniques, but it does not apply to the therapy of drug-abusing adolescents. Biological and social interventions and the type and frequency of psychotherapy, including possible family and marital therapy, should also be discussed. The outcome of treatment will not be known until the adolescent is really able to remain dry. If marijuana is used intermittently, it is likely to be used more regularly under additional stress.

The goal of therapy is not, as many people believe, the creation of happiness but is to help the individual cope more competently with frustrations.

Even when family therapy is not recommended, the relationship between the family's or the parent's life-style and the adolescent's drug or alcohol abuse becomes evident in therapy:

A 15-year-old boy was brought in by his parents for treatment. He had smoked two to three marijuana cigarettes daily for about a year. He would often smoke in the house when his parents were out and then lie to them about what he had been doing. In one session he said, "I had a nice weekend," but he looked uncomfortable. The therapist commented that the way he appeared seemed to contradict what he said.

"My mother was away for the weekend and my father and I watched the Indy 500 on TV. He gave me beer, and we both got buzzed."

"Would that have happened if your mother had been at home?"

"Oh no, she's the moral member of the family. She called, and I guess we were rather loud on the phone. She wondered whether Dad had been drinking, but he denied it."

The father, however, had always grounded his son whenever he was caught lying. Thus the therapist clarified for the boy that he seemed to do what his father did rather than what he said. The boy wrongly thought that he was defying his father; actually he was behaving like his father. The patient spent the next 20 minutes recounting many similar family and personal episodes.

If successful outpatient interventions are impossible, in some states, parents still have the right to insist that their child— if under 17—be put in a situation in which drugs are not available. If this is impossible, then nothing can be done.

Residential care in group homes, halfway houses, drug abuse centers, and therapeutic schools may help those who are motivated to stop abusing drugs and who are trying to deal with an underlying developmental impasse. But those with serious personality problems, biologically based mood disorders, attention deficit disorders, and schizophrenia require interventions that may include sophisticated psychiatric hospitalization.

ALCOHOL

Society is, almost terrifyingly, tolerant of alcohol abuse from middle adolescence onward. Middle-class parents often buy kegs of beer for their teenagers' parties. Such parents usually are more concerned that their children not drink and drive or not drive with a drunken friend than that they not drink at all. This injunction may thus be taken to mean that it is acceptable to use alcohol if one does not drive.

Many parents seem to equate adolescents' current alcohol use with that common two to three decades ago. At that time it was relatively unusual for adolescents aged 15 or 16 to get drunk every weekend. This has now become so common that it has become accepted by the adolescent's peer group and, unwittingly, encouraged by the parents. For adolescents in the 1950s, drinking did not begin until age 17 to 19, and certainly it was unusual for youngsters of 13 and 15 to drink at all (Blatt and Hills 1968). By 1984, of those high school students surveyed, 67 percent of those in grades 10 to 12 reported that they had used alcohol in the past month, and 39 percent reported drinking at least five drinks in the two weeks prior to the survey. This compares with the approximately 5 percent who smoked marijuana daily (National Institute on Drug Abuse 1985).

Clinical studies indicate that the incidence of alcohol abuse has continued to rise and that now alcohol apparently is abused equally by both boys and girls. Furthermore, alcohol and marijuana use are not mutually exclusive.

Alcohol, as with other drugs, is used experimentally, intermittently, or regularly, and it may become part of a progressive drug-use syndrome. Alcohol, unlike marijuana, is still fraught with formal social, intrafamilial, and religious symbolism and rituals which have a long history in the West. For example, French children often have wine with their meals, and American adolescents may occasionally have a beer with their parents.

The adolescent abuse of alcohol and the incidence of adolescent alcoholism still vary among ethnic and national groups. At one time alcohol abuse was rare among Jews, but this is no longer true; alcohol is now used by all adolescent groups.

After an episode of drinking, a blood alcohol level of over 0.2 mg per liter leads to impaired coordination, slurred speech, poor judgment and sometimes loss of impulse control. Automobile accidents and fights caused by drunks are common.

Chronic intoxication, besides creating social and vocational impairment, increases family stress. Parents are likely to handle their inability to prevent such abuse by withdrawal, disregard, or criticism. Sometimes techniques of control that are chronologically inappropriate reinforce the patient's self-devaluation. "Grounding" may be appropriate for a middle-stage adolescent; it cannot control the behavior of a boy in grade twelve. Removing the family car may indeed be necessary, but a society that fails to provide adequate public transportation makes this intolerable.

An adolescent's interpersonal relationships will change with chronic abuse. All of his or her friends will tend to be alcohol or marijuana abusers or both. Chronic intoxication is also made worse by a concomitant abuse of marijuana.

Alcoholism, at least partly determined by genetic sensitivity (Elmasian et al. 1982), is considered primary when it appears to be genetically determined (Goodwin 1974). Offspring of a genetically vulnerable parent may inherit the vulnerability but may also be identifying with the parent's behavior. In secondary alcoholism, or "problem drinking," alcohol is used as a tranquilizer and a sedative (MacKay 1961). Alcohol used by a mood-disturbed adolescent may be secondary problem drinking, but it may also be primary alcoholism. In a study of 300 male Irish alcoholics, 106 were diagnosed as having an affective disorder. In 34, the mood disorder preceded the alcoholism, and in 72, the alcoholism was diagnosed first (O'Sullivan et al. 1983).

Primary alcoholic adolescents do not appear satisfied with one or two drinks but always seem to need to become overtly toxic. There are two types of primary alcoholic drinking: intermittent binge drinking, which occurs whenever alcohol is available, although it is not generally sought; and chronic drinking, which occurs when the drinker seeks out alcohol and then drinks until intoxicated.

Problem drinking may be used to try to cope with both chronic difficulties and acute trauma. In chronic difficulties, people may drink to avoid emptiness, boredom, or feeling "nothing." In acute trauma, people may drink to forget a loss: a parent through death or divorce, or a friend through death or separation.

Primary Alcoholism

Little or nothing is known of the neuroendocrinology or body chemistry of primary alcoholism. Typically, adolescents who suffer from this syndrome rapidly develop symptoms. There is no preliminary period of light drinking, because when these youngsters start drinking, they cannot stop until they are drunk. Unless they are binge drinkers, when alcohol is not available, they will crave it.

Primary alcoholism may first appear in early adolescence and, in some ways, is as difficult to treat as is marijuana abuse.

Young people may incorporate into their personalities a craving for alcohol that is as great as the urge for sex. They talk about both in much the same way; that is, being intoxicated becomes as important as having an orgasm. Alcoholic adolescents of this type are unwilling to consider not drinking. Educational, social, and sexual difficulties and blackouts all seem irrelevant and generally produce no genuine motivation for change.

Liver damage may appear in this age group before there is any evidence of an organic brain syndrome.

The younger is the adolescent who becomes alcoholic, the more difficult will be the treatment:

> Terry, an adopted child, was first seen in an adolescent treatment center at the age of 16. She had been in outpatient treatment for the last three years because of thefts from her parents, marijuana abuse, and defiant behavior. At no time did she tell her previous therapist that she was using alcohol. But whenever she got the opportunity she always got "buzzed." She stole money from her parents to buy liquor. Although she had been drinking regularly for three years, she had kept her drinking secret from both her therapist and her parents.
>
> Terry's referral for inpatient diagnosis was because the outpatient care had failed, not because of her alcoholism. As soon as she entered inpatient treatment, she attempted to get the children who were living at home to buy her liquor. When her therapist inquired about her drinking, she immediately admitted that she abused it. On asking as to why this had not been brought up with her previous therapist, she said that the therapist had never asked. When Terry had once casually mentioned that she had had something to drink, the previous therapist tried to understand with her the reasons for this. This Terry saw as the therapist's not taking her drinking seriously: "she did not make me stop."

After many months of inpatient care, Terry's later outpatient treatment did not succeed, as she saw nothing wrong in her using alcohol, and adults' disapproval only forced her to be dishonest. Terry was then sent to a residential treatment center in the hope that if she could not drink, her personality might develop. If she could develop a sense of self, independent of alcohol, she might begin to use the supportive techniques available to older adolescent alcoholics. As soon as Terry turned eighteen, she signed out of the treatment center. Her family, in an attempt to get her to return voluntarily, refused to let her come home. On her return to the city, she then went back to the adolescent treatment center, not for help with her alcoholism, but to buy time so that she could "get a job and find somewhere to live." Although very bright, she had not read a newspaper while in the residential center and was unaware that unemployment was high among teenagers. She indicated that all the time she was in residential care she had craved alcohol and that she did not intend to give it up—but "I won't get drunk this time" (a statement she had made many times before).

Terry had become alcoholic at age 13, and her need for alcohol was as acceptable as that for sex. Her internal preoccupation with alcohol meant that she was not significantly involving herself with people and that her personality development was thus impaired. Terry retained as a young adult many of the attitudes that might be appropriate for an early adolescent. However, her personality did develop somewhat in the absence of alcohol: Terry joined Alcoholics Anonymous one year after her return home and later married another recovering alcoholic. Four years later, she was dry, as was her husband, a skilled carpenter. She also was an effective mother to her year-old son.

When alcoholism starts in middle adolescence, the prospects for recovery seem brighter than when it starts earlier. It also appears that binge drinkers have a better prognosis, as they are not so internally preoccupied with the need for a drink. The difficulty of therapy is that because the wish for alcohol depends on its availability, alcoholism may not be seen as a problem:

> Carla, age 16, was in treatment for behavior that included self-mutilation, suicidal threats, a poor school record, temper tantrums, and a sort of mindless promiscuity. She suffered from a mood disorder that responded to a combination of lithium carbonate in therapeutic doses and a tricyclic antidepressant.
>
> Carla stayed overnight with a girl friend and there drank a bottle of vodka and ended up in a hospital emergency room. She then

revealed that this had happened twice before and that "I always drink that way." She did not see this as a problem.

With such an adolescent who "found" binge drinking in middle adolescence, the treatment was less difficult:

Alison first began to use alcohol when she was 15. Both of her parents were alcoholics, but they both had stopped drinking. Alison came to an adolescent treatment center after three episodes that had required hospitalization. She had consumed several pints of liquor and had become acutely toxic. In one of these episodes, she nearly died. She was also an intermittent user of marijuana. Alison had many doubts about her own worth, which was related to her abandonment by her natural father when she was four years old.

By the age of 18 Alison was in college and well understood that she could not drink alcohol: "I went with some girls to a singles' bar last night. It was a meat market, and I did not like it. I did not mind drinking 7-Up, although the others all drank beer."

Alcohol abuse beginning in late adolescence seems to have the best prognosis:

Alan was a 19-year-old who began to drink at the age of 17. He always drank to intoxication.

When Alan had taken the college entry tests, he had been hung over and so was not at his first-choice college. He sought treatment because "I am always drinking; my fraternity brothers get stoned only on weekends." A brief supportive intervention helped him join Alcoholics Anonymous, and a year later he was still dry.

Alcoholism in early and middle adolescence may not be taken seriously by adults because the child's withdrawal symptoms are often not as acute as with older adolescents and adults. Acute hallucinosis (DTs) is very rare before the age of sixteen or seventeen. Likewise, early and middle adolescents who become addicted to heroin, without external suggestion, are likely to be symptom free when the drug is withdrawn.

Most alcoholic programs for adults include facilities for daily individual and group counseling services as well as formal education in medical issues and alcoholism. Patients are also encouraged to attend Alcoholics Anonymous meetings. However, adequate treatment facilities for the intoxicating disorders of adolescents are generally scarce (Bean 1982).

Alcoholic youngsters in therapy do not usually agree to stop drinking because of emotional attachments to their families and therapeutic personnel. If they do agree to stop, it is because of anxieties about the consequences of their drinking and this is rare until late adolescence and young adulthood. Young alcoholics have difficulty realizing that they have a problem, and alcohol only reinforces their feelings of omnipotence, their poor time sense, and concrete thinking. Thus they cannot understand emotionally the necessity of stopping.

Disulfuram (Antabuse) has been used with adolescents, but again, the psychology of this age period causes difficulties, and the drug has a rare side effect: it may produce a temporary psychosis. Further, the omnipotence of disturbed alcoholic adolescents and their wish to experiment may lead to the use of alcohol while they are taking Antabuse. In addition, especially for early adolescents and those whose emotional maturity is at that level, such external control is not tolerable. Adolescent patients also generally stop taking Antabuse when they leave the hospital.

Secondary Alcoholism or Problem Drinking

Regular alcohol use by adolescents who are not primary alcoholics is symptomatic of emotional problems. Without alcoholic regression, some adolescents may not be capable of involving themselves emotionally with others and so need alcohol to lubricate sexual and social relationships.

Adolescent problem drinking may represent an identification with the parents' alcohol abuse. Like marijuana, it may be used as an attempt to cope with stress. An acute loss—of self-esteem or people—and the chronic internal desolation, boredom, and emptiness, feelings that typically occur in adolescents who suffer from emotional deprivation and mood disorders all may lead to problem drinking.

Secondary alcoholism, as well as primary alcoholism, is associated with delinquent behavior (Millman and Khan 1982). Problem drinkers may appear to suffer from a borderline-like syndrome because of their impaired capacity to be empathic, their failure to develop an age-appropriate tolerance of frustration, and the affective turbulence produced by alcohol.

Allowing for a variation in the age of onset, problem-drinking adolescents are generally easier to treat than are primary alcoholics. The craving for alcohol is the result of psychophysiological reinforcement rather than cellular sensitivity, and so middle and late adolescents are more able to accept clarifications of their use of alcohol:

> Ron had used so much alcohol between the ages of 14 and 17 that he already showed signs of liver damage. He had been having blackouts for one year before treatment. He absconded after four weeks in the hospital, feeling acutely distressed, as he believed his parents did not care about him. Although he drank on that occasion, he did not get as drunk as he had in the past. He was discharged from the hospital after eight weeks and was in once-weekly supportive therapy for four months. Two years later he was still dry.

The treatment of secondary alcoholism requires resolution of its underlying causes and abstention from alcohol. A suicidal, depressed, problem drinker needs facilities that can provide for specific treatment needs. These include the possibility of continuous therapeutic care as both an inpatient and an outpatient. In addition, nonspecific care that helps reinforce personality growth is needed. A 21-day program for the treatment of alcohol dependence is thus likely to be inadequate. Identity as an alcoholic may be reinforced by placement in a chemical dependence program, and for secondary alcoholics, this is a questionable practice. When their basic difficulties have been resolved, secondary alcoholics may still use alcohol occasionally, but this is never true for primary alcoholics.

Physicians and nurses are said to be generally disinterested in the diagnosis and treatment of alcoholics (Westermeyer, Dohney, and Stein 1978). In regard to preventing alcoholism, it has been said that the only certainty is the squandering of taxpayers' money (Selzer 1980).

HALLUCINOGENS

The most commonly used synthetic hallucinogen is lysergic acid diethylamide, or LSD 25. It was found to be hallucinogenic in 1943, along with other drugs, such as psilocybin from Mexican mushrooms and the seeds of the morning glory plant. Adolescents give these drugs exotic names such as "Mr. Natural" and "Window Pane." Other hallucinogenics are chemically synthesized, the most commonly used of this group being MDA (3.4-methylene dioxyamphetamine).

LSD 25 affects brain biochemistry and is quickly absorbed when taken by mouth. In about two hours, half of the drug ingested is still present in the bloodstream. In the human brain, it takes about two hours to reach its peak, and its effects last about 12 hours. This suggests that it links up with chemical substances usually present in brain cells. LSD also passes very readily across the placenta, and so if pregnant women take it, their infant will become psychotoxic.

The usual dose of LSD is 20 to 100 mcg, although adolescents have been known to take ten times that amount. Repeating the dose while on an LSD trip may increase the duration of the hallucinatory experience, but it does not enhance its intensity.

For most adolescents, LSD produces changes of mood, changes in the perception of the world, visual hallucinations, and changes in body image. Sometimes youngsters feel extraordinarily omnipotent, and tragedies have occurred because while "tripping," adolescents have thought they could fly:

A psychiatrist was called by one of his patients to the apartment of a 16-year-old friend. He found the place in a shambles. A boy was standing on a window ledge on the fifth floor announcing that he was going to fly. The doctor sat by the window for two hours talking to the boy, who finally came into the room.

As the boy was being taken to the hospital by the paramedics, a noise was heard in the bathroom. His naked girl friend was cowering in the corner. According to her, she and the boy were having intercourse when suddenly he got up and began to tear the room to pieces. She fled, terrified, and locked herself in the bathroom for safety.

LSD causes initial insomnia, although mild fatigue is common after using it (Hoffer and Osmond 1967). Later, REM (dream) sleep is enhanced. Cardiovascular effects include increased blood pressure and a rapid pulse. Hairs become erect. Toxic side effects, or "bad trips," create a feeling of being alienated from oneself and cause acute panic reactions, sometimes acute paranoia, with a perception that the whole world is hostile. Individuals on bad trips may become acutely agitated, destructive, or, sometimes, catatonic. They appear terrified and often have no sense of their own body boundaries. They may impulsively be destructive, especially as they are likely to distort bright objects seen behind glass.

Some persons show the effects of apparently chronic use after only one to five toxic episodes. In heavy users, LSD can be associated with chronic and possibly irreversible visual disturbances which are mediated centrally as well in the retina (Abraham 1983). Others may take the drug 50 or 60 times or more without such episodes. Many chronic users appear to isolate words from emotions and often are circumlocutory. What some intelligent adolescents say may almost seem to make sense, but after some minutes the listener suddenly realizes that the thoughts do not hang together: the adolescent's confusion is really being projected onto the listening adult. These boys and girls are often aware of their inability to get in touch with their own feelings. As one boy said, "I feel as if I am taping a message to myself; I don't feel anything." They too are often aware that their thoughts do not hang together: "I am about to say something and halfway through the idea, I don't remember where I was, and I cannot get the idea back." These youngsters are commonly known to their friends as "acid heads." In an acute hallucinatory episode, an adolescent may be brought by his or her parents or friends to a hospital emergency room.

Phencyclidine, or PCP, is a drug that was popular among adolescents in the 1970s but this is no longer true in the 1980s. After a brief flurry as a postoperative pain killer in the 1960s, it is now used as an animal tranquilizer. Drugs sold in the street as the active ingredient in marijuana, THC (tetrahydrocannabinol), are almost always PCP. It is also not unusual for marijuana bought on the street to be contaminated with PCP. The drug is commonly sniffed. The effect of PCP that is most appealing to individuals suffering from emotional deprivation syndromes is bodily warmth. One user described the sensation as similar to "being wrapped in a delicious warm cotton blanket." Tingling, floating sensations are common and pleasurable. Hallucinations are rare, but the perception of bodily distortion is striking: the body is tiny; it has no weight; one can float. Space and time are distorted, a striking effect in a generation that suffers from an instability of both.

Usually about 2 to 3 mgs of PCP are taken in one dose. The high begins in about five minutes and usually lasts from four to six hours, though in some individuals it may last for as long as 48 hours. The drug's half-life is a week or more. Side effects may include gross distortion of muscle activity, rigidity, jerking of the limbs, agitated and repetitious movements, exhibitionistic masturbation, and inappropriate laughing and crying. Such individuals may be totally out of touch with reality for up to two weeks. Hospitalization is necessary, and the treatment of choice is haloperidol (Haldol), 2 to 5 mgs, twice daily. Users of PCP are sometimes described by their friends as "crystallized." They are dull and lethargic and cannot concentrate.

Even though some researchers have found no evidence of frontal lobe damage in polydrug abusers (Brandt and Doyle 1983), it is clear from clinical studies that evidence of organic brain damage is fairly common after a variable number of hallucinogenic episodes. One previously academically successful boy reported that he could not multiply six times six but had to add them together. The capacity to make abstractions seems to become impaired, and highly concrete thinking is common. "Flashbacks" are common with all the hallucinogens, but particularly after about 15 to 50 exposures to LSD (Abraham 1983). Flashbacks are recurrent acute hallucinatory episodes in the absence of further drug ingestion. They may have a genetic basis, may be precipitated by psychological stress, may be a type of conditioned response, or may follow the use of another hallucinogenic drug such as marijuana:

> One boy in a hospital had flashbacks whenever his parents were going to visit him. He was anxious about their criticisms, but when he resolved some of his conflicts about his parents, the flashbacks disappeared.

An example of a conditioned response is as follows:

A British physician took LSD, using herself as an experimental subject to study the etiology of schizophrenia. While she was toxic on LSD, the church bells were ringing. She reported getting flashbacks for one year, which occurred whenever she heard church bells.

Of all the drugs on which intense psychological dependence is possible, LSD and PCP appear to be the most dangerous. They create a craving for their use that appears to last long past the time when any aftereffects of the drugs are evident. As with alcoholism, the earlier a child begins using these hallucinogens, the harder it is to deal with the craving:

Paul, age 16, was admitted to an adolescent treatment center because of irrational behavior at home and school, school failure, and the daily use of marijuana, which he could not stop. He gave a history of having used LSD about "100 times." He also was the local dealer of LSD and MDA.

Initially, Paul could not concentrate in school and felt as if his inner world was being explored by both himself and others. He was markedly out of touch with his own feelings. Psychological tests indicated a learning disability. Five months later, Paul was functioning well in the treatment center's school, wrote beautiful poetry, and all evidence of a learning disability had gone. Paul remarked, "I won't have any trouble staying off pot, but if anyone offers me acid, I know I'll take it. I think about it every day and remember how beautiful the experience was."

Treating Acute Toxic Hallucinogenesis

Many institutions deal with violent patients by strapping them down or injecting large doses of tranquilizers such as chlorpromazine (Thorazine). These techniques, however, worsen the psychosis of LSD and other hallucinogens. The ideal technique of handling such young people is to engage them physically and verbally in a process that has become known as *talking down*.

This technique is reassuring to acutely psychotic individuals, whether their psychosis is due to panic, drug toxicity, mania, or schizophrenia. In this process, the patient is physically held down on a bed, the floor, or an examining table by three or four individuals who ensure that he or she cannot be hurt. Ideally one member of the team is of the opposite sex to the patient. The team members stroke the patient to help clarify body boundaries, and in a quiet way, the patient is reassured.

Some individuals are reassured by having their bodies touched and stroked, the equivalent of cuddling a frightened child. LSD, however, can exacerbate homosexual anxieties, and so a misguided cuddling equivalent by an individual of the same sex as the patient can produce panic.

Medication has been used with LSD toxicity, but it makes diagnosis and, ultimately, accurate specific interventions very complicated, as the treating clinician may not know exactly what drug has been taken. For example, 50 mgs of chlorpromazine will end a trip after adequate liver function has been ensured. Diazepam (Valium) in small doses of 5 mgs by mouth relieves the tension associated with LSD toxicity but does not oversedate the patient.

Our clinical experience is that the recovery from the effects of toxic states produced by chronic LSD use takes 6 to 12 months. Those who are genetically vulnerable may precipitate schizophrenia by using the drug. Some adolescents who become psychotoxic for a prolonged period after one dose of hallucinogen may be in this group, the illness presumably being precipitated by the biochemical insult to the central nervous system. Some adolescents become overtly psychotic on two or three doses of hallucinogen. Each hallucinogen is said to produce specific side effects. Psilocybin produces visions rich in color, and mescaline makes the individual feel free of earthly cares and particularly affects hearing, smell, and taste.

COCAINE

The use of cocaine, derived from the coca plant, was unusual in adolescents until the present decade. It is still believed by many young people to be nonaddictive, and the only factor that seems to limit its use is its price. *Freebasing*, or smoking cocaine, is made possible by a mixture of cocaine and ether. Smoking of "crack," a pure form of the drug, is the most addictive. When freebase is inhaled, it induces a euphoric state of great intensity (Perez-Reyes et al. 1982). Smoking also increases the blood pressure and pulse rate more than does an injection of cocaine hydrochloride, and the craving for a repeat dose in "recreational" users is greater. Affluent young adults and adolescents are smoking crack with increasing frequency.

Cocaine is distributed differently from marijuana. Dealers do not carry the drug with the hope of making a sale; it has to be specially ordered. Its use is therefore planned, and except when it is given away at parties, it is rarely used impulsively.

Cocaine is usually inhaled (sniffed). Because of its expense, to ensure that none is wasted and that every grain is used, it is often arranged in lines for sniffing from glass or mirrored table tops. Adolescents seem to enjoy this preliminary ritual:

One boy described his coming high school graduation as follows: "The coke dealers are swarming around the school, and the kids who want to be thought of as special are buying it. I guess their hotel rooms will be full of glass." The psychiatrist did not quite understand the latter's comment and asked, "Why glass? You mean they want kinky sex and watch it on the ceiling?" The patient looked at his therapist rather pityingly: "No, glass tables. You need them to make lines of the drug."

It is still rare for cocaine to be pure. Usually it is cut with a variety of substances, often mannitol, which is inert, or sometimes analgesics such as Tylenol. On occasion, amphetamines are included. Generally, the purity of street cocaine ranges from 30 to 70 percent, and the average dose of cocaine is from 10 to 50 mgs.

Pure cocaine's stimulant effect lasts about 30 minutes, much less time than that of the amphetamines. It is thus difficult to know whether the side effects reported after cocaine use are due to the drug or its contaminants. After injecting the drug, some users become acutely anxious and paranoid, and others become briefly acutely psychotic.

Daily use interferes with eating and sleeping; concentration is difficult; and users become hyperirritable. One boy lost 20 pounds in four weeks. One 12-year-old child described his parents, who were apparently addicted to freebasing:

> "They go into the basement and stay there for hours. If the phone rings, they don't answer. I don't want to interrupt them because mother looks dopey and just yells at me."

Students who become addicted may spend all their money, including their school fees, on cocaine, and business persons have been known to go bankrupt. Many deal the drug in order to support their habit, and prostitution is a common solution.

Decongestant nasal sprays are often used to cover the nasal drip that develops in those who chronically inhale. Cocaine has the notorious reputation of producing a "saddle" nose, caused by the destruction of the nasal cartilage, but this is rare.

In high doses, cocaine can cause seizures, depression of the medullary centers of the brain, and death from cardiac arrest.

Treating Cocaine Abuse

Those who become dependent on a cocaine high find it difficult to give up if the drug is available. One study reported that 15 mgs of methylphenidate daily relieved the craving behavior and toxic withdrawal symptoms of a woman who used two ounces of cocaine a week (Khantzian 1983).

Cocaine overdosage requires the inhalation of oxygen, and convulsions may be treated by injecting a short-acting barbiturate (25 to 50 mgs of sodium pentothal). Indural (Propranolol) injected intravenously has also been used to treat cocaine overdosage (1 mg/1 min. intravenously for 8 min.).

It is becoming increasingly common for adolescents to be referred for treatment of cocaine abuse, although only late adolescents appear to refer themselves. Cocaine is also mentioned more and more by affluent adolescents in treatment, and it is reported as enhancing orgasm.

Those who are psychologically vulnerable can become dependent on cocaine extraordinarily quickly, especially those adolescents who find it difficult to make trusting relationships in middle adolescence when emotional involvement with those outside the family becomes important:

> At the beginning of his vacation from boarding school, Harry, age 16, met a girl, age 18, whom he had known as a child. She introduced him to cocaine, and four weeks later he had spent all his earnings as a busboy and $1,000 he had stolen, on the drug.

The analogy with the binge drinking of primary alcoholism is striking. On the other hand:

> Fifteen-year-old Lisa had used cocaine every weekend for one year. She commented, "I would wait for Friday to come around, and by Wednesday, I wanted it so much I got no work done at school. I used to steal liquor from my dad to take the edge off until I could get coke."

Both adolescents showed no overt withdrawal symptoms when hospitalized, and both denied craving the drug. But they both agreed that when under stress they thought about it, talked to peers about it excessively, and, when discharged to outpatient therapy, knew that if cocaine were offered, they would be likely to take it. Attendance at Narcotics Anonymous groups did not seem to be helpful to them or other middle-stage adolescents.

THE AMPHETAMINES

When the use of mood-changing drugs spread out of the black ghetto and the jazz world in the United States to the white population, the first drugs to be widely abused were the amphetamine derivatives. Before 1955, these drugs had some following among students who wanted to be able to cope better with examinations. By 1960, the use of amphetamine-barbiturate mixtures was common in large cities in the United States and in Britain. Because nowadays the middle class is less apt to use amphetamines than is the lower socioeconomic class, those middle-class adolescents who use amphetamines are more likely to be severely psychologically disturbed than are lower-socioeconomic-class adolescents. Stimulant pills used by British working-class youth have special names such as "black bombers" (Durophet) and "purple hearts" (Dexamyl). In the United States, stimulants share the term *speed*, and at the present time these drugs are not used as commonly as they once were. A change from ten years ago, it is unusual nowadays in clinical practice to see an adolescent who uses only speed.

The amphetamines were introduced into the youth culture indirectly by physicians and the pharmaceutical industry. They were widely prescribed for various, somewhat unrelated, conditions (Bett 1976), and by 1958, something like 3.5 billion tablets, and by 1970, 10 billion tablets had been sold. This family of drugs has no clinical value, except perhaps for hyperactivity in children with an attention deficit disorder. Prescriptions for amphetamines are now illegal in many states.

The abuse of amphetamines surfaces usually only when adolescents show toxic symptoms. The previous failure of such adolescents to master the tasks of this age period apparently are rarely a cause for adult concern. In large doses, the typical symptoms of amphetamine use are tachycardia, peripheral vasoconstriction and dryness of the mouth. Transient euphoria and sleeplessness are also common. Amphetamines taken over several days produce extreme fatigue. Phenmetrazine (Preludin) and the amphetamines both can cause psychosis. Forty-two cases of individuals who became psychotic after a single dose of amphetamines and 32 after several doses have been reported (Connell 1958).

Some individuals die from amphetamine overdosage. Though abnormal electrocardiographs have been reported in adolescents, most adolescents appear not to suffer permanent cardiovascular damage. Necrotizing angiitis, the destruction of blood vessel walls, has, however, been reported in young drug abusers who use methamphetamine alone or with heroin or LSD (Citron 1970).

In an amphetamine psychosis and that caused by sniffing solvents, the individual typically is paranoid:

A 15-year-old boy ran away from a school for delinquent boys and, "blocked" on speed, was later picked up by the police. The police called the principal of the school, who collected the boy in his car. As the principal was driving back, the boy suddenly tried to wrench the steering wheel from his hands, screaming, "We must get out. We are being attacked by a gang of murderers who are firing machine guns at us from the sidewalk."

Amphetamines in high doses affect sexual functions and inhibit erections in males.

There is often an alternation between the heavy use of amphetamines and then abstention. It is during this withdrawal phase that violent behavior is common. Adolescents who are toxic on amphetamines may also be dangerous to others. Sometimes depression may occur, and during such episodes, because of feelings of inadequacy and low self-esteem, users may attempt suicide.

Treatment of an amphetamine psychosis includes protecting the patient and others, but there is no need to prescribe antipsychotic medication unless the condition persists. Indeed, the drug is cleared more rapidly by acidifying the patient's urine through the use of ammonium chloride.

Some adolescents sniff powdered caffeine, or No-Doz, a popular drug that can be purchased over the counter. It is reported to give a pleasurable, rapid, but short-acting high.

THE BARBITURATES AND METHAQUALONES

Barbiturates ("downers"), methaqualone (Quaaludes or "ludes"), and diazepam (Valium) continue to be used widely. In the 1980s, Quaaludes became the chemical most widely used by adolescents. Although the general use of Quaaludes has been declining, their occasional use is still popular with both high school and college students.

In clinical practice it is uncommon to see heavy regular use of methaqualone. This drug is not usually taken alone (Gerald and Schurian 1973), and it has the reputation, with no real evidence, of being an aphrodisiac. Girls who are "downed out on ludes" are thought to be more sexually available, and boys, more potent. In England, the drug is known as "Mandrax" when it is combined with diphenhydramine; in the United States, this has led to one street name for Quaaludes, "Mandrake."

Methaqualone is a longer-acting drug than are most barbiturates. Its site of action in the brain is similar to that of barbiturates and alcohol. Alone, it does not usually cause breathing difficulties and heart failure, but Quaaludes with alcohol, or "luding out," is a common cause of drug-related toxicity and death:

> One 16-year-old boy ended up in the local emergency room when he drank half a bottle of liquor and took three Quaaludes. He became unconscious and could not be aroused by his panic-stricken friends. He was then admitted to the adolescent clinic, and his long history of drug abuse and concomitant theft was revealed.

Overdosage of methaqualone leads to restlessness, delirium, and perhaps convulsions. Its side effects include headaches, dizziness, diarrhea, chills, and fever. It interferes with REM sleep and thus may cause fatigue for several days after its use.

The three major barbiturates available to and used by adolescents are short acting: secobarbital ("reds," "red devils," "downers"), phenobarbital ("yellows," "yellow jackets," "tuinals"), and a combination of these known as "rainbows." Long-acting barbiturates such as nembutal are rarely used unless stolen from pharmacies, although sometimes the children of physicians distribute them to their friends. Like Quaaludes, barbiturates are not taken by adolescents as a regular drug of abuse. Older adolescents and young adults who are polydrug abusers and deeply embedded in the drug culture may inject both amphetamines and barbiturates. The injection does not generally appeal to adolescents but has been seen occasionally in emotionally promiscuous, deprived girls.

As with alcohol, users of barbiturates occasionally become violent. For instance, barbiturate use is reported in 6 percent of all suicides (Schwartz 1972). Chronic barbiturate use, like chronic alcoholism, produces poor memory, slow speech, and emotional lability. It is as dangerous for an adolescent to drive an automobile after having taken barbiturates or Quaaludes as after having ingested alcohol.

The treatment of chronic barbiturate abuse is to wean an adolescent from the drug in a hospital setting, as acute overdosage is a medical emergency. Rapid withdrawal of both barbiturates and methaqualone can lead to convulsions.

HEROIN

The heroin epidemic is continuing in the United States, but heroin use is still uncommon among early and middle adolescents.

Heroin addiction causes particular therapeutic problems. Addicts may be withdrawn from the drug as outpatients if they are sufficiently motivated. A five-day course of methadone has been popular, in which the dosage depends on the amount of heroin previously taken. Methadone maintenance is still employed, but it is used illegally on the street to check withdrawal symptoms and may affect the newborn infants of treated mothers (Brust 1983). If an addict's motivation is doubted or if the patient is an adolescent, hospitalization or placement in an appropriate therapeutic community is always necessary. From clinical observation, early and middle adolescents who use heroin do not become as physiologically addicted as do late adolescents and adults. If it is not suggested to younger adolescents that they might get withdrawal symptoms when they can no longer obtain heroin, they often will not. Unless liver function tests can be given, it is probably unwise to give chlorpromazine to abate the possibility of "cold turkey." Chlordiazepoxide hydrochloride (Librium), in doses of 25 to 50 mg tablets three to four times daily, facilitates withdrawal. Librium should not, however, be given to young adolescents until there is symptomatic evidence of withdrawal. Naltrexone can be used intermittently but is not recommended for longer-term maintenance.

Programs focusing only on withdrawal—a brief period of hospitalization, for example—are much less successful than are programs in which the patient's character defenses are challenged, along with clear expectations, high staff control, and enough time in treatment (Bale et al. 1984). Society's refusal to pay for adequate treatment has a tragic effect on the outcome of young addicts, and mental health laws that give adolescents the right to refuse treatment are equally disastrous.

FAMILY RELATIONSHIPS AND DRUG ABUSE

In drug abuse, as with other psychiatric symptoms, there is a relationship between the implicit and explicit messages that parents give to their children and the children's explicit behavior. Sometimes parents say that they do not wish their children to take drugs, but they act as if they do:

> Larry, a 15-year-old schoolboy, was hospitalized because of his aggressive antisocial behavior. He began to abuse amphetamines at the age of thirteen. He was first given them by his doctor-father because he slept excessively when having to study for an examination. The boy felt that his father was "always giving me pills" and used this behavior to justify his own drug abuse.

> The father was told about this by the psychiatric social worker and asked not to give the boy drugs. During a visit to his father, the boy complained of headaches. The latter immediately gave him some aspirin. The same day the boy absconded from the hospital and was picked up by the police one week later in the company of other drug-abusing youngsters.

The unconscious provocation of drug use is not unlike the unconscious provocation of aberrant sexual behavior (Johnson and Szurek 1956). Common parental responses are ignorance, denial, helplessness, anger, and despair. Many parents are unaware that their children abuse drugs or alcohol. If they suspect abuse, their child will usually lie. If the child continues to get good grades in school or to keep his or her part-time job, the child's denial of abuse will be reinforced. It is probably impossible to resolve early adolescents' difficulties associated with drug abuse without adequate family intervention. If the child is over the age of 16, an inability to assist the family can usually be overcome by increasing the frequency of therapeutic contact with the youngster. If, for example, a boy of 16 has a mother who cannot part with her dependent child, whose drug abuse keeps him in an infantile state, and if the mother is unable or unwilling to be helped, then psychotherapy will need to be more frequent.

DRUG ABUSE DURING TREATMENT

Drug abuse is a particular problem in the treatment of mood disorders and schizophrenia. Marijuana interferes with the efficiency of antidepressants, and the effects of alcohol are made worse by tranquilizers. Medication is generally not advised for acute confusional states until their cause is clear. Recovery may also be spontaneous.

Before the current pandemic of drug abuse began, a conscious motivation for therapy became more likely by middle adolescence. But now, adolescents who abuse drugs are often consciously unmotivated for therapy, even into young adulthood. Chronic drug abuse generally interferes with psychological maturation; concrete thinking persists; and the capacities to tolerate frustration and to be able to look at oneself remain impaired.

In the initial stages of outpatient therapy, drug-dependent adolescents may be able to stop abusing drugs if they are seen daily. Such psychotherapy is possible only when a therapist is able to make a meaningful alliance with a patient. Once the drugs are withdrawn, adolescents may be able to continue not to take them because of their initial idealization of the therapist. To enable the therapy to continue, however, adolescents must recognize that their idealized perception of the therapist is unreal, that it represents their own wish to remain omnipotent. The frustration in this understanding is the point at which efforts at outpatient psychotherapy may break down. Destructive acting out of the wish for omnipotence will follow, and then the drug taking may resume.

The therapeutic dilemma is that on the one hand, the therapist must use the omnipotence that the patient has given to him or her. On the other hand, he or she must carefully weigh the ending of this phase of treatment. As the patient begins to realize that the therapist is not all-powerful, the patient's hostility becomes apparent. Only if this hostility is correctly interpreted can the patient stay dry.

Drug-dependent adolescents tend to have a harsh, weak superego that is not powerful enough to control their discharge of impulses. If this superego is projected onto the therapist, the patient will attempt to escape from the treatment, as from his or her own internal conflicts.

The consciously unmotivated drug-dependent adolescent who cannot stop taking drugs will certainly need to be treated in a setting in which drugs are not available. Sometimes a treatment center can contain the youngster, and sometimes psychiatric settings that can exercise greater control are indicated. Drug-dependent adolescents may appear to be unable to make emotionally meaningful relationships until the drugs are removed and they dry out. During the opening phases of treatment, the underlying causes must be diagnosed. The effects of abuse may make the assessment of treatability difficult for several weeks.

Drug toxicity may be the storm center in which an adolescent who would have mastered difficulties by means of spontaneous self-righting mechanisms may falter. In psychotherapy, accurate and well-timed comments do not necessarily control acting out, and continued drug abuse may destroy the value of psychotherapy.

Professional help is less and less available. Insurance policies have restricted outpatient and inpatient benefits, and so few can afford such treatment. The government has similarly reduced its funds.

Drug abuse has complicated adolescent personality development, and in regard to treating adolescents, it has made some apparently unreachable. The majority of disturbed adolescents, provided that they can be kept away from drugs of abuse and alcohol, can be helped.

REFERENCES

Abraham, H. D. (1983). Visual phenomenology of the LSD flashback. *Archives of General Psychiatry* 40:884–889.

Bale, R. N., Zarcone, V. P., Van Stone, W. W., Kuldan, J. M. (1984). Three therapeutic communities: process and two-year follow-up results. *Archives of General Psychiatry* 41:185–191.

Bean, M. (1982). Identifying and managing alcohol problems of adolescents. *Psychosomatics* 23:389–396.

Bett, W. R. (1976). Benzedrine sulphate in clinical medicine: A survey of the literature. *Post Graduate Medical Journal* 22:205–206.

Blatt, M. M., and Hills, D. R. (1968). Alcohol abuse and alcoholism in the young. *British Journal of Addiction* 63:183–191.

Brandt, J., and Doyle, L. F. (1983). Concept attainment, tracking and shifting in adolescent polydrug abusers. *Journal of Nervous Mental Diseases* 171:559–563.

Brill, H. (1969). EEG abnormalities in marijuana overdosage. *Proceedings of the New York State Narcotic Addiction Control Commission.*

Brust, J. C. M. (1983). The non-impact of opiate research on opiate abuse. *Neurology* 33:1327–1331.

Carrol, B. J., and Curtis, G. C. (1976). Neuroendocrine regulation in depression. *Archives of General Psychiatry* 33:1039–1064.

Citron, P. B. (1970). Necrotising angiitis associated with drug abuse. *New England Journal of Medicine* 283:1003–1011.

Connell, P. H. (1958). *Amphetamine Psychosis.* London: Chapman and Hall.

DeRopp, R. S. (1957). *Drugs and the Mind.* New York: St. Martin's Press.

Elmasian, R., Neville, H., Woods, D., Schuckit, M., and Bloom, F. (1982). Event related brain potentials are different in individuals at high and low risk for developing alcoholism. *Proceedings of the National Academy of Science* 79:7900–7903.

Gerald, M. S., and Schurian, P. M. (1973). Nonmedical use of methaqualone. *Archives of General Psychiatry* 28:627.

Goodwin, D. (1974). Drinking problems in adopted and nonadopted sons of alcoholics. *Archives of General Psychiatry* 31:164–169.

Grinspoon, L., and Bakaler, J. B. (1976). *Cocaine: A Drug and Its Social Evolution.* New York: Basic Books.

Hoffer, A., and Osmond, H. (1967). *The Hallucinogens.* New York: Academic Press.

Johnson, A. M., and Szurek, S. A. (1956). The genesis of antisocial acting out in children and adults. *Psychoanalytic Quarterly* 22:323–343.

Johnson, L. D. (1982). Drugs and the Nation's High School Students: Six Year National Trends. Rockville, MD: National Institute on Drug Abuse.

Kandel, D. B. (1982). Epidemiologic and psychosocial perspectives on adolescent drug abuse. *Journal of the American Academy of Child Psychiatry* 21:348–353.

Khantzian, E. J. (1983). An extreme case of cocaine dependence and marked improvement with methylphenidate treatment. *American Journal of Psychiatry* 160:784–785.

Lumberger, L., Silberstein, S., Axelrod, J., and Kopin, J. (1970). Marijuana studies in the disposition and metabolism of Delta 9 tetrahydrocannabinol in man. *Science* 170:1320–1322.

MacKay, J. R. (1961). Clinical observations of adolescent problem drinkers. *Quarterly Journal of the Study of Alcohol* 21:124–134.

McMillan, D. E., Harris, L. S., Turk, R. F., and Kennedy, J. S. (1970). Development of marked behavioral tolerance to 1 delta 8 tetrahydrocannabinol in the pigeon. *Pharmacologist* 12:258.

Miller, D. (1973). The drug dependent adolescent. *Adolescent Psychiatry* 2:70–97.

———. (1974). *Adolescence: Psychology, Psychopathology, and Psychotherapy.* New York: Jason Aronson.

Millman, R. B., and Khan, E. T. (1982). Alcohol and adolescent psychopathology. In *Alcoholism and Clinical Psychiatry*, ed. J. Solomon. New York: Plenum.

National Institute of Drug Abuse (1985). Use of Licit and Illicit Drugs by American High School Students. 1975–1985. National Institute on Drug Abuse. Rockville, MD.

O'Sullivan, K., Williams, P., Daly, M., Carroll, B., Clare, A., and Cooney, J. (1983). A comparison of alcoholics with and without coexisting affective disorders. *British Journal of Psychiatry* 143:133–138.

Perez-Reyes, M. D., Guiseppi, S., Ondousek, G., Jeffcoat, A. R., and Cook, C. E. (1982). Freebase cocaine smoking. *Clinical Pharmacology and Therapeutics* 32:459–465.

Schwartz, J. (1972). Barbiturates. *Texas Medical Journal* 68:54.

Schwartz, P., Fletcher, J. M., and Sutler, L. S. (1977). Neurophysiological, intellectual and personality correlates of chronic marijuana use in native Costa Ricans. In *Chronic Cannabis Use*, ed. R. L. Dornbush, A. M. Freedman, and M. Fink. New York: Academy of Sciences.

Selzer, M. L. (1980). Alcoholism and alcoholic psychosis. In *Comprehensive Text Book of Psychiatry*, ed. H. Kaplan and A. M. Freeman. Baltimore: Williams and Wilkins.

Shapiro, J., and Wynne, E. A. (1981). Adolescent alienation: evaluating the hypotheses. *Social Indicators Research.*

Stefanis, C., Boulougonis, A., and Liakus, A. (1976). Clinical and psychological effects of cannabis in long term users. In *Pharmacology of Marijuana*, ed. M. C. Brunde and S. Szara. New York: Raven Press.

U.S. Department of Health and Human Services. (1981). *Fourth Special Report of the U.S. Congress on Alcohol and Health* (ADM). Washington, D.C.: U.S. Government Printing Office.

Weisberg, P. S. (1979). Group therapy with adolescents. In *The Short Course in Adolescent Psychiatry*, ed. J. R. Novello. New York: Brunner/ Mazel.

Westermeyer, J., Dohney, S., and Stein, B. (1978). An assessment of alcoholic care for the hospital patient. *Alcohol* 2:53.

Winnicott, D. W. (1953). Transitional objects and transitional phenomena. *International Journal of Psycho-Analysis* 36:89–97.

Wynne, E. A. (1979). Facts about the character of young Americans. *Character* 1:1.

11

Treating Antisocial Adolescents in the Correctional System

Although all the behavioral disturbances to which disturbed young people are prone are, in a sense, antisocial in that they inflict pain on others, are developmentally destructive, and are pathologically gratifying to the adolescent, a number of children, in addition, break the law. If they are found guilty, they are deemed *delinquent*, a social rather than a medical term. Adolescents who are termed delinquent usually have no conscious complaints about themselves. They inflict pain on others and may justify this with a variety of rationalizations. Theft does not matter because the insurance companies will pay; the victims are affluent, or they belong to a different ethnic group. Violent behavior is acceptable.

In 1975, 35 percent of violent crimes were committed by males aged 15 to 20, who represent 8.5 percent of the population (Marohn 1982). In 1973, over half the juvenile court judges in the United States found as the most pressing problems they faced,

inadequate facilities for detention and shelter care pending disposition. Fifteen percent saw more knowledge about the right way
to handle cases and better facilities for testing and psychological
evaluation as most needed (Fox 1981).

Although the facilities for adolescents in the correctional
system are inadequate, this is a result of their not being allocated
rather than their not being available. Paradoxically, there are
now more than enough available professionals, but currently,
society is unwilling to decide whether it is worthwhile to rehabil-
itate antisocial adolescents.

Therapeutic services in the correctional and health care
system should follow the same principles. A residential experience in a psychiatric setting or in a correctional setting should
be isolated from the community as little as possible. If a correctional setting is to be therapeutic, discharge should not mean
losing the significant people of that institution. Unfortunately, in
many such settings, their geographical placement or lack of
funds means that the residents cannot continue their relationships with the same professionals in the institution, the family, and
the larger community.

The educational deficits of delinquent males have been well
recognized (Wolff et al. 1982), but there are generally very few
therapeutic educational environments that identify learning
needs, blocks to learning, and current educational capacity (Nichtern 1974).

The deficiencies of the correctional system are well known.
New York's so-called reform schools vary according to age, sex,
race, and degree of the residents' troublesomeness, as well as the
institution's security, amenities, and per-capita expenditure. The
only apparent constraint is that not one school can provide even
minimal mental health treatment for the seriously disturbed
children it receives (Fox 1981).

Those who work in such systems are often well aware that
they cannot offer the treatment that is needed. Bureaucratized
child care is constantly under pressure from diminishing funds or
confusion as to what the organization's goal should be. Such
difficulties are dealt with by arranging a disposition on the basis
of the antisocial behavior's severity, although it is clear that
ethnic group and social class may determine the type of placement used.

Depending on the underlying disturbance's severity, trial in adult courts and automatic incarceration in adult prisons for those found guilty do not improve outcome. It appears that the more antisocial the behavior is, the more likely it is that labeling will be regarded as sufficient to determine the subsequent "treatment."

The typical profile of a delinquent adolescent who has been involved in a violent crime may include the following: the adolescent has acted in ways that are dangerous to the self; has had suicidal thoughts; is accident prone; has committed intentional, marginally intentional, or accidental suicidal actions (Miller 1982); and has self-mutilated. Danger to others, including anger, belligerence, negativism, and affective and predatory assaultive behavior are usual. These behavioral symptoms may be present with psychological symptoms and signs that are often not recognized, as well as hallucinations, delusions, and gross difficulties in interpersonal relationships. An inability to obtain satisfaction and comfort from performing expected social activities is to be expected, and peer and other relationships are shallow. The individual's capacity for self-expression may be limited.

Typically, such young people fail to reach their academic potential, may refuse to go to school, and have school phobias or disciplinary problems. The unemployment rate is high for those who have left or dropped out of school, and if work is available, it is often poorly performed. Emotionally impoverished, these young people then seek excitement and realistic gratification from theft, planned or otherwise, breaking into homes, mugging, and thefts from parked automobiles. The ability to use leisure time constructively is minimal or absent. Sexual dysfunction is not rare and as with those in psychiatric hospitals, the abuse of drugs or alcohol is common.

TREATMENT IN THE JUVENILE
JUSTICE SYSTEM

Perhaps because of the difficulties in understanding and treating the delinquent and violent adolescent, psychiatry has generally focused only on the care of those who are overtly mentally ill or suicidal.

Even in psychiatric hospitals, violent young people who do not easily make relationships are particularly difficult to help. They tend to disrupt therapeutic settings, often by intimidating both staff and other patients, and they succeed, for a variety of reasons. One reason is that most adolescent treatment centers, although they are better staffed than adult psychiatric hospitals, are still not sufficiently equipped to provide well-planned specific and nonspecific care. Adolescents who respond to stress by means of violent behavior disrupt the world outside themselves, and many end up by being temporarily contained rather than treated. Both the psychiatric and the correctional systems fail to assess adequately the delinquent's treatability and often cannot decide how to return a productive youngster to society. The goal of juvenile corrections is still reform, but the reconviction rates remain depressingly high.

It is unlikely that the juvenile justice and correctional systems will change much, but constructive change in two areas is possible. Early diagnosis, before institutional care becomes necessary, might enable skilled necessary biological intervention. The overall social system of institutions could develop a clear, honest concept of their goal and how it is to be achieved. If the goal is only to protect society temporarily, at the risk of returning more violent individuals to the community, this should be clear. Adult jails are the adolescent "gulags" of Western society and cannot be rehabilitative.

If delinquents are to be placed in a closed institution from which society is protected by fences, guards, or distance from cities, a minimum realistic goal is to inculcate in the inmate a sense of socially acceptable masculinity or femininity. To achieve this goal, an institution should provide for the adolescent relationships with both men and women. The adults should be acceptable identification models who are able to be empathic and firm without being coercive. They should occupy a role in the institution that has meaning as being valuable in the larger society. If the staff's only role is as guards who merely observe, this behavior is an unacceptable identification model for the inmate, who needs to learn to be productive in the community at large.

The staff need to understand that adolescents' respect for the physical care of their own bodies is an important way of respecting their integrity and obtaining a sense of self-worth. Resources to make this possible thus need to be provided. All staff should understand which of their own values are based on social or ethnic class; ethnocentricity is no excuse for ignoring developmental needs. In racially prejudiced societies, it is inevitable that racial tensions from the community at large will spill into the institutional system, and the implications of this must be faced.

Ideally, a correctional system should forbid all forms of violence and try to teach the youngsters a respect for others. Furthermore, the buildings' architectural design should convey this while at the same time protecting the community at large.

Education that encourages creativity and imagination is especially needed because of the boredom that many disturbed adolescents experience. The search for excitement is one cause of antisocial behavior, and so such adolescents should be taught how to earn a living and should be trained in skills valued by the community. Hours of idleness are of no value and are developmentally destructive. Remedial education should be available for those who are below grade level and who are learning disabled. Education should be vocationally realistic: any adolescent who leaves a correctional institution unable to earn a living represents a failure by the institution.

The institutional system should have as its goal socially acceptable productivity and environmental mastery. It should reinforce mutual caring and teach young people to be empathic. Controls should be comprehensible consequences for unacceptable behavior rather than arbitrary punishment. Such controls should depend on interpersonal relationships with valued staff and the production in the social system of a life-style that reinforces some types of behavior and forbids others.

Psychological treatment should be made available only if it is directed toward reinforcing these goals. Group counseling should encourage honesty, reinforce empathy, and limit anger to interpersonal relationships with designated staff counselors. Although family, group, and individual counseling are seen as being useful in corrections, often the goal of these interventions may not be clear, nor may they use appropriate techniques.

At the present time, the severity of the crime for which the

youngster has been adjudicated guilty determines whether community treatment or institutional care—with a varying length of
stay and location of incarceration—should be used. Progressively
more coercive and restrictive environments tend to be used as
this sieving technique fails, and eventually 14-year-old youngsters may be tried as adults and incarcerated in adult jails. The
general purpose, depending on the crime, has been to use the
least restrictive intervention, but this ignores the necessity of a
biopsychosocial diagnosis. Even when such a diagnosis is made,
juvenile court judges are not generally trained to use the information.

The same type of violent event, with a multidetermined
biopsychosocial cause, has a different prognosis in different adolescents: the severity of their crime is only one determinant.
Although acting out is inevitable in any successful intervention,
any type of counseling is of little value if the adolescent does not
trust the counselor. If drug abuse, theft, or violence continues in
the institution's underground life, this will imply that the authority system's values are inconsistent and worthless.

The way the system "ought" to be able to function but
currently cannot is demonstrated from the report of a consultation with an adolescent in a juvenile correctional setting:

> Charles, who became a state ward after a homicidal attack on his
> brother, was a rather small, chunky, black boy of 16. He was
> referred for an opinion because while at a juvenile correctional
> setting, he had not been able to cooperate with the staff. Except
> for an hour or two a day when he went to school, he had been
> isolated for two months in his room. During this time, he day-
> dreamed, but he denied having had hallucinations. He had refused
> to talk to anyone.

> When Charles was thirteen, after an evening when he became
> intoxicated on a mixture of alcohol and other drugs, he stabbed
> his brother with the latter's knife. This was reported to the police
> by the hospital to which the brother was admitted as a patient.

During the diagnostic interview, Charles gave a long history
of having been moved from place to place. He had not done
satisfactory work in school; he had used cocaine, hashish, alcohol,

and some heroin; he had run away from a group home in which he had been placed after the violent episode; and he had then ended up in the juvenile correctional system:

> Charles indicated that he did not trust anybody in authority. He saw the counseling groups as useless. He trusted only two people, his mother and a girl friend. He claimed that the latter had been a counselor at the group home where he had lived for a while. He said he had had a sexual relationship with her. With ill-concealed, but unconscious, anger, he indicated that she was white.

> Charles reported that he became violent with people only when they attacked him; then he hit them to the point that he felt safe. He denied loss of control, but his violence was always excessive for the provocation. When he was not taking drugs, he described himself as feeling depressed and empty. His unrealistic goal was to get his high school equivalent and go on to college, but he apparently abandoned this idea in the course of the interview.

The psychiatrist asked how he could talk so easily, and Charles replied that he "liked" the doctor and thought that he "did not bullshit," that he could trust him. The psychiatrist felt that the boy needed to be cared for, perhaps an indication of the boy's disturbance; healthy adolescents do not arouse this feeling in adults.

Charles did not show any sign of a thought disorder. He was using language superior to that to be expected of a boy with a reported IQ of 87, which suggested that he might have an undiagnosed learning disability. At the end of the interview, with a good deal of sadness, he asked the interviewer if he could see him again.

The diagnostic conclusion was that this was a manipulative boy who had little sense of himself as a person. He could talk freely of his capacity to be angry, his emptiness, and his propensity to withdraw under stress. His violence was affective rather than predatory and would probably require biological intervention. He was thought to have a borderline personality and to be suffering from a low-risk, Class III violent syndrome (Miller and Looney 1976).

Four types of intervention were recommended: diagnostic,

social, biological, and psychological. The diagnostic intervention would be to determine whether there was central nervous system pathology, that is, whether clinical examination and biological investigations showed evidence that he suffered from a type of mood disorder that might respond to medication. With a low-average IQ, Charles verbalized at apparently a higher level. Because he had a history of school failure, he needed to be assessed for a learning disability and a possible attention deficit disorder.

Charles had little sense of his own identity and had poor controls over his own impulsive and violent behavior. The severity of his personality difficulty also needed to be assessed, particularly his capacity to make meaningful interpersonal relationships. The fact that he behaved in one psychiatric interview with seductive frankness did not mean that he could make a significant relationship with an adult.

The role of Charles's family in his disturbed behavior, both historically and phenomenologically, also needed to be understood, as it would indicate whether within a residential setting, frequent therapeutic contact with his mother and siblings in some type of family treatment was necessary. His social environment at home would indicate whether and when he could return there; if he did not stop abusing drugs, his prognosis would be poor.

Even though Charles needed an environment that could protect society from him, an ideal correctional setting would need to consider the following if the intervention was to be successful:

1. What type of relationship could Charles make? Could he make new identifications with individuals? Could he relate only within social networks? Could he use any type of therapy, supportive or expressive? Was there an indication for group therapy or family therapy as a specific intervention, or should the therapy be only nonspecific?
2. What consequences should follow antisocial behavior in the residential center that would be comprehensible to Charles? How much control would he be able to exercise over himself?

3. What type of remedial educational and vocational training was indicated?

4. Could Charles function without a well-structured day? How much creative interaction was needed to help him deal with his inner boredom? It was clear from his history that Charles's school system had never offered him much creative and imaginative stimulation.

5. The setting would also have to provide and maintain biological intervention.

The final recommendation might well be that Charles needed to be in an environment in which he could establish relationships with adults whom he felt were consistent and caring. A special, supportive relationship might be needed with a psychologically skilled adult. In this his attitudes toward reality would be a particular issue. The time spent with him should not be longer than his attention span. All this was, of course, unavailable.

ENVIRONMENTAL TECHNIQUES TO ENHANCE PERSONALITY DEVELOPMENT

A reasonable goal for antisocial adolescents is to reinforce their drive toward socially acceptable autonomy. This means that the individual's sense of worth should be enhanced, the goal being the development of maturationally appropriate productivity. A corollary is to help such adolescents develop an acceptable sense of personal, ethnic, and social-class identity (Miller 1969), relative freedom from infantile attachments and a capacity to tolerate frustration, control antisocial behavior, and be loving.

A reasonable technique for a therapeutic correctional system then could be to provide for all adolescents in their care adequate educational and vocational activities and socially acceptable outlets to help sublimate antisocial and violent impulses. The staff would need training both to understand and to respect the developmental needs of their charges, including their need for bodily integrity and privacy. The social organization should be able to contain that symptomatic behavior that offers destructive outlets for instinctual satisfaction, thus corrupting personality development.

Without security, severely disturbed damaged and damaging individuals will rarely be helped. If they are to develop inner controls, they must be "held," psychologically and literally. Control based on social isolation, physical restraint, and chemical sedation is not helpful to fragmented personalities, as these may reinforce the propensity to affective aggression.

A setting that aims to be therapeutic should be able to provide gradations of external security. When control is physically necessary, it should be by people rather than punishment. Some disturbed and delinquent adolescents must live in a specially created, secure environment with staff who can structure a developmentally appropriate life-style. Adolescents' confinement needs to last until the behavioral difficulties have ceased and the youngster has developed sufficient internal controls to function in a socially acceptable way. The ability to live in the community at large and control self-destructive or other violent behavior depends on relationships established in the therapeutic setting; ideally these should continue until no longer needed. Those who need specific medication should be able to accept responsibility for using it.

The ideal treatment center should have a therapeutic nexus of people and activities available when the youngster is in a controlled, closed setting and, later, in a group home, foster home, or with parents. Ideally, all treatment centers, correctional or otherwise, should be accessible to the larger community in which the adolescent normally lives. This is the case in the Netherlands, where a treatment center for "psychopathic delinquents" is in the center of Rotterdam.

The approach to care should support the healthy side of the adolescent's personality, by offering impulse control, socially acceptable outlets for violent wishes, and opportunities for creativity and imagination in play and work.

The ethos of a setting for antisocial and potentially violent adolescents is that violence is not acceptable. The environment has to be one in which the staff are felt to be in control and to be caring. The setting requires:

1. The acceptance of an individual for long-term care in a therapeutic environment with a multidisciplinary staff whom the inmate perceives as able to perform socially meaningful tasks; to be a personal counselor or a guard is not enough.

2. The youngsters should be given graduated degrees of responsibility, and no adolescent should ever be allowed to control another.

3. The ethos and staff structure of a planned environment will form a framework within which care and control become interdependent aspects of treatment.

4. Educational facilities—remedial, compensatory, and developmental—should be available to the individual on a year-round basis.

5. Recreational facilities, both indoor and outdoor, should be remedial as well as challenging and appropriately competitive.

6. Social interventions with the family and the community at large should be offered to all the inmates.

Against this background, which requires a sophisticated architectural design so that a closed building can give a feeling of openness and comfort, satisfactory treatment is possible.

INDIVIDUALIZED DIAGNOSTIC SERVICES

Although a psychosocial environment that reinforces healthy personality development will help some adolescents, without specific individualized services, the successful treatment of many in corrections is difficult when the cause of their delinquent behavior is more than a developmental problem.

A psychological diagnosis, with a generalized statement of psychodynamic causes and psychotherapeutic recommendations, is rarely helpful in planning treatment in the correctional system, as even specific recommendations may be ignored. The following

report was written by a visiting psychiatrist on a violent, disturbed boy in a correctional setting:

> I saw this boy at the request of his group leader. He has been
> in G. for several weeks and previously had been in a reception
> unit. He is currently on Mellaril. This medication was started
> because of apparent evidence of hallucinations and bizarre and
> violent behavior. He is a potentially explosive boy who has consid-
> erable difficulty in dealing with the realities of the outside world.
> He frequently acts in a highly inappropriate and bizarre manner.
> He was committed to this unit for rape. Since being here he has
> shown no ability to function within, or get help from the group
> structure, which is the characteristic of this setting.
>
> When I saw him today, he came across in an extremely
> passive and compliant way; he talked of his robbery but did not
> mention the rape. When we discussed difficulties within the
> group setting, he said they were related solely to the fact that he
> prefers to have an individual adult supervisor rather than have
> boys his age make any decision about him.
>
> He suffers from a schizophrenic reaction of relatively long-
> standing duration. At the moment it is apparently adequately
> controlled by Mellaril. His problems are such that the group
> structure here will not be of help to him. On the other side of the
> coin, it is very difficult to involve him in a situation which will be
> helpful to other boys on his unit. I think his stay here has proven
> beyond any doubt that this is not the place for him. An early
> discharge from this agency would be in order.
>
> Unfortunately, there are few places in the state where boys
> like him can get any meaningful help. A relatively long term
> psychiatric institution seems at the moment to be the most realis-
> tic alternative. In a useful psychiatric setting for such a youth, a
> decision would be made as to whether the prescribed medication
> was the appropriate biological intervention. Vocational training is
> as important in a hospital as elsewhere, as are arrangements for
> family visits and contact with the world outside the institution.

Although this was the fifth such recommendation made by separate psychiatrists, the boy was not placed in a psychiatric hospital.

Treatment recommendations should list both the nonspecific and specific individualized services that should be offered:

Steve was a tall, husky, blond, 17-year-old white male who had been in a residential setting for 18 months. He had been in various placements over the past five years because of truancy, drug abuse, and antisocial behavior. His mother and sister lived some two hundred miles away from his current placement.

Steve was referred to determine both his readiness for discharge and whether or not he had any neurological deficits. The reason for his failure to respond to a "positive peer counseling" approach was also an issue.

Steve was seen for an outpatient psychiatric evaluation, which consisted of six one-hour sessions with a psychiatrist, a physical and neurological examination, an electroencephalogram, skull X rays, and two, three-hour sessions of psychological tests. His counselor was seen by a social worker for one hour. Steve's mother was contacted in two extended telephone conversations, his present maladjustment having a long history:

Steve recalled having cut school almost from the day he first started. He generally got along well with his teachers but mostly he never went to class, he pointed out, because of fights after school.

By the fifth and sixth grades, Steve was admiring the youngsters who were on the fringe of the school society, particularly those who used alcohol and cigarettes. Steve grew very rapidly, and because he was the biggest boy in his grade, he was the butt of many fights. He recalled that by the time he was 12 or 13, he would sneak out of his home without permission, steal bicycles and money, and break into and enter houses.

Steve had an extensive history of drug abuse, including hallucinogens and marijuana. He reported a variety of frightening experiences on LSD. "There were creatures, things like monsters. . . . I'm running after them with a chain saw. . . . I cut off their arms and their legs." Also: "There are people running after me, and I have a machine gun, and I shoot them in the head, and they go after my father a lot. . . . They are not people that I know; they are just things. . . . There are no faces. . . . They are monsters or animals. . . . I take out a knife, and I cut their throats, and they become piles of flesh and bones, all crushed."

Because of his disturbed behavior, Steve had had a variety of placements and finally was sent for an extended stay to his present placement, whose goal was "positive peer counseling." The setting had moderate educational resources and some recreational facilities.

Steve sexually assaulted his sister during a Christmas vacation. He had been angry with her for going out with older, married men and for disobeying their mother. He had attempted to reason with her, but "she would not listen." He described the assault as being like a dream: "In my dreams, I am afraid of losing control, and I get aggravated. She was only an object. I have hit her before, but it was not like this. I really hurt her."

Steve went on to describe how when they were in the kitchen, he got angry, forced her to go to his room, slapped her once or twice, and, then, having an erection, penetrated her and remembered ejaculating. She then got dressed and left home, and he left to get drunk.

Steve also reported situations in which he became extremely jealous of other young people, particularly those whom he saw teasing those who were weak. He admitted that he was very afraid of fighting because "when I fight with someone, I am afraid I will really hurt him. Someone has to hold me on the ground so I will not kill something. Something comes over me; I just cannot stop." He went on to explain that when he got angry, he wanted to stamp on someone's face until it disappeared.

Steve's personal history included the following:

Steve's mother divorced his father because of his affairs with various women and his fathering several illegitimate children. The mother described her husband as a powerful man who terrorized the family. He was overly strict, spanked Steve numerous times, beat him with a belt, and at times left him with welts. These beatings would take place for no apparent reason. Steve's mother related how frightened she was and how she could not interfere. Steve never talked back but would cry quietly.

During Steve's early years, his mother recalled having felt depressed and very sorry for herself. She felt she could not protect Steve from his father's anger, but she also would punish her son by pulling his hair or making him stand in the corner.

Steve's mother stated that she had had no difficulties with Steve as an infant. She remembered his destroying things. She used to spank him occasionally. Steve's memories of his early life was of relatives coming to visit and his feeling left out.

The general impression of Steve's early life is that there was little consistent nurturing because of his mother's depression. She was terrified of his father and could not protect Steve from his capricious physical abuse.

One of the few trouble-free times that Steve remembered was when he was on the football team; he said that he enjoyed the activity of physical punishment, both giving and receiving it. Steve perceived himself as being possibly crazy: "Maybe I have bad nerves." In describing his anger, he said "It is hard to say. I want to swing out; I just go into a rage. I feel like an animal, as if I am in a torment and I want to torment an animal. I want to strike back."

Steve viewed himself as primarily heterosexual; he currently had a girl friend whom he idealized. He believed that if he could return home, he could perhaps marry her, and they could live on a farm together and adopt children.

Steve described his sexual experiences when he was drunk: "I am nasty and angry and mean; I do everything. I do oral sex. It is more animalistic than human. It is like I was an animal."

Steve hoped that physical relationships that could be connected with love and affection would make things better for him.

Psychological tests and clinical examination revealed Steve as highly preoccupied with violence and that he had to keep reminding himself that it would not work. He sought external control. He did not see others' violence controlled when he was small and now had little control of his own. He had a highly unstable personality, and from time to time he lost touch with reality.

Steve was diagnosed as a Class II risk, violent individual. He dehumanized as easily as he was dehumanized and, under stress, found affective violence acceptable. There was also a great deal of evidence that because of Steve's personality structure, he was capable of homicidal acts. He was considered a dangerous individual because he had minimal control of his own violence, which was acceptable to him. He became violent when frustrated because people would not do as he wished. Females were particularly vulnerable, although he could also be violent with male peers. In addition, alcohol made Steve more likely to be violent.

Steve was thus a primitive young man with little sense of his own worth as a person. He was not capable of warm loving relationships that would make demands on him. With external controls, he could maintain a facade of adequate social function but appeared capable of only minimal feelings of affection, sadness, and satisfaction. He experienced physical sensations that are the precursors of emotions but did not feel loving and secure:

> Nonspecific treatment should be in a secure hospital setting, because of Steve's potential for impulsive and dangerous activity. This setting should be able to offer both open and closed care. Whatever Steve's level of responsibility for himself, whether in a secure hospital or in a group home, he needs the opportunity to keep the human relationships he makes in the hospital. The hospital milieu must be responsive to individual needs and not be a rigid institutional structure. The staff must include strong adult males who can at the same time be controlling and caring and offer protection when it becomes necessary.

> Group counseling and the ability to monitor relationships with peers must be available. The goal of these groups should be to convey that one does not have to act in the same way that one feels, that it is necessary to understand the feelings of others.

> The vocational program should try to provide Steve with a career that could serve as a useful outlet for his aggression and through which ultimately he might earn a living.

The recreational program should be aimed at helping Steve sublimate his violent impulses, become aware of his own strength, and gain self-esteem.

The individualized program should make available the appropriate biological interventions. Psychotherapy should begin in a way that would allow Steve to form a relationship that feels real to him. He must perceive the therapist as being useful and able to value both his or her own self-worth and, thus, Steve's. The therapy initially should be supportive, so as to help Steve make appropriate reality decisions. Once Steve comes to trust the therapist and identifies with him or her in being able to look at himself, the therapist might be able to use expressive as well as supportive techniques. These should be aimed at helping Steve understand his violence.

Steve may learn controls through the processes of identification, but without adequate biological intervention, it is not believed that psychotherapy would be helpful, either in a group or with an individual. When Steve leaves the protection of the institution because he is no longer dangerous and antisocial, he must be able to maintain a relationship with the same therapist. He should not be isolated from the whole therapeutic system. The institution's educational, recreational, and vocational services should continue to be available to Steve when he begins to live in the community.

Although none of this was made available, it is believed that such reports confront the judiciary with the inadequacy of the system to which they commit juveniles. They should be aware that adequate care is possible.

PROBLEMS IN DELIVERING THERAPEUTIC SERVICES

Most institutions that treat violently disturbed adolescents seem understandably interested in producing conformity to their social system's demands. Although the goal of nonviolent behavior is reasonable, the relationship between inmate conformity to institutional norms which may be societally aberrant and acceptable behavior thereafter is unclear.

In treatment, disturbed adolescents need to behave from time to time in an infantile and regressive way. The staff may have to remind early adolescents to brush their teeth and take showers, and the children may need snacks and hot drinks before bedtime.

Adolescents who suffer from personality disorders may start to behave in an unacceptable way during their recovery, at the point when a period of depression associated with a personality change is imminent. It is as though the loss of a capacity to behave impulsively creates a sense of inner deprivation, and further impulsive behavior may be an attempt to recapture this experience. As the treatment progresses, poor impulse control and an inability to tolerate frustration may, after a period of apparent conformity, give way to a further period of unacceptable behavior. This is a manifestation of an adolescent's struggle for autonomy, not necessarily an indication that the intervention has failed. The development of adolescence in a previously postpubertal individual may create rebellious behavior, which is part of the striving for independence.

In some correctional centers, there are problems when young people develop a trusting therapist–client relationship with a member of the staff. In three separate counseling groups conducted over three years, a psychiatrist worked with groups of adolescents over issues of trust. Each year the groups failed. In each group, the adolescents began to talk freely of events occurring in the institution. They revealed episodes of homosexual assault, staff brutality, and drug abuse. If no action was taken, the adolescents would perceive the therapist as collusive; if the therapist tried to take action but failed, they would see him as helpless; if the therapist intervened successfully, they would perceive him as omnipotent. Furthermore, revealing these problems to the institutional authorities would have broken the inmates' trust. In addition, the adolescents regarded the therapist—because he was employed by the institution—as being as responsible as were the rest of the staff.

Successful therapy is possible only if the therapist makes

clear that trust means that nothing will be done to hurt the youngsters. But when the institution's social system is antidevelopmental, this is impossible.

STAFF DEVELOPMENT

The staff members of most residential centers have different capacities, but all need emotional support and respect. The staff should, at the least, know the institution's explicit philosophy and how it agrees with the implicit institutional messages given to the inmates.

Many attempts at training the staff fail because they do not take into account the value system of the institution's power figures (Miller 1964). The staff should be trained with goals that have the approval of the system's authority figures. Middle management develops an emotional stake in functioning in known and predictable ways and they may consciously obstruct change. Change agents should first work with this group rather than with lower levels of management (Miller 1964).

CONCLUSION

Psychological medicine has failed to affect significantly the treatment of delinquent antisocial adolescents. This failure to use adequate care has, moreover, allowed some to claim that psychiatry and rehabilitation have little or nothing to offer delinquent adolescents (Kaufman 1975). Punitive social responses, which tend to reinforce the likelihood of violence, thus have become the norm, and social policy has begun to eliminate competent medical care from reaching these antisocial and psychologically disturbed young people.

REFERENCES

Fox, S. J. (1981). *Modern Juvenile Justice. Cases and Materials.* 2nd ed. St. Paul: West Publishing.

Kaufman, A. (1975). *Report to the American Bar Association* (abstract). American Bar Association, Chicago.

Knesper, D., and Miller, D. (1976). Treatment plans for mental health care. *American Journal of Psychiatry* 133:45–50.

Marohn, R. (1982). Adolescent violence: Causes and treatment. *Journal of the Academy of Child Psychiatry* 21:354–360.

Miller, D. (1964). Staff training in the penal system: the use of small groups. *Human Relations* 19:151–164.

———. (1965). *Growth to Freedom: The Psychosocial Treatment of Delinquent Youth.* Bloomington: Indiana University Press.

———. (1969). *The Age Between: Adolescents in a Disturbed Society.* London: Hutchinson.

———. (1982). Adolescent suicide. *Adolescent Psychiatry* 9:327–363.

Miller, D., and Looney, J. (1976). Determinants of homicide in adolescents. *Adolescent Psychiatry* 4:231–254.

Nichtern, S. (1974). The therapeutic educational environment. *Adolescent Psychiatry* 3:432–434.

Wolff, P. H., Waber, D., Bauermeister, C., Cohen, C., and Faber, R. (1982). Neuropsychologic studies of adolescent delinquent boys. *Journal of Child Psychology and Psychiatry* 23:267–279.

12

Adolescent Sexual Disorders

Sexual disorders, except for transsexual disorders, rarely have biological causes. The violent behavior produced by neuroendocrine disorders may include sexual activity but more usually inhibits sexual interest.

Sexual intercourse reinforces sexual identity: it is a way of being loving; it releases sexual tension; and it satisfies regressive and infantile needs. This is apparent in the biting, sucking, and cuddling associated with sexual activity. For some adolescents, sexual activity is the only time when they are hugged and cuddled.

The general interest that girls show in boys' sexuality is also supportive of their (the boys') self-esteem. Boys may like to pretend that girls are not discussing how "cute" they are, but those who are sexually active, or wish to be, make it clear in the way they dress and carry themselves that they are seeking female attention.

Boys and girls who lack self-esteem may use promiscuous

sexual activity to try to meet the needs that result from developmental and emotional deprivation. Young males whose self-image is modified by having an absent father—whose only apparent role was to impregnate their mother—may use sexual activity to reinforce their sense of manhood. Such boys may see impregnation as the only valid image of masculinity. But other young fatherless males may refuse to involve themselves with women at all, either sexually or emotionally.

There is no evidence that those who postpone their sexual experimentation or involvement are developmentally hindered. They are still able to become loving adults. In Western culture, in the middle class, heterosexual behavior typically begins to appear toward the latter part of middle adolescence. Lower-class youth, with some ethnic exceptions, become sexually active earlier (Schofield 1964). Examples of these exceptions are that in Ireland in small towns and villages, heterosexual relationships are socially inhibited until adults reach their mid-20s. Some religious groups discourage sexual activity until marriage becomes possible. Adolescents seemingly cope with this unless their peer group has contradictory goals:

A 16-year-old Orthodox Jewish boy was referred to a psychiatrist because he was repeatedly stealing his father's automobile. He was a member of an ultrareligious group that forbade masturbation and would allow no contact with the opposite sex until marriage. While the youth attended a religious school, he was asymptomatic. He was moved to a private school because his father wanted him to have a better education. The conflict between his peer group's acceptable behavior and his internalized standards led to his symbolic attack on his father by stealing his automobile.

Similarly:

A 15-year-old girl, whose parents were members of the Apostolic Church of God, sought treatment for headaches and anxiety attacks after a family move. She had had to change to the local public school from the church-run school she had previously attended. She found the sexual interests expressed by the girls at her new school "disgusting" but clearly had conflicts about them.

When young males remain celibate for religious reasons, their masculine identity comes to depend on the reinforcement of other attributes: empathy, service to others, vocational success, and physical prowess. Those who join religious orders in order to resolve sexual anxieties may fail to complete their training, or they may show many symptomatic difficulties, especially with alcohol.

Children exposed to the sight of adults having sex and those who are victims of a sexual assault attempt to resolve their anxieties by playing games that have clear sexual implications. As adults, these children may become sexually inhibited or promiscuous.

PROMISCUITY IN ADOLESCENCE

When promiscuous behavior is socially sanctioned, it allows young males to engage in basically self-referent masturbatory behavior with others. Usually this is heterosexual. As these adolescents mature, they come to view this as boring. Thus, socially sanctioned early and middle adolescent promiscuity may eventually be replaced by long-term heterosexual relationships.

In the homosexual community, promiscuous sexual behavior generally seems to continue for much longer than it does for heterosexuals, although there are no known comparative statistics that can validate this.

The development of homosexual relationships, particularly when they begin in middle and late adolescence, is complex. For young males, physical appearance does not remain a primary issue when they have once established a long-term heterosexual relationship; other qualities become more important. But the physical appearance of young homosexual males tends to be valued for a much longer time. The cultural criterion is apparently the appearance of youth, with genuine affection often taking second place. If this is the primary criterion—physical appearance and looking youthful—sexual activity is likely to remain self-referent and promiscuous. Additional stimulants may then be used to increase the excitement of orgasm, either different sexual experiences, such as sadomasochistic behavior, or drugs.

SEXUAL VIOLENCE AND ABUSE

Sexual violence is not unusual among adolescents. Gang bangs—the mass rape of one girl by several boys—are often reported in clinical practice. And the sexual abuse of younger children by older siblings is more commonly seen in clinical practice than is abuse by adults.

Adolescents may also be victims of adult rape, especially when boys are placed in adult prisons; girls are more often victims of rape in the community at large. Adolescents may also sexually victimize one another. Incestuous relationships between siblings or fathers and daughters are reported fairly frequently. Father–son incest may also be seen, but mother–son incest is extremely rare.

In 1984 and 1985 there was a flurry in the United States of reported cases of child sexual abuse by adults in day-care centers. This rapidly became a media event, although it remains unclear what the actual incidence of such abuse might be. Two-thirds of those children who are molested are willing partners (Gibbens and Prince 1963). According to a study of 28 children from the rural southern United States, who had been molested by fathers or father surrogates, all required psychiatric care (Johnson 1974). Adolescents who sexually abuse children are usually nonempathic and may be extremely anxious about their sexual involvement with their peers:

> Thirteen-year-old Dan was sent to a psychiatric hospital because he sexually assaulted one boy and two girls, aged five to seven. Dan said that he did not have intercourse with them because "my penis is too big and might hurt them." However he enjoyed playing with the children's genitalia and had his first ejaculation while doing this. He remarked, "I like doing it with smaller children because they won't criticize me or get mad at me."

It had not occurred to Dan that he might in some ways emotionally damage these children, and he was quite shocked when this was put to him as a possibility. Dan was a schizophrenic boy with a marked thought disorder.

A similar problem was reported by a 15-year-old girl:

Caroline was accused of sexually assaulting two small girls, aged three to five. At the age of 12 she had been forced into a prostitution ring run from a state children's home. The incident took place while she was living with a foster family. There were 14 people living in a six-room house. The two children concerned both had witnessed intercourse between their mother and her boy friend. Caroline insisted that while she was lying on the bed, the children approached her. She was asked why she allowed the five-year-old to perform cunnilingus on her. She replied, "It felt safe."

Caroline had little or no capacity to make trusting relationships and was an impulse-ridden, angry girl who was unable to be empathic. For example, she could not understand why the neighborhood was incensed with her.

ADOLESCENT PREGNANCY

The child resulting from an adolescent pregnancy is subjected to a significant degree of medical and psychological risk (Roosa, Fitzgerald, and Carlson, personal communication, 1980). Even though, with good care, infant mortality in adolescent mothers can be as low as that for older women, such care is generally not available to adolescents. Adolescent mothers have a higher incidence of premature babies—those weighing less than five pounds at birth—than do older women. The adolescent mother's separation from the baby, because it is premature, then decreases the likelihood of satisfactory mother–infant bonding. There is then a statistical likelihood of later child abuse (Adams-Tucker 1982). Babies tend to be underaroused or overstimulated by adolescent mothers. And because early mother-to-infant verbal communication helps determine the baby's later capacity to handle language, the children of teenage mothers are then less likely to reach their academic potential.

Nine months after the delivery of an illegitimate child, only 60 percent of mothers in a black ghetto population reported that they saw the child's father (Ewer and Gibbs 1975), although the percentage of married adolescents has risen from 3 percent to 17 percent. In a study of adolescent fathers in a Los Angeles clinic, the majority were over nineteen years old (Pannor, Evans, and Masarik 1971), and in lower-class groups this age generally implies adulthood.

There is no statistical evidence that adolescents who impregnate girls or become fathers are in any way less well adjusted than are those who, though sexually active, do not do either of these. Not all sexually active males impregnate their partners, however, so there is an attitudinal difference between males who are ready to risk their partners' becoming pregnant and those who do not.

Some adolescent males perceive the successful conception of an infant as reinforcing their sense of masculinity. Among some social classes and ethnic groups, the birth of an illegitimate baby may make its father feel guilty, although a boy's inability to make a girl pregnant may also be felt as a failure of his masculinity. After a child is born, these adolescent males are likely to have little contact with the mothers or their infants (Pannor et al. 1971).

The teenage mother is likely to have a preexisting emotional difficulty or to have her emotional development hindered by the experience of pregnancy. One-third of early adolescent mothers live below the poverty level, and those who first give birth in early or middle adolescence are four times more likely to be at this level than is the adult population. Besides the poverty's lessening the likelihood of the young mother's receiving an advanced high school education and acquiring marketable special skills, early pregnancy in most communities interrupts school, work goals, and career plans (GAP Report 1986). A pregnant adolescent girl also is likely to experience multiple psychological stresses which impede the development of a secure sense of self. As well, the infant's needs interfere with the necessary self-involvement of adolescence.

Generally, early adolescent mothers are unable to mother well and are likely to become overwhelmed with guilt and anger. Inevitably, such a girl becomes more dependent on her nuclear family, which slows her achievement of autonomy. Adolescent pregnancy may be a syndrome of psychological failure, but it almost certainly obstructs the development of emotional maturity (Card and Wise 1978).

Perhaps because the psychological price inflicted on adolescent mothers is so high, most of the problems of illegitimacy, its prevention, and its care are focused on them. But despite the problems created by becoming a teenage mother, abortion appears to create even greater psychological problems among adolescents than among adults.

Illegitimate pregnancy might be prevented if it were known which girls were likely to be sexually active and if they then used contraception. Nowadays the prevention of conception tends to be seen as a female responsibility. If a girl without a regular partner is not to signal easy sexual availability, contraception in unplanned intercourse should be a male responsibility. Premarital abstinence is not likely to be achieved by simplistic solutions offered by society, nor was it produced by fear of genital herpes.

Ignorance of how conception takes place is widespread among both boys and girls. A random selection of 20 middle-class adolescent males in an inpatient psychiatric practice were asked if they knew when girls were likely to be fertile; most did not. A significant number of unmarried females in middle and late adolescence do not know the time during the menstrual cycle when the risk of their becoming pregnant increases.

Forty-three percent of all males between the ages of thirteen and nineteen are said to be heterosexually active (Furstenberg 1976), but in a selected cohort of socially conformist middle- and upper-class males aged 15 to 17, this figure was only 10 percent (Offer and Offer 1974). The number of sexually active young people among less conformist groups must then be considerable. It is not surprising, then, that in 1979, there were approximately 600,000 pregnancies in unwed adolescent females (National Center for Disease Control 1978), and there is no evidence that this figure is dropping.

Illegitimate conception is most likely to be prevented, in the short run, by encouraging the use of contraception. The problem is that many adolescents interpret being told that contraception is desirable as adults' giving permission for extramarital intercourse.

Many sexually active adolescent males do not use contraceptives themselves and discourage their partners from doing so, even if they are so inclined. There has, however, been remarkably little study of the psychology of these adolescent males, who are likely to impregnate their sexual partners. Perhaps if this was understood, attempts at prevention might be more successful.

Sexual behavior may be classified on the basis of frequency. Those who engage in regular sexual intercourse are active in the maximum number of occasions in which this is possible with willing partners. The frequency may vary from three to four times monthly to two to three or more times weekly. Regularly heterosexually active adolescent males usually report having intercourse more than once during each sexual contact. Most adolescent males who engage in this behavior have a history of multiple sexual partners.

Intermittent sexual intercourse is typical of those adolescents who are willing to engage in such behavior but, for a variety of psychosocial reasons, may not be able to find sexual partners. Some deny that sexual activity is particularly important to them, or they engage in relationships in which they seldom have sexual intercourse.

Occasional sexual intercourse is typical of those who have the appropriate motivation but no willing sexual partner and may take the opportunity when it occurs, for example, under group pressure at a party. Alcohol abuse is common under such circumstances. The attitude of the larger social system, that is, peers, parents and extraparental adults, and social class and/or ethnic ethos, may be important to facilitating or preventing this type of behavior.

Promiscuity can be defined as sexual activity with partners with whom there is little or no emotional involvement, as opposed to extramarital intercourse with a partner with whom one has a stable and meaningful emotional relationship.

The adolescent fathers of illegitimate children are generally not available as research subjects, nor are most adolescent males who engage in heterosexual activity. Epidemiological questionnaires asking the frequency of contact are notoriously unreliable (Schofield 1964), as adolescents may distort their answers and may reply on the basis of either fantasy or negative feelings about adult authority (Miller 1974).

Heterosexually active adolescent males are available for personality study in depth usually only when they are given psychological examinations, having been caught in an antisocial activity, are being seen and examined by professionals for routine physical examinations, or are suffering from a minor physical disability. A young male who has had some emotional conflict that necessitates professional counseling may also be available for such a study.

THE DEVELOPMENT OF FEMALE SEXUAL IDENTITY

Sex is the biological and physiological basis for male and female development, and gender is the degree of masculinity or femininity. The wish to become a mother has been thought to represent a fundamental aspect of feminine identity. This is culturally reinforced from infancy onward in little girls' doll play. By the age of two, girls are aware of the differences between the sexes, and they fantasize being the woman of the house (Gulensen and Roiphe 1976). When mothers are comfortable with their own femininity and convey this to their daughters, girls have greater confidence in their own bodies. This reinforces their sense that women are to be valued, and the love and attention of their fathers enhances this sense of feminine worth. The wish for a baby is apparent from the age of two onward, and it may also be present in boys. This may represent the wish to be like the ideal and idealized mother.

A girl's attitude toward men as individuals to be loved is based both on the awareness of the explicit and implicit interactions between her parents and on the relationship between her father and herself. If girls internalize at an early age the awareness that childrearing requires the parents of both sexes, they are not likely to accept the idea of being a single parent.

The wish to be pregnant is not the same as the wish to be a mother. Some girls perceive becoming pregnant as desirable, as it make them feel whole, human, and alive. The baby inside them cancels out the feeling that one is internally empty, which is part of adolescent depression. Thus, a depressed adolescent mother may see her unborn infant as an individual who will make no demands. It is clear that many depressed girls who become pregnant fantasize that their baby will nurture them, rather than the reverse.

Sexual activity may have different meanings at different stages of adolescence. Early adolescent girls who have inter-course often do this as the emotional price to be paid for contact comfort (Hatcher 1973). Many have not really internalized an awareness that having intercourse is likely to lead to impregnation. This lack of emotional knowledge is reinforced by the fact that the infrequency of ovulation is likely to make such young-sters relatively sterile:

> A bright 15-year-old girl had been sexually active since the age of 13, after having been seduced by a 20-year-old man. In a clinical interview, she was asked whether she might be pregnant. She denied this but then revealed that she had had intercourse seven days earlier, and she had not yet had a period. When asked why she was so sure, she indicated that although neither she nor her partner used contraceptives, she had never been pregnant; there-fore there was nothing to be concerned about.

Sexually active early adolescents are seeking new sensa-tions, often related more to bodily comfort than to orgasm. Often, the goal is to satisy their male partners, and so in a primitive way, they are acting out a fantasy of father–mother and father–daughter relationships.

The middle adolescent girl who comes from a social group that disapproves of such behavior often has intercourse to assert her independence and femininity. This is essentially an act in which rebellion is confused with independence. But when preg-nancy supervenes, greater dependency ensues. Pregnancy during this developmental phase is often associated with the fantasy that the girl will become a more successful part of the father–mother–child bond than did her own mother; the fantasy now is that at least she will have the exclusive attention of males. It is as if the price to be paid for the idealized love of her father, and to remove such affection from her mother, is to become pregnant herself.

Late adolescent girls who are sexually active in a monoga-mous relationship often become pregnant with the goal of obtaining a commitment from the impregnating lover. The pregnancy is often consciously accidental, but the girls' wish is to be married. According to clinical observation, girls who were themselves conceived out of wedlock may identify with their mother's behavior and become pregnant in a similar way. Sometimes pregnancy occurs in relation to loss (Schaffer and Pine 1972), and sometimes it is part of an omnipotent fantasy that all problems can be solved in this way.

Although the wish to be a mother and pregnant clearly develops before the age of three, with the idea that the unborn is inside one, understanding the significance of intercourse as a necessary preliminary to impregnation comes later. All children know at an emotional level that babies come as a result of an interaction between a man and a woman and have learned the anatomical differences between them. Sometimes children are told this by their parents when they ask, and sometimes they learn at school, either in sex education classes or from peers.

THE DEVELOPMENT OF
MALE SEXUAL IDENTITY

The assignment of sex at birth is the first step in establishing the identification of oneself as male or female (Tyson 1982). A male baby is given verbal and nonverbal messages that indicate the family's concept of manhood. In the early part of the second year, a boy becomes aware that he has a penis and genitals and then begins self-stimulation. The boy then begins to realize that he has an organ that can give him pleasure.

In order to feel secure in his masculinity, a boy has to weaken his initial identification with his mother and concentrate on identifying with his father. This does not mean that both parents do not have similar qualities: productivity, loving tenderness, and sensitivity to the feelings of others are, or should be, in the identity of both males and females. Clearly, boys never totally abandon their identification with a nurturing mother, and girls model themselves to some extent on their father. Nevertheless, by the second year of life a child should be making his or her primary identification with the same-sex parent. The first obvious moves are in physical modeling. By the age of 12 to 14 months, it becomes important to a boy to see his father urinating, and upright urination is probably a boy's first step in assuming a masculine role. Masturbatory play seems to begin at 14 to 18 months. If fathers are not present and a boy is relating only to his mother and perhaps other women, the first order of business in being male, that is, to reinforce the psychological push to avoid merging with the mother, is more difficult, and the boy is likely to be more feminine in his orientation (Stoller and Heidt 1982).

In developing a sense of masculinity, little boys must move from identifying with their mother, that is, imitating her household tasks and often expressing a wish to bear children (Ross 1975). As they recognize that they are physically different from girls, boys must deal with an envy of their mother's capacity to bear children, and so they often have fantasies of anal birth. Fathers play an increasingly important role in helping boys move from their initial identification to a more masculine one. They encourage socially acceptable masculine attitudes (Stoller 1979), and they help produce a male gender role identification. If small boys perceive males as impregnating their mothers and then leaving, that will be their model of a sexual male. The more often that fathers are available to participate in the generalized aspects of masculinity, from upright urination to masculine play, the more that boys will internalize a socially acceptable model of masculinity.

The father's presence is crucial, not just because he provides a direct role model for his son, but also because the child then becomes aware of the relationships between men and women. It is clear how devastating can be separation by death, divorce, or absence. This is especially true if no other male is consistently available as a model of masculinity. The general quality of the father's role in relation to his son, in everything from the games they play to being a loving masculine figure, encourages boys to become self-reliant and independent. Fathers who are overrestrictive may produce in their sons a passive orientation, although these boys may eventually identify with the parental attitudes of being overcontrolling and rigid.

Children also make significant attachments to their siblings, to whom they should also bond and become dependent. Boys may relate to their sisters in an overassertive, "masculine" way, although ultimately they may become highly protective; sisters may be a "little mother" to their siblings.

By the age of three or four, boys will attempt to assert their masculinity with their mothers and sisters, perhaps by expressing the wish either to be husbands or fathers (Solnit 1979). Although boys before the age of five may envy their father because of the size of his penis, they do not understand its role in procreation. But by the time boys have gone through puberty, they are aware that they can, like all males, produce seminal fluid, and its production is a significant seal to a sense of manhood.

There is no evidence that early male sexual behavior, which includes intercourse, is necessarily related to any type of emotional deprivation, nor does it indicate a developmental impasse. The idea that male adolescents who have intercourse are psychologically deprived (Futterman and Livermore 1967) is not necessarily true. However, because solitary masturbation, two or three or more times daily, is a function of emotional deprivation and conflict, the same may be true of sexual intercourse that is masturbatory in its quality:

Ted, a 15-year-old boy, had been seduced by a neighborhood couple when he was 11 and had had regular intercourse with the wife, observed by her husband, until this was discovered when he was 14. His mother was alcoholic and had left the family when he was ten. He came for treatment of his drug abuse, but his concept of relationships with girls was "I fuck them." He engaged in minimal preliminary sexual play and was extremely promiscuous. After he had had intercourse, he would then leave his sexual partner and usually not see her again.

In therapy, Ted first came to understand that he was doing no more than masturbating with a female; he was not relating to her as a person. Then he began to see himself as really needing psychological assistance.

There is no statistical evidence that males are specifically motivated to impregnate females and create children (Ewer and

Gibbs 1975). From clinical evidence, however, it is clear that the need for such procreation is often related to the need of some men to establish a secure masculine identity.

Many boys begin heterosexual activity to the point of intercourse in early adolescence. Social class and ethnocentricity are important to determining the age of first intercourse (Schofield 1964). It is almost certain that the maximum use of contraceptives among males does not exceed 50 percent and is probably less. Black and Hispanic males, in a study that made no allowance for social class (Finkel and Finkel 1975), reported a higher frequency of intercourse and a lower use of contraceptives than did whites.

The reason for an adolescent male to put a high priority on either premarital chastity or the use of contraceptives is almost certainly related to family attitudes toward responsibility and mutual caring. There have been, however, no studies on the reason that some males have this attitude and others do not. The fear of impregnating their sexual partner is the reason given by many young males for abstaining from intercourse, but sometimes it is clear that this is a rationalization for anxiety over performance. Nevertheless, some adolescent males obviously feel responsible for the well-being of a sexual partner, and it is highly likely that family attitudes have taught them this. Some adolescents combine a capacity for empathy with a conviction that even one episode of sexual intercourse may produce pregnancy. This omnipotence may explain why some who seem to be casually irresponsible in their use of drugs, alcohol, or violence are highly responsible in regard to their sexual behavior.

In early and middle adolescence, males may use sexual intercourse to facilitate the development of their self-worth. This, however, can also be reinforced by socially appropriate creative, imaginative, cognitive, and physical activities; young males need to feel that their nonsexual productivity is socially valued and available. If these reinforcements are tenuous or missing, the likelihood of aggressive or regressive techniques to maintain a sense of self is more likely. Active heterosexual behavior is one way that an otherwise psychosocially impotent young male can reinforce self-worth and may explain the greater frequency of heterosexual intercourse among economically deprived youth, compared with that of their middle-class peers (Schofield 1964). In late adolescence, intercourse often seems to be a significant way in which a young male can confirm a sense of himself as an autonomous person with a capacity to be loving.

MASTURBATION IN THE DEVELOPMENT OF MALE SEXUAL IDENTITY

Masturbation is important to males' personality development. As infants, they recognize that genital stimulation is satisfying, and infants of both sexes may use masturbation to soothe and gratify themselves (Tyson 1982). In addition, the two-year-old male's pleasure in urinating often is associated with genital stimulation (Fenichel 1965).

Masturbation becomes a highly significant developmental act at the onset of puberty. It then no longer just provides excitement and self-solace but also represents a reaffirmation of masculinity. Masturbation becomes a method whereby genital excitement is now allied with fantasies about sexual involvement. Early adolescent masturbation is a way station on the road to loving adult sexuality, but it also has other psychological functions. When puberty arrives, erections become more frequent, which arouse in a young male the awareness that a part of his body is out of control. Masturbation is one way that the uncontrollable can be controlled. As the masturbatory act helps control tumescence and detumescence, penile erections are no longer an event that arouses anxiety as well as gratification. With the act of masturbation, aggressive and sexual fantasies become separated from each other, and unconscious oedipal fantasies are now reworked.

Among middle-class males, masturbation may continue more or less regularly until early adulthood. It is then replaced by either periods of abstinence or regular sexual involvement. In adult males, masturbation occurs as a self-solacing activity, usually under conditions of deprivation and stress.

Male sexuality is initially more experimental than loving. But with emotional maturity, intercourse becomes part of a loving sexual act. The self-reference of masturbation thus becomes other-directed intercourse.

Lower socioeconomic groups regard solitary masturbation during early adolescence as infantile, and its continuation thereafter is often thought to have a derogatory, homosexual connotation. The psychobiological need for sexual tension relief nevertheless continues. The solution is to establish an essentially masturbatory relationship with others, and so a girl's vagina becomes a masturbatory stimulant for a boy's penis. Mutual satisfaction or caring has generally little or no relevance.

Self-referent early and middle adolescent males who are heterosexually active are unlikely to use contraception. As an additional complication, psychologically immature males equate potency and fertility. The more insecure a young male might be about his masculine identity, the more he will believe this equation.

Sexually active early adolescent girls are quite unlikely to become pregnant, as regular monthly ovulation does not occur for approximately three years after menarche. Some sexually active males thus find their inability to make a girl pregnant as a threat to their sense of masculine potency. They then reinforce this by suggesting to themselves and their partners that they have a magical control over their own fertility. They may also attempt to deal with their anxiety by becoming promiscuous, their goal being to impregnate. In psychoanalytic literature, male heterosexual activity with many partners is seen as a "Don Juan" type of behavior, associated with a longing for male companionship and a dread of homosexuality. Although this may be present in some adolecent males, nearer to their consciousness is the feeling that if they cannot make a girl pregnant, they are less of a man.

The girl's irrelevance as a significant other person is demonstrated by early adolescent language. Just as derogatory words are used for masturbation; so are they used about girls who are masturbatory objects. For example, lower-class males in Britain refer to masturbation as "wanking." A wanker, originally, was an inadequate seaman in the British navy (Miller 1974), but the word has come to mean weakness and incompetence. A girl who is used by boys for the masturbatory act is called a "slag" and is not looked upon as a girl with whom one would want to become permanently involved. In the United States, boys "jerk off," and a "jerk" is an individual who is regarded as weak, incompetent, and stupid. Girls who are the objects of male exploitation are commonly called "sluts."

Early and middle-adolescent males also assess their masculinity by comparing themselves with others. Violent behavior, "macho" talk, and antisocial activity, and, more acceptably, athletic prowess and, among middle-class groups, intellectual achievement all are compared. In addition, males in all social classes compare their physique and genital size. Sometimes the comparison is of the length of the penis during erection, sometimes the strength of the urinary stream, and sometimes the distance that they can ejaculate. There is an obvious unconscious homosexual preoccupation in these comparisons. In violent youth involved in gang activities, this comparison may also lead to gang rape. Young males may use a "gang bang" to assert their masculinity to other males, to demonstrate their contempt for women, and to satisfy themselves as to their own potency.

Because masturbation is self-referent, the likelihood of empathic involvement with a partner is minimal. When masculine identity is weakened by either a societal failure to meet developmental needs or a personality disturbance, the drive to impregnate may be reinforced.

It is reasonable to assume that the more a young male's sense of worth is weakened, the more likely he is to seek to demonstrate his masculinity to himself and others by making a girl pregnant. When such an individual finds himself unable to impregnate a girl, his inner anxiety is enhanced, and his attempts to impregnate a girl increase. Not only do such young males not use contraception themselves; they also actively discourage the practice in their partners. Condoms, particularly, are not used, as they are said to interfere with satisfaction. And many young males insist that if they have intercourse with a girl on the "pill," it is not as satisfying as if they have intercourse "naturally":

One 14-year-old boy with some motivation to prevent conception described how he impregnated his girl friend. He said that he tried to have intercourse with her with a condom, but he did not like it, and so, "I tore it off and then I had intercourse, and then she became pregnant." He said this with ill-disguised satisfaction.

When his partner becomes pregnant, a young male's sense of potency is assured: at this point, the girl may well have fulfilled her role and is then likely to be abandoned.

Early childhood experiences may reinforce an adolescent male's wish to impregnate. Lower-class black males in the United States are reported to have intercourse first at a mean age of 12; Hispanics are nearly 13; and whites are nearly 15.

Many impoverished black and Hispanic fathers are forced to live away from their spouse and children partly because of regulations governing the payment of welfare and aid to dependent children (Stack 1975). If the model of masculinity presented to boys is to impregnate and then disappear, this might further explain why consistent fathering is less likely among the economically depressed. One would thus expect that with the rising divorce rate, male adolescent impregnation would become more prevalent in white middle-class culture. All the evidence, as manifested by an increase in illegitimate births, is that there is such an increase in illegitimate conception. Because middle-class women are more likely to have abortions than poor women are, this increase is probably more dramatic than the statistics indicate. From clinical observation, the age of first intercourse is now earlier for middle-class males.

The increase in the divorce rate is thus likely to produce a different model of acceptable male sexuality. Fathering is not necessarily associated with living with one's children, and masculinity is unduly associated with the concept of impregnation.

A single-parent mother is often felt as too intrusive and too powerful, even if she is not. Another effect of not having a father is to make boys unwilling, either emotionally or physically, to engage themselves with girls, because they believe that women are too intrusive. This suggests that the number of males who do not marry or establish permanent emotional relationships with women will increase, as will the number of those who are homosexual. But there is as yet no firm study that can confirm this hypothesis.

ILLEGITIMATE PREGNANCY AND ADOLESCENT LOVE AFFAIRS

It is not unusual for adolescent boys and girls to become infatuated with each other. These youngsters are often offspring of apparently intact nuclear families and may be from any socioeconomic group. They may have an uncertain sense of a separate self but do not show their emotional disturbance in socially defined disorders of behavior. They may resolve their need for infantile attachments by a pseudomature heterosexual involvement. Such young people spend all their free time with each other and effectively isolate themselves from their peers.

Although the family may appear to be functional, the adolescents involved in such intense relationships usually have experienced a variety of nurturing deficits. These are not generally young people from obviously depriving families, but it often appears that they retain an intense need for nurture. They seem to remain in the same psychological position as does the small child who cannot leave his or her mother without a teddy bear or blanket. The "transitional objects" (Winnicott 1958) of adolescence may be drugs of abuse, religious cults, or an intense emotional attachment to a member of the opposite sex. Because ultimate personal autonomy requires the withdrawal of infantile attachments, in the process of secondary separation and individuation these young people become intensely involved in relationships which enable them to emotionally withdraw from their parents. Such adolescents may feel acutely depressed when not in the presence of the chosen boy or girl. This may be so intense that when such a relationship is terminated, the "bereaved" partner may become overwhelmed with depression. In those to whom it is acceptable, attempts at suicide are not unusual:

A 17-year-old boy became acutely suicidal when his girl friend of three years told him that she did not wish to continue the relationship. He was hospitalized in a panic state, suffering from an acute identity confusion, and he saw death as his only solution.

A similar situation:

A 15-year-old boy made two suicidal attempts in the course of one week. At the age of thirteen and a half, he had become involved with a girl friend with whom he had maintained a relationship until one week before the episode. He was a big boy and looked about two years older than his chronological age. He had had intercourse for about a year, and the girl was his only attachment. She told him that she was getting bored with the relationship and wished to end it. At this point, he took a dose of his father's tranquilizers and sedatives. He was taken to a hospital and then was sent home. Two days later he repeated the episode.

Such girl friends are, in a sense, the coat that the boy wears to make himself more of a man; in his turn the boy allows the girl to feel separate from her mother. The need in boys is less to prove their masculinity than to create a sense of self. Although the young male may seem to be involved in heterosexual behavior, he is also receiving from his girl friend the nurture that he requires in order to prove an inner sense of total integrity.

If a boy comes from a social group in which solitary masturbatory activity is psychologically or socially forbidden, he then is likely to be sexually active, and the risk of impregnation is great. If in addition, a boy needs to use fertility to prove his potency, pregnancy also is likely. Even if proving his sexual potency is not a paramount issue, intermittent intercourse is not unusual in such relationships, although perhaps only in times of deprivation and stress. If under such circumstances, a girl refuses to have intercourse, a boy may become sexually aggressive:

One boy of 16 reported that he had had intercourse with his girlfriend the night before. He said, "She had refused to have sex with me for the last six weeks because she was afraid of getting pregnant. So I got her real wasted, and I then screwed her. I did not use anything."

Although he was apparently fond of his girlfriend, he had no sense of guilt about this behavior. His sense of deprivation was such that he felt entirely justified in meeting his own needs.

Girls involved in such relationships often appear to have strong mothering needs and are often a year or two older than their boyfriends. Because of this, a number of them see themselves as being responsible for preventing conception. Thus pregnancy is not common in these relationships. In addition, many are relatively celibate involvements in which sexual intercourse is quite rare and occurs only under special circumstances.

When these transitional relationships are asexual, they are highly idealized, as an intimate sexual involvement with an emotionally significant other person may be felt as emotionally threatening. If there is intercourse—and then pregnancy—in these idealized relationships, the young couple will support each other during an abortion, or they will marry. The marriage, however, usually turns out to be disastrous. If one or the other partner matures and becomes more autonomous, the other partner may be discarded, like a teddy bear by a three- to five-year-old. If a baby is born, his or her demands may be felt as an intolerable threat, particularly by the immature young father. He thus is likely either to flee from the demands on him or to respond aggressively. He cannot tolerate his wife's satisfying the infant's mothering needs and thus will abandon a perceived depriving female and a threatening infant.

Some boys who use girls as masturbatory, self-gratifying objects may also need these more involved relationships in order to develop a sense of autonomy. Pregnancy is then very likely. The adolescent mother, who is almost certainly unable to tolerate frustration, often becomes an abusing parent. When immature males make these relationships when a child is already present, they are also likely to abuse their spouse's children.

Adolescent males who impregnate their girl friends are not necessarily psychologically deviant. Just as a healthy late adolescent may choose to use masturbation as a preferred sexual outlet and then become a heterosexually active and loving adult, early and middle adolescents who have had masturbatory relationships with girls may eventually mature.

Adolescents in inpatient psychiatric treatments are particularly likely to form intense relationships with patients of the opposite sex. When this happens, both may develop a pseudomaturity; their behavioral difficulties may disappear; and they may make an apparent but unreal recovery from their psychological difficulties:

> John and Carol were patients in an adolescent treatment center. They became extremely attached to each other while living on the intensive treatment unit. They continued this in the partial hospitalization program and as outpatients. John was a big, well-built boy of 15 when the relationship began. Carol was 16. They began to have intercourse when they were outpatients, and Carol got herself a diaphragm.

> They both had been drug abusers, and both gave this up. Neither, however, was able to improve their underachieving school performance. John was unable to envisage leaving home to go to school, and Carol continued to be petulant and infantile with her mother.

Both, however, terminated their treatment. John returned for help at the age of 19, having found himself unable to work in college. He had one further bout with drug abuse but with the help of Narcotics Anonymous was now dry. At the same age, Carol became involved with a married man of 32.

PREVENTING ILLEGITIMATE CONCEPTION

One important issue is to make contraceptive advice available in health clinics, especially in high schools in underprivileged neighborhoods. Another issue is whether males can be persuaded to accept the idea of using contraceptives. There is evidence that with competent sex education, girls are considerably more willing to use contraceptives, but there is less evidence that this has had any effect on adolescent males. A recent drive in the United States to inform parents when their children—under seventeen—seek contraceptive advice could reduce the incidence of its use. In Western culture, sexual activity is an integral part of the drive for autonomy and generally involves secrecy from the parents.

Emotional support is necessary for girls who have an abortion. Although follow-up studies in adult women show little or no psychological sequelae to an abortion, there is clinical evidence that many adolescent girls become depressed at the time that the baby would have been born and may conceive again at this time. Girls with low self-esteem often become pregnant with the idea that this at least is something they are able to do. Their pregnancy seems to have the same meaning to them that intercourse does to a devalued male. Not only is it gratifying, it is something that they can do successfully.

If girls become pregnant in an attempt to resolve their feelings of emptiness, worthlessness, and misery, an abortion, particularly one that is encouraged by their parents, is likely to make them feel that the world agrees that they are worthless. These young adolescents, providing that they receive competent prenatal and postnatal obstetric and psychological care, will have a better personality development if they carry their baby to term and then release it for adoption.

An abortion performed as a social convenience often means that the experience is likely to be repeated:

> Kathleen was a 16-year-old girl who was referred for psychological help after two suicidal gestures, in which she had overdosed with aspirin and cut her wrists. She was an adopted child and felt that not only was she worthless but that she was a nuisance to her parents. When drunk one night, she was impregnated by a 21-year-old man who had fed her liquor. This was her first sexual experience. Her parents assumed that she would have an abortion, and she denied any doubts about this wish. After the abortion, she became highly promiscuous and again became pregnant. She again had an abortion and then made the suicidal gestures. She said that her father had pressured her to have an abortion.

It was apparent that Kathleen's guilt about the first abortion made her repeat the conception; by delivering a healthy baby, she could repair the damage. In her second abortion, as in her first impregnation, she behaved as if she were helpless against an overpowering male.

In an ideal caring society, a social policy that forbids legal abortions might be justified, but at the present time such a policy will protect neither adolescents nor their offspring. If an abortion is recommended, competent obstetric and psychological care should be offered, but an abortion should not be an automatic response to adolescent pregnancy.

Males need to establish a sense of self-worth in ways other than by becoming a father. Exhortation to celibacy or education in contraceptive techniques does not reinforce masculine identity; rather, indirect techniques are necessary. Adolescent males must be secure in their masculine identity without needing to impregnate.

Children whose concepts of masculinity and femininity have been distorted by the fragmented roles of their parents can mature by making significant emotional relationships with nonparental adults. Their ethos should be that loving behavior does not automatically imply impulse gratification, whether sexual, violent, or drug abusing.

For those who are able to make such meaningful emotional involvements, adolescence offers a second chance for mature development. Those significant adults who subscribe to an ethos that may be different from the family system need to be aware of the emotional significance of what they say and do. They should recognize that if they want to influence the young, the latter may ultimately reject them, not vice versa.

Those parts of the social system that cater to young people, such as schools, churches, and youth organizations, should clarify their goals. The young need models of both sexes who are both sexually and vocationally successful and who clearly respect the integrity of others.

Even in an adequately nurturing nuclear family, if models outside the family are not available to reinforce identity, then a firm sense of self cannot be achieved. If adolescents do not value the integrity of others, despite an adequate child-rearing experience, and if their community finds sexual activity to be permissible, then the frequency of such activity will probably increase.

REFERENCES

Adams-Tucker, C. (1982). Proximate effects of sexual abuse in childhood: Report on children. *American Journal of Psychiatry* 139:1252–1256.

Blain, H. P. (1976). Masochism: the ego ideal and the psychology of women. *Journal of the American Psychological Association* 24:157–191.

Bulikian, H., and Goldman, A. (1971). A study of teenage pregnancy. *American Journal of Psychiatry* 128:735–758.

Card, J. J., and Wise, L. L. (1978). Teenage mothers and teenage fathers. *Family Planning Perspectives* 10:192–205.

Ewer, P., and Gibbs, J. (1975). Relationships with putative fathers and use of contraception in a population of black ghetto adolescent mothers. *Public Health Report* 90:417–423.

Fenichel, A. (1965). *The Psychoanalytic Theory of Neurosis.* New York: W. W. Norton.

Finkel, M., and Finkel, D. (1975). Sexual and contraceptive knowledge, attitudes and behavior of male adolescents. *Family Planning Report* 7:256–260.

Furstenberg, F. (1976). *Unplanned Parenthood.* New York: Free Press.

Futterman, S., and Livermore, J. (1967). Putative fathers. *Journal of Social Casework* 28:176–178.

Gibbens, T., and Prince, J. (1963). *Child Victims of Sexual Offences.* London: Institute for the Study and Treatment of Delinquents.

Group for the Advancement of Psychiatry. (1986). *Teenage Pregnancy: Impact on Adolescent Development.* New York: Brunner/Mazel.

Gulensen, E., and Roiphe, H. (1976). Some suggested revisions concerning early female development. *Journal of the American Psychological Association* 24:29–57.

Hatcher, S. (1973). The adolescent experience of pregnancy and abortion: A developmental analysis. *Journal of Youth and Adolescents* 2:53–102.

Johnson, C. L. (1974). Child Abuse in the Southeast: Analysis of 1172 Reported Cases. Athens, GA: Regional Institution on Social Research.

Miller, D. (1974). *Adolescence: Psychology, Psychopathology and Psychotherapy.* New York: Jason Aronson.

National Center for Disease Control. (1978). *Mortality and Morbidity Weekly Report* 27:460–461.

Offer, D., and Offer, J. (1974). Normal adolescent males: the high school and college years. *Journal of the American College Health Association* 22:209–215.

Pannor, R., Evans, B., and Masarik, F. (1971). *The Unmarried Father*. New York: Springer Publishing.

Reider, N. (1968). The unmarried father. *American Journal of Psychiatry* 18:230–237.

Ross, J. M. (1975). The development of paternal identity: a critical review of the literature on nurturance in boys and men. *Journal of the American Psychological Association* 23:783–818.

Schaffer, C., and Pine, F. (1972). Pregnancy, abortion and the developmental levels of adolescence. *Journal of the American Academy of Child Psychiatry* 2:511–536.

Schofield, M. (1964). *The Sexual Behavior of Young People*. London: Longman.

Solnit, A. (1979). Psychosexual development: Three to five years. In *The Basic Handbook of Child Psychiatry*, vol. 1, ed. J. Noshpitz. New York: Basic Books.

Stack, C. (1975). *All Our Kin: Strategies for Survival in a Black Community*. New York: Harper and Row.

Stoller, R. J. (1979). Fathers of transexual children. *Journal of the American Psychological Association* 27:837–866.

Stoller, R. J., and Heidt, G. H. (1982). The development of masculinity: a cross cultural contribution. *Journal of the American Psychological Association* 30:20–61.

Tyson, P. (1982). A developmental line of gender identity, gender role and choice of love object. *Journal of the American Psychological Association* 30:61–87.

Winnicott, D. (1958). *Transitional objects and transitional phenomena*. In *Collected Papers: Through Pediatrics to Psychoanalysis*. New York: Basic Books.

13

Self-Starvation Syndromes

"It's like the women's magazines: on one page they tell you how to diet; on the other, they tell you how to cook." (Anorectic patient aged 16)

The amazing proliferation of centers to treat eating disorders is a measure of both medicine's marketplace approach and societal reinforcement. Both pediatric and psychiatric literature indicate a determined effort to find specific biological interventions that can resolve self-starvation syndromes. Some have said that the goal should be to seek a better biological classification of eating-disordered patients (Goldberg, Halmi, and Eckert 1979). There is as yet no evidence that anything other than psychosocial conflict is the reason for the specific symptoms of self-starvation in those who might otherwise present other types of difficulty. Self-starvation syndromes, like most other behavioral disorders, have biopsychosocial causes. The starvation, however, then produces further biopsychological effects.

Not all excessive weight loss is due to anorexia nervosa: it may occur in athletic young males who misunderstand the need for adequate food intake. But in those who suffer from anorexia nervosa, running may manifest a symptomatic need for excessive exercise (Chapman 1983).

The principal self-starvation syndromes are anorexia nervosa and bulimia. These syndromes may exist together or separately. People may also try to get thin by abusing over-the-counter laxatives. Many patients with bulimia have a normal weight (Herzog 1982), and some deliberately vomit so that they can eat what they like.

Many individuals who eat compulsively induce vomiting or use purgatives. One 15-year-old remarked gleefully: "I don't care what people think! I eat what I like and then get rid of it by throwing up."

Some who binge have abnormal EEGs (Green and Rau 1974), although there is, however, no conclusive proof that phenytoin is of any value in this condition (Johnson et al. 1983b).

The biological causes of self-starvation syndromes include neuroendocrine disturbances—particularly those associated with mood disorders—and the schizophrenic syndromes. Nowadays, when these are associated with food and bodily delusions, eating disorders are particularly likely. Starvation syndromes are also seen in those who suffer from tuberculosis, malignancies, endocrine dysfunctions—particularly panhypopituitarism—thyrotoxicosis, and pituitary tumors.

In some individuals, no known biological cause can be found. Some have conversion disorders (Garfinkel et al. 1983); some are phobic, some depressed because of emotional deprivation; and others suffer from personality disorders, including histrionic and borderline characters.

Anorexia nervosa has been said to occur independently of these syndromes (Bliss and Branch 1960), but this theory is questionable. The reinforcement of the perception of control of the self and others, with consequent omnipotence, distorts personality development. The biopsychological causes of eating disorders are not specific. When anorexia nervosa occurs in those suffering from borderline personalities, it may be used to maintain control over anxiety, even if the cost is death. With these, as with all other symptom complexes produced in borderline individuals, the choice of symptom cannot be explained on a psychological basis alone. The syndrome's "success" in maintaining equilibrium in an individual who feels threatened with overwhelming tension helps perpetuate it. This is reinforced by the psychological response to starvation, which initially produces symptoms that enhance feelings of being in control of the world and the self.

ANOREXIA NERVOSA

Anorexia nervosa has been called a "dance macabre" among the psychological syndromes. Young people may starve themselves to death in a sea of plenty. It was probably first mentioned in the thirteenth century in a description of Princess Margaret of Hungary, who died at the age of 25 (Konradyne 1973). It was also described in the medical literature by Morton in the seventeenth century and later by Gull (1874). In recent years, along with bulimia, the incidence of anorexia has become pandemic among relatively affluent groups. It does not generally occur among the economically deprived. It is statistically more common among girls (Halmi 1974) and is reported to have a mortality rate of between 3.6 and 6.6 percent (Kalucy 1977).

Although anorexia may appear suddenly, there often has been an insidious dietary preoccupation for a long time before the illness becomes evident. Typically, the illness occurs in "the best little girl in the world," often a bright, personable child who has never given any particular trouble to her family, her friends, or her school. There usually is no previously diagnosed illness and no history of a thought disorder. The characteristic features of the primary syndrome are the pursuit of thinness in the struggle for an independent identity, the delusional denial of excessive thinness, a preoccupation with food, hyperactivity, and a striving for perfection. The syndrome is associated with hypothermia and intolerance to cold; abdominal pain and constipation; vomiting, agitation, or lethargy. Sometimes a systolic murmur is present, and there may be evidence of petechial hemorrhages.

Depending on the degree of starvation, there may be a decrease in thyroid test values; abnormalities in cortisol and growth hormone secretion; decreased gonadotrophins; hypercarotenemia; other evidence of hypothalamic dysfunction and deviation of blood urea nitrogen (Schwabe et al. 1981).

A distortion of body image seems to be specific to anorexia nervosa. Body-image distortion is often related to the preoccupation of being enslaved and exploited both by one's own body and by others. In other syndromes of self-starvation, the patient does not see herself as being attractive when emaciated. Only in anorexia nervosa will a girl consent to put on a swimsuit and feel acceptable when she has so starved herself that she is androgynous in appearance and clearly emaciated. Only in anorexia nervosa is the tension associated with diffuse anxiety replaced with the feeling of being "fat." The attempt to control the experience of anxiety is difficult, if not impossible, but fatness can be magically relieved by refusing to eat.

The psychological conflicts that appear in anorexia nervosa seem not to be specific. Some see the illness as related to oedipal conflicts and the acceptance of sexuality (Kestenberg 1972). Others see the syndrome as occurring in those for whom the problem is control over a sense of helplessness and the establishment of a sense of autonomy. The helplessness is partially dealt with by projecting it onto others who may be perceived as powerful, especially parents and therapeutic personnel.

It is reasonable to conclude that the choice of anorexia nervosa symptoms represents a psychosocially determined path to resolve many biopsychological conflicts. For those with problems developing a sense of autonomy, self-starvation symptoms are a particularly effective way of retaining a hostile dependence on their parents, particularly their mothers. But the symptoms may produce enmeshment rather than the reverse. All anorectic patients show conflicts over issues of control, but self-starvation is only one of several ways that vulnerable individuals may attempt to gain mastery over themselves and their immediate environment. Problems of identity, especially those presented with a denial of a wish to be sexual, may be present in those with anorexia. This is also a typical conflict of those who have histrionic personalities but who do not self-starve. Particularly competent and competitive children whose identity confusion is reinforced because they are unsure whether they are loved for themselves or for their abilities may develop eating disorders, but they too may deal with their conflicts in other ways.

In all eating disorders, the issue of control is projected onto food. Self-starvation, bulimia, and excessive purgation become issues over which the control battle is fought with both the family and the self.

In bulimia, vomiting appears to be an attempt to control a chaotic eating pattern (Johnson and Berndt 1982). Bulimic patients feel that when they allow themselves to eat, they lose all sense of control, and so they then will binge. Many who self-starve have the same anxiety.

Although it may be unclear why some use eating disorders to try to resolve conflicts, it is clear why once the syndrome is adopted, it is likely to continue. Self-starvation gives anorectics an experience of control both over the self and over the reactions of others. By controlling the uncontrollable, they can project their helplessness and can obtain a false sense of mastery. Anorectics can also deal with the bodily induced helplessness produced by pubertal changes: in females, amenorrhea, and in males, increasingly infrequent erections can come to mean that one's body is finally under control. Because starvation in itself increases the sense of omnipotence with this dynamic reinforcement, anorectic patients become terrifyingly omnipotent: they have bodies that do not need food, and if they die, they will survive. Furthermore, because individuals who feel helpless also very easily can feel tormented, they need to resolve their confusion about this issue by making this experience real. The projection of helplessness onto others ultimately produces punitive responses. That is, both their families and the therapeutic personnel may make real the adolescent's fantasized experience of persecution.

Behavioral techniques of increasing isolation as a response to weight loss (Maloney and Klykylo 1983) replay family attitudes of rejection and coercion. The denial of nutritional needs, the pleasure in refusing food, and the unusual handling of food (Feighner 1972) all reinforce the negative response of both family and therapeutic personnel to the syndrome. In addition, when these youngsters induce emesis, use cathartics, and exercise excessively (Lippe 1983), all may produce coercive environmental responses, which are enhanced by the patient's denial of illness. Approximately 93 percent of all individuals who suffer from anorexia nervosa deny their illness (Rollins and Piazza 1978), and the 4 percent of all sufferers who are boys are the most resistant to treatment (Sours 1974).

FAMILY AND SOCIETAL ISSUES

Two-thirds of the patients in Bruch's (1982) series of studies were girls, often with older-than-average parents. The family constellation surrounding anorexia nervosa is typical of that seen in all psychosomatic illnesses. In particular, the patient has a sense of being enmeshed in the family: there is excessive parental overprotection, rigidity, or dishonesty over moral and other issues, and an inability by the family to solve interpersonal conflicts (Minuchin 1978). These are usually controlling rather than impulsive families (Miller 1980).

As with all psychosomatic symptoms, the patient's problems commonly appear to regulate the family system. For example, a marital conflict may be converted into a family conflict over caring for the child. The patient may force separating parents to come together over issues of survival. Again, none of this explains why one individual and not another will develop the symptoms of anorexia. Perfectionistic individuals with identity problems are seen as having other psychosomatic illnesses and many other psychological syndromes.

It is not unusual for borderline personalities to become anorectic or to adopt other symptom complexes.

A mother who cannot allow her child a sense of separate self (Sours 1974) will not necessarily produce a child who self-starves.

The triad of disturbances in cognitive development described by Bruch (1973) do not explain the reason for the syndrome's appearance. That is, the disturbance of appetite and the misinterpretation of bodily stimuli are the results of starvation, and the inability to have age-appropriate sexual feelings is not unique to anorexia nervosa.

In neuroendocrine mood disorders, there is often an inexplicable fluctuation of mood, daily, hourly, or even more frequently. Again this experience is partially controlled by anorectic symptomatology, but there are many other ways in which it can be controlled.

The actual choice of symptom is probably related to implicit family and societal conflicts over food and weight. It is common for anorexia to appear in families that have been highly preoccupied with issues of diet, health foods, and overweight. Although this has no statistical significance, four of a group of six boys who suffered from anorexia nervosa all had parents who worked in the food industry. It is not unusual for anorectic girls to have mothers who have conflicts about cooking. Often these mothers have returned to school or to work, and so their homemaking tasks have become more onerous. Thus it is as if the daughter refuses to eat so as to obey an implicit message from the mother who no longer wishes to cook. When this maternal situation is combined with a controlling father and societal conflicts over thinness, the land is fertile for the development of anorectic symptoms.

Often the symptoms appear to begin by chance in an adolescent with conflicts. Typically, the quiet, good child who is relatively ignored by the family at mealtimes begins to diet because of social pressures. When at family meals, the child's failure to eat is noticed, he or she suddenly becomes the focus of the family's attention. If the individual has internal conflicts over issues of helplessness, control, and sexuality, this will reinforce the self-starvation.

Many adolescent girls who suffer from self-starvation syndromes may appear to be victims of group contagion. Often high school girls are intensively preoccupied with their weight. Such groups have a leader who shares the larger group's conflicts over weight and sexual attractiveness and who encourages group dieting. The members of this group who become anorectic are likely to be those with preexisting biopsychosocial vulnerabilities, especially those who have family conflicts over autonomy, who are confused about their sexual and personal identities, and who are highly preoccupied with issues of helplessness. Such individuals become both the group's messengers to the adult world about the group's conflicts and the internal controllers of the group itself. Anorectic adolescents then are used by their peer group: those who are starving are both devalued and protected. The peer group is seemingly tolerant of their increasing starvation, as are the patients' families, until it becomes apparent that their condition is serious. Then the peers become highly preoccupied with feeding their starving members and with their own diets.

Anorexia nervosa is not a disease of poverty. Children of the poor with conflicts over identity, sexuality, control, and helplessness rarely present themselves with self-starvation as a significant symptom.

THE EFFECTS OF STARVATION

Weight loss that occurs in less than three months, greater than 25 to 30 percent of estimated body weight, begins to produce serious physiological effects. The same applies to a loss of 35 to 40 percent occurring in a longer time period. Bradycardia, hypotension, hypothermia, and listlessness indicate a life-threatening danger.

There is no primary hypothalamic abnormality that causes anorexia nervosa, and the effects on hypothalamic function are secondary to food deprivation (Drossman, Untjes, and Heizer, 1979). An increase in plasma growth hormone with a decrease in luteinizing hormone, follicle-stimulating hormone, and thyroid hormone (T3) all are clear evidence that there is interference with hypothalamic function. Sometimes the administration of thyroid release hormone (TRH) or glucose causes a paradoxical rise in serium growth hormone (Macaron, Wilber, and Green 1978).

Weight change does not only create disordered hypothalamic function; it may also produce secondary pituitary dysfunction. There may be a kwashiorkor-like syndrome, with very low serum protein. At this, the patient may continue to lose weight even after adequate nutrition has begun: it is as though the body is devouring itself.

Amenorrhea occurs with lanugo hairs. The heart rate may slow to less than sixty beats per minute and may result in heart block and death.

Besides the physiological symptoms of starvation, its psychological effects influence the development of personality. Starving individuals lose their ability to feel hungry and so do not know when they are empty and when they are full. Starvation produces a psychological regression, a narcissistic preoccupation with the self, and often psychoticlike thoughts. When starvation is intense, acute confusional states are common. Starvation is associated with hyperacuity and hypersensitivity, which both may create a feeling of being special. The bodily changes of starvation influence the perception of one's body image, but what differentiates anorexia nervosa from other eating disorders is the perceptual distortion that the weight loss produces beauty.

Some individuals who suffer from mood disorders present themselves as having anorexia nervosa. Others suffer from self-starvation but are aware that their weight loss has made them unattractive; they are honest about their failure to eat and do not secretly exercise.

The maturational age of individuals when anorexia nervosa appears is significant. If the syndrome occurs just before puberty, it will then interfere with the development of adolescence. In middle adolescence, identity cannot be consolidated, and in late adolescence, sexual conflicts may not be as apparent in those in whom anorexia has occurred earlier.

ANORECTIC SYNDROMES AND MOOD DISORDERS

One symptom of mood disorder is an appetite disturbance, and in a psychosocial conflict, this can easily produce profound self-starvation. These adolescents do not see themselves as being more comfortable if they "lose another two or three pounds" but are acutely aware of their own inappropriate appearance.

Sometimes depression may be present in adolescents with identity confusion, and it is then not unusual to have a mood disorder along with the anorexia nervosa:

> Alice, age 16, had a history of intermittent excitement each year, which lasted for about three months. This was first noticed when she was approximately 15-months-old. Her paternal grand-mother had been hospitalized for depression, and her mother was also depressed.

> When Alice was eight, a 16-year-old male babysitter had intermittently sexually assaulted her over a period of about one year. At age 13, she dated a boy of 17 who attempted to neck with her. She became very frightened and so decided to eliminate her breasts. After a 25-pound loss, from 100 pounds, she was admitted to the hospital. She was excited, grandiose, and omnipotent and, within two weeks, became overtly depressed. She had marked affective lability.

> An appropriate dosage of lithium carbonate ended Alice's mood swings, but she continued to feel that she must be as asexual as possible. Her weight returned to normal, but therapy was needed for her chronic sexual confusion and anxiety.

BULIMIA

Disordered eating among young women is now so common that it is easy to overdiagnose both bulimia and anorexia nervosa. In an Australian study, 63 percent of the subjects described binge eating from time to time, and among this group, 13 percent weighed either less than 80 percent of their standard weight or more than 120 percent (Abraham et al. 1983). Bulimia is characterized by the self-perpetuating practice of binge eating followed by various methods of purging, including self-induced vomiting and the abuse of cathartic and diuretic drugs. It is a condition in which patients deny having control over their eating. For at least six months, they will have been binge eating and then inducing vomiting at least once a week. Bulimia is associated with a morbid fear of fatness but not necessarily with gross underweight. However, some adolescents who remit from anorexia nervosa may later develop bulimia: 25 percent of bulimics have such a history (Fairburn and Cooper 1984). This is more likely if therapy has produced only symptomatic relief in anorexia nervosa:

> Pamela was admitted at the age of 13 to an adolescent treatment center with self-starvation, a perception of being fat whenever she was stressed, and a loss of 25 percent of her estimated body weight. She was the younger of two siblings of parents who were on the verge of divorce. Her father was a sympathizer with the American Nazi party and was alternately effusive and depressed. Her mother was a retiring and withdrawn bank teller. Pamela was found to have a mood disorder and a borderline personality. Her father was then discovered to have a bipolar illness. Pamela became extraordinarily dependent on the hospital, and two of her psychotherapists gave up, feeling unable to deal with her intractable symptomatology, her "refusal" to leave the hospital, and her persistent nastiness. A third therapist finally managed to involve the patient in both individual and family therapy, and after over a year in hospital, Pamela returned home, started school, and continued in three-times-weekly outpatient therapy. She went through a flurry of marijuana abuse and sexual promiscuity and became intermittently bulimic. Her therapy continued for three years, and there was one episode of attempted suicide when she overdosed on imipramine, which usually controlled her depressed mood when given with lithium. She did not cope well with the transition from high school.

Binge eating is typically associated with the ingestion of high-calorie, easy-to-eat food. The binge ends with pain, sleep, or vomiting. It is often secretive and is associated with repeated attempts to lose weight. The physical effects of repeated vomiting include enlargement of the parotid gland, rectal bleeding, irregular menstruation, alopecia, and an erosion of dental enamel. Laboratory examination may show hypokalemic alkalosis and increased serum amylase three days after a binge.

Most of the studies of bulimic patients have suggested that even if they have anorectic symptoms, they will have a later onset, a higher incidence of familial obesity, and a more chronic outcome than will most sufferers from anorexia nervosa (Casper et al. 1980, Strober 1982). In adolescents bulimia is clearly so gratifying that they find it as difficult to abandon as do those who abuse marijuana. It is now less easy to differentiate different types of eating disorders. Among those adolescents who self-starve, some are also bulimic and indulge in occasional purging behavior, others always purge themselves after bingeing, others purge themselves with a normal diet on a daily basis. Adults whose symptoms began in young adulthood show more clearly differentiated syndromes. Of those adult patients studied, a majority do not seek psychiatric help, although many have an impaired life adjustment (Johnson et al. 1983a).

The medical complications of these symptoms may be profound. A potentially fatal complication of binge eating after starving is acute gastric dilatation with abdominal distention and severe pain. Another complication is post-binge pancreatitis, which carries a 10 percent mortality rate. For bulimic patients high calorie foods with high salt content also increase the risk of arteriosclerosis. Vomiting is most commonly induced by the patients sticking fingers into their throats; sometimes, however, individuals may insert a toothbrush or press their necks. Lacerations of the throat and bruising of the neck may then occur. The most dangerous effects of vomiting are a rupture of the esophagus and the resulting possibility of severe pain and bleeding while the patient vomits.

Salts are lost when the patient vomits potassium, chloride, and hydrogen ions. Symptoms of this are weakness, constipation, frequent drinking and urinating, abdominal pain and easy fatigue. Sometimes ipecac may be swallowed to produce vomiting. This can cause serious cardiac complications.

Laxative abuse is increasingly common. The laxative abuser does not eliminate unwanted calories, but weight loss can be caused by dehydration. As in vomiting, chronic laxative abuse affects salt balance, and similar complications then occur. One of the most disturbing complications of abuse is what is known as "cathartic colon." The colon becomes an inert tube and feces cannot be eliminated without increasing doses of laxative. As with laxative abuse, diuretics may also be taken in secret. Sometimes adolescents may see physicians for the symptoms associated with salt depletion and hide the abuse of their own bodies.

TREATING BULIMIA

Between 5 and 19 percent of female college students have bulimia (Pyle et al. 1983). Highly organized supportive group treatment with adults and a relatively short-term follow-up with
12 group meetings may reduce symptomatic bulimic behavior
(Johnson et al. 1983b), but this technique does not seem to help
adolescents. In adolescent eating disorders of any type, group
treatment with patients with the same symptomatology is not
helpful. According to the reports that these patients give of their
relationship with one another, they compete over weight, diet,
and the frequency of their bingeing and vomiting. Group treatment thus may reinforce the false identity of being "anorectic,"
"bulimic," and "eating disordered." The treatment of bulimia is
the same in principle as that of all adolescent maladjustments:
the symptoms must be controlled, and the underlying biopsychosocial causes treated. If these are related to biologic depression,
the binging may stop when tricyclic antidepressants are given.

Problems of Treatment

Self-starvation syndromes become difficult to treat when the
symptoms cannot be controlled within the context of the interpersonal relationships that an individual may have with the family, significant others, peers or adults or therapeutic personnel.
Difficulties arise also when the patient does not respond to the
appropriate psychopharmacological interventions. This especially
applies to those whose eating disorder is a primary symptom in
mood disorders and schizophrenia.

   The intensity of the anorectic symptoms indicates whether
or not hospitalization is necessary. The patient may deny the
need to eat, both verbally and by action. This denial may be
accompanied by an unrealistic level of exercise, bingeing, vomiting, and food hiding. The effects of starvation may be apparent,
but they are denied. Indeed, the patient may comment that with
the loss of just a few more pounds, he or she will be satisfied.

   The physiological effects of starvation are likely to be apparent in those who require hospital care. Depending on how long it has lasted, there may be hypoplasia of bone marrow, hypercarotonemia, hypercholesterolemia, and a low sedimentation rate. An electrocardiograph examination, besides indicating a lower pulse rate, may also show ST depression, flat T waves, and a lengthened QT interval.

An indication for urgent intervention is a halving of the pulse rate and/or a shift from a state in which the youngster is hyperactive and convinced that the loss of weight is appropriate to a state of lethargy and general apathy.

The interfamilial and social environments may become psy-·chonoxious for the self-starving patient. Family psychopathology that joins the patient in denying the severity of her illness can lead to the patient's death. Some families, perhaps in response to the anorexia, begin to behave as though they would like to destroy their child. One family proposed resolving their child's serious loss of weight with a voyage in the Caribbean on a sailboat; another spent so long looking for a suitable hospital that when their 15-year-old daughter was admitted, she was unable to metabolize food satisfactorily and was an acute medical emergency.

The pathological family interaction that results from anorectic behavior cannot always be rapidly resolved, despite the optimism of some (Minuchin 1978). Children of invasive parents who cannot allow them to have any emotional or physical privacy may have to be taken from their families, either completely or at certain times, in order for the children to survive. Thus, intractable cases whose symptoms are not significantly alleviated in outpatient care require hospital treatment.

Hospital Care

This may be in a pediatric unit or an adolescent psychiatric inpatient setting which is part of a general hospital. Ideally, such a psychiatric treatment center should provide comprehensive and continuous high intensity care in a critical care unit with available less intensive care in a partial hospital and then in an outpatient clinic. Sometimes symptoms can be contained with weekend pediatric hospital care (MacDonald 1984) and sometimes with partial hospitalization along with any necessary biopsychosocial therapy. Sometimes in out-patient care families can be taught behavior modification techniques, but the developmental risks of this approach seem inordinately great; that is, they may greatly impede the adolescent's struggle for autonomy.

The quality of the therapeutic social system must be known if the treatment is to be successful. A general pediatric ward often is served by several attending physicians, each of whom may have his or her own way of treating anorexia. Some may concentrate on diet; some may focus on weight; and some may use minor tranquilizers, sedatives, or antidepressants without a formal diagnosis of depression. The nurses often must work under many house officers. In a social system in which positive reinforcement is rare, the staff may easily become coercive. Psychiatric units often do not offer satisfactory medical care, and it is doubtful in many of these settings if the developmental needs of the adolescents or adults who suffer from emotional disturbances, including anorexia nervosa, can be met. Free standing psychiatric hospitals in which crisis medical care can not be provided should not treat syndromes in which life-threatening events may acutely occur.

Adolescent medical wards under the direction of a staff physician who is responsible for the treatment of all patients, as well as similarly staffed adolescent psychiatric wards would seem to offer the best environment in which to treat anorectic adolescents when hospitalization is indicated.

A hospital experience should provide a continuity of therapeutic relationships and meet the patient's specific and nonspecific treatment needs (Knesper and Miller 1976). If a holding environment (Winnicott 1955) can be created, tension will be alleviated, symptoms will be treated, and specific therapeutic interventions will become more effective.

The therapeutic staff should be able to differentiate between the symptoms of psychological illness and those created by the developmental impasse that they produce. The staff need to understand that those patients who have starved themselves may not know when they are hungry and when they are full and that their eating patterns have to be reestablished. This requires sensitivity by the staff so that the patient is not infantilized, coerced, or ignored. As well as skilled nurses, physicians trained to resolve specific conflicts should be able to provide the appropriate medications and physical care.

Managing Severe Self-Starvation

When anorectic adolescents who have lost at least 20 percent of their estimated body weight or are steadily losing weight despite outpatient intervention are admitted to critical care, they should be told that if they can gain at least one-half pound a day, they can take part in all of the treatment center's program activities, which should be generally stimulating and enjoyable. But if they do not gain weight or if the gain is excessive—usually because large quantities of fluid are ingested—given the risk to their health that necessitated their admission, they will have to stay in bed.

Most adolescents cannot tolerate more than four thousand calories daily and so cannot be expected to gain more than one-half pound daily. Stuffing an individual with more than this makes them susceptible to bulimia and does not reinforce their trust in the staff to control their gorging and loss of control. The patients are weighed daily but are not told their weight as this encourages dietary manipulation.

Those who require bed rest will require adult supervision while awake. Because it is well known that ancillary symptoms are common in anorexia nervosa, to leave the child alone may be perceived as giving him or her permission to vomit, to exercise excessively, not to stay in bed, or to cheat with weight by drinking excessive amounts of fluid.

This adult should be a good companion, play board games with the patient, and assist with schoolwork. Nevertheless, the child may see the special supervision as persecutory, as all but the most depressed strive for autonomy and privacy. But the continuous presence of a caring adult essentially motivates the child to become free from what is felt as intolerable dependence.

While on bed rest, the adolescent is not restricted from contact with peers or forbidden to have visits from parents. Peers are essential message carriers from the environment and thus reinforce the patient's desire to be able to get out of bed. With this regimen and with individual psychotherapy from a therapist who is not concerned with environmental management, the patients in our therapeutic system usually begin to gain weight within three to five days. Of all the anorectic patients admitted to our treatment center since 1979, only two have required intubation. Both had been tube fed before psychiatric hospitalization in our center; one had eroticized this experience and was admitted with the tube in place.

Weight gain is thus achieved by an implicit technique of operant conditioning accompanied by positive reinforcement. Other than bed rest, no technique of social deprivation is used. Food is an indirect issue. If the patient becomes anxious about excessive food intake, food may be offered on individual trays. The amount that ought to be eaten is offered with a food supplement if necessary. The patient then knows that protection is possible. We do not believe that isolation can ever be helpful.

Psychotherapy

A physician who is not the patient's psychotherapist can best manage the patient's weight gain and responsibility for daily behavior. Anorectic patients should not be accepted for outpatient therapy by non-medically trained psychotherapists without the patient's physical condition's being regularly supervised by a knowledgeable pediatrician. Too many such patients admitted to hospitals have been allowed to become dangerously ill. The desired frequency of medical supervision should be determined by the pediatrician, not the family, the patient, or the psychotherapist.

In our center, a pediatrician trained as a child psychiatrist manages the patients' lives with them. The psychotherapist helps resolve the patients' conflicts so that they can rejoin their age-appropriate developmental track. Problems of projection, helplessness, denial, and control of the environment by dietary manipulation can be dealt with only by a therapist who is not directly involved in these maneuvers.

Psychotherapists cannot be preoccupied with the management impasse that the patients may create by dieting, as this will become an intolerable therapeutic resistance. The patients' omnipotence is immense: with smiling insouciance, a 15-year-old girl of 5 feet, 5 inches said that she considered her ideal weight to be 70 pounds. She remarked, "I know you think that is dangerous, but I don't feel that is true."

Usually patients are seen in expressive-supportive psychotherapy three times weekly. The supportive therapy helps clarify to the patients how they are attempting to control their environment. Patients admit that most of their emotional energy is spent on a preoccupation with weight, diet, and feeling fat. The therapist needs to become allied with that part of the patient's personality that struggles to make an emotional involvement with the world outside this sterile self. The patient feels helpless with this preoccupation but omnipotently feels that within it there is a magic answer. Both the omnipotence—"I know you can help me. My parents have known about you for years but could not find you," said one 15-year-old—and the helplessness—"All you do is take my parents' money, you don't do anything"—are projected onto the therapist. Behind both is infinite rage.

The psychotherapy of anorectic patients must be adequate; a recommendation of only once-weekly supportive therapy will starve the patient of emotional nourishment just as they are starving themselves of food.

The therapist should clarify the patient's complaint of persecution and begin to address problems of helplessness. These patients will also have sexual conflicts and have failed to resolve oedipal issues. Many have little sense of autonomy and appear as borderline personalities. These patients will have difficulty abandoning these symptoms, as they are exchanging certainty for uncertainty, as well as the security of omnipotent control, or its fantasy, for the uncertainties of living.

Therapy has many cognitive overlays, and the therapist must agree with the patients that the price of emotional involvement with others is risking loss and pain. As they begin to recover, they become aware of their emotional dependence. One youngster confessed, "I don't like my mother. It makes no sense, but I cannot do anything without her permission. It makes me mad."

The goal of family therapy—which in our center is usually offered by the psychotherapist—is the disengagement of the patient from the family (Story 1982). It begins as the patient shows some sense of autonomy and is designed to focus on how the patient has become trapped in the family and how the patient's illness has become the focus of family conflict. Family therapy may not be possible if parents refuse to share parenting or if their own conflict is so great that their narcissistic involvement with each other means that they cannot emotionally involve themselves with their child. Some parents may so need a disturbed child that they are unable to resolve this issue. This is particularly likely with parents who themselves suffer from borderline personality syndromes or undiagnosed and untreated mood disorders.

A particular problem for the family is when their daughter is clearly out of physical danger but is not yet ready to involve herself in any meaningful way with age-appropriate relationships, particularly with members of the opposite sex. At this point the parents have a safely dependent daughter, and this may be enormously appealing to them. Their daughter's ambivalence about continuing therapy and allowing herself maturational age-appropriate intimacy with others adds to the parents' reluctance to part with a dependent child. This is when they may want to terminate the therapy. Typically this occurs before the return of the menstrual cycle. Girls who dread the appearance or return of menstruation often become intolerably anxious at this time. This lack of bodily control becomes a focus for the patient's projected fear of a disintegration of personality controls, and a recurrence of symptoms at this time is common.

Sometimes the patient's therapy is terminated before menstruation has restarted, when her weight is stable and with stated demands for autonomy, but the prognosis for successful adult adjustment is impaired when this happens. However, if the patient continues treatment, when she has accepted the inner helplessness associated with menstruation, conflicts concerning her sexual identity are likely to surface. Some adolescents who decide that they no longer need any therapy may, however, return later with a more conscious motivation to resolve their inner conflicts.

Eating disorders thus have many causes. Those who self-starve or become bulimic with a careless disregard for their physical well-being always have serious personality problems, even though there may also be significant biological dysfunction or family chaos. The psychotherapist cannot become preoccupied with managing the symptom, for to do so would be to turn the symptom over and over. Therapists should use symptoms appropriately, as a ticket of admission to the patient's inner disturbance. Often the patients, even though quite young, have been multiply exposed to economically depriving and government-supported fantasies of an instant cure; many health-maintenance organizations contract for a maximum of fourteen days in a psychiatric hospital. Thus iatrogenically patients are distrustful of psychotherapy and therapists.

There are two main problems: the developmental impasse that creates vulnerability to the symptoms of eating disorders and the developmental arrest that is created by the disorder itself.

There is no evidence that adolescents who suffer from behavioral syndromes should be treated in special centers that ignore their different causes and behave as if the speedy relief of symptoms is all that is required. This may work for some, and the magic of a special clinic or center for a cluster of symptoms is appealing. The vested interest in eating disorders created by problems of payment and in the medical and psychological establishment is the same as for drug abuse, delinquency, and sexual dysfunction. The problem is that few treatment centers are biopsychosocially sophisticated, and few recognize developmental differences as significant and emotional maturity as a realistic goal.

REFERENCES

Abraham, C. F., Mira, M., Beumont, T. D., and Pierre, J. V. (1983). Eating behaviors among young women. *Medical Journal of Australia* 2:225–228.

Bliss, E., and Branch, C. H. (1960). *Anorexia Nervosa: A Multidimensional Perspective.* New York: Hoeber.

Bruch, H. (1973). *Eating Disorders.* New York: Basic Books.

———. (1982). Perceptual and conceptual disorders in anorexia nervosa. *Psychiatric Medicine* 24:187.

Casper, R., Eckert, D. E., Halmi, K. A., Goldberg, S., and Davis, J. M. (1980). Bulimia: its incidence and clinical significance in patients with anorexia nervosa. *Archives of General Psychiatry* 37:1030–1035.

Chapman, J. (1983). Excessive weight loss in the athletic adolescent. *Journal of Adolescent Health Care* 3:247–252.

Drossman, D. A., Ontjes, D. A., Heizer, W. D. (1979). Anorexia Nervosa. *Gastroenterology* 77:1115–1131.

Fairburn, C. G., and Cooper, P. J. (1984). The clinical features of bulimia nervosa. *British Journal of Psychiatry* 144:238–246.

Feighner, M. (1972). Diagnostic criteria for use in psychiatric research. *Archives of General Psychiatry* 26:57–63.

Garfinkel, P. E., Kaplan, A. S., Gamer, D. M., and Darby, P. L. (1983). The differentiation of vomiting/weight loss as a conversion disorder from anorexia nervosa. *American Journal of Psychiatry* 140:1019–1022.

Goldberg, S. G., Halmi, K. A., and Eckert, E. D. (1979). Cyproheptadine in anorexia nervosa. *British Journal of Psychiatry* 134:67–70.

Green, R. S., and Rau, J. H. (1974). Treatment of compulsive eating disorders with anticonvulsant medication. *American Journal of Psychiatry* 131:428–432.

Gull, W. (1874). Anorexia nervosa. *Transactions of Clinical Society of London* 7:22–28.

Halmi, K. A. (1974). Anorexia nervosa: demographic and clinical features in 94 cases. *Psychosomatic Medicine* 36:18–26.

Herzog, D. (1982). Bulimia: the secretive syndrome. *Psychosomatics* 23:481–487.

Johnson, C. L., and Berndt, D. J. (1982). Preliminary investigation of bulimia and life adjustment. *American Journal of Psychiatry* 140:774–777.

Johnson, C. L., Stuckey, M. K., Lewis, L. A., and Schwartz, D. M. (1983). Eating disorders. A descriptive survey of 316 cases. *International Journal of Eating Disorders* 2:3–16.

Johnson, C. L., Stuckey, M. K., and Mitchell, J. E. (1983). Psychopharmacological treatment of anorexia nervosa and bulimia: review and synthesis. *Journal of Nervous and Mental Disease* 171:524–534.

Kalucy, R. S. (1977). An approach to the therapy of anorexia nervosa. *Journal of Adolescence* 1:197–201.

Kestenberg, E. (1972). *Le Faim et le Corps*. Paris: Presses Universitaires de France.

Knesper, D., and Miller, D. (1976). Treatment plans for mental health care. *American Journal of Psychiatry* 133:45–50.

Konradyne, G. (1973). *Margitsziget*. Budapest: Kossath Nyonida.

Lippe, B. (1983). The physiological aspects of eating disorders. *Journal of the American Academy of Child Psychiatry* 22:108–113.

Macaron, C., Wilbert, J. F., and Green, O. (1978). Studies of growth hormone, thyrotropin and prolactin secretion in anorexia nervosa. *Psychoneuroendocrinology* 3:181.

MacDonald, J. (1984). Personal communication.

Maloney, M. J., and Klykylo, M. D. (1983). An overview of anorexia nervosa, bulimia, and obesity in children and adolescents. *Journal of the American Academy of Child Psychiatry* 22:99–107.

Miller, D. (1980). Family maladaptation reflected in drug abuse and delinquency. In *Responding to Adolescent Needs*, ed. M. Sugar. Jamaica, N.Y.: Spectrum Publications.

Minuchin, S. (1978). *Psychosomatic Families*. Cambridge, Mass.: Harvard University Press.

Pyle, R., Mitchell, J. E., Eckert, E. D., Halverson, P., Neuman, P., and Gold, G. (1983). The incidence of bulimia in freshman college students. *International Journal of Eating Disorders* 2:75–85.

Rollins, N., and Piazza, F. (1978). Diagnosis of anorexia nervosa: a critical reappraisal. *Journal of the American Academy of Child Psychiatry* 17:126–137.

Schwabe, A. D., Lippe, B. M., Chang, R. J., Pops, M. A., and Yager, J. (1981). Anorexia nervosa. *Annals of Internal Medicine* 94:371–381.

Sours, J. A. (1974). The anorexia nervosa syndrome. *International Journal of Psycho-Analysis* 55:567.

Story, I. (1982). Anorexia nervosa and the psychotherapeutic hospital. *International Journal of Psychoanalytic Psychotherapy* 9:267–302.

Strober, M. (1982). The significance of bulimia in juvenile anorexia nervosa. An exploration of possible etiological factors. *International Journal of Eating Disorders* 1:28–63.

Winnicott, D. (1955). *Maturational Processes and the Facilitating Environment*. New York: International Universities Press.

Subject Index

Abortion, 72, 283, 299
Accidental suicide, 186–187
Acting out, 7
  environmental stimulation of,
    35–37
  in families, 53
  medications and, 99
  nature of, 34
  in play, 124
  by substance abusers, 251–
    252
Acting up, 34
S-adenosylmethionine, 101
Administrative psychotherapy,
  109–111. *See also*
  Supportive therapy
Adolescence
  developmental distortions of,
    38–39
  stages of, 29, 174
Adolescence, early
  acting up versus acting out
    during, 33–35

alcohol abuse during, 233–236
characteristics of, 29–31, 174
delinquency during, 66
emotional crises of, 30–31
hero idealization in, 31–33
outer-directedness of, 29–31
self-concept in, 29–30
sexual activity during, 286,
  290–291, 292, 293
substance abuse during, 66
Adolescence, late
  alcohol abuse during, 235
  description of, 174
  sexual activity during, 286–
    287, 291
Adolescence, middle
  alcohol abuse during, 234–235
  delinquency during, 66
  description of, 174
  sexual activity during, 286,
    290–291, 292, 293
Affective rage syndrome, 124,
  129

Stress
  identity and, 39–40
  societal stimulation of, 36–37
Stress, reactions to
  acting out, 35
  affective violence, 158–159
  dehumanization, 20
  depression, 144–145
  HPA system, 145
Substance abuse, 197–255. *See
  also* Drug experimentation
  developmental needs and, 59–
    60
  extraparental relationships
    and, 213
  frequency of, 198–199, 203
  groups vulnerable to, 212–214
  prevention of, 66–67, 69–71
  societal attitudes toward, 4–5,
    59
  during therapy, 78, 251–252
Substance abuse, behaviors
    affected by
  acting out, 34–35
  learning, 226
  sexual activity, 222, 226, 247
  suicide, 178–179, 185–186, 197
  violence, 224, 247
Substance abuse, etiology of,
    199–200, 205, 207
  family relationships, 54, 58–61,
    68, 213, 250–251
  helplessness, 39
  mood disorders, 100–101, 142,
    206–209
  personality conflicts, 204–206
  sexual anxiety, 209–214
  social class, 198
Substance abuse, treatment of,
    91, 108, 110, 217–255
  for alcohol, 230–238
  for amphetamines, 245–247
  for barbiturates, 247–249
  for hallucinogens, 238–242
  for heroin, 249–250
  for marijuana, 217–230

  for methaqualone, 247–249
Substance abusers, classification
    of, 198
Suicidal behavior
  accidental death versus, 188
  clinical evaluation of, 188–191
  conditions associated with,
    183–184, 185–186
  frequency of, 119, 169–170,
    194–195
  parental denial of, 85, 173–174
  religion and, 170
  treatment of, 84–85, 189, 191–
    195
  warning signs of, 179–181
Suicidal behavior, determinants
    of, 170–179
  biological, 164, 178–179, 182
  psychological, 146–147, 164,
    174–178, 181–182, 186, 189,
    295–296
  social, 170–174, 182–183, 184–
    185
Suicidal behavior, types of, 179–
    187
  accidental, 186–187
  group, 184–185
  intentional, 179–184
  marginally intentional, 185–
    186
Suicide. *See* Suicidal behavior
Supportive therapy
  administrative, 109–111
  uses of, 103–105, 148, 315,
    320
Symptoms, behavioral,
    importance of, 2–3
Systematic desensitization, 108

Talking down, 241–242
Tarasoff v. *Regents of the University of
  California*, 131
Television viewing
  negative impact of, 67, 126–
    127
  in treatment settings, 95

Testosterone, 157
THC (tetrahydrocannabinol),
    197, 222, 239
Therapist
  idealization of, 251
  as identification model, 110
Thioridazine (Mellaril), 102
Time disturbances, 149
Token economies, 108
Transference neurosis, 106
Transitional objects, 295
Treatment. *See also specific type*
  continuity of care during, 92–
    94, 194
  developmental issues affecting,
    11–23
  family role in, 60–61, 81–84
  nonspecific social needs and,
    96–98
  planning of, 89–114
  right to refuse, 83–84
  socially oriented, 112–114
Trust, capacity for
  assessment of, 76–77
  child-care social policy and, 67
  depression and, 149
  developmental issues affecting,
    11–15
  suicidal behavior and, 176–177

Unipolar illness, 140, 141, 179

Valium, 197
Violence, definition of, 120–121.
  See also Violent behavior
Violent behavior, 119–138
  aggression versus, 120–121

ambivalence and, 17–18
assessment of, 127–131
attention deficit disorders and,
  153
definition of, 120–121
dehumanization and, 128–129,
  134–136
delinquency and, 257–258
in families, 53, 85–86, 130–131
incidence of, 119–120
internalization of, 41–42
as learned, 124–125
mortality rate for, 194–195
prediction of, 128, 131–133
prerequisites for, 121
prevention of, 73
during puberty, 28
social acceptance of, 124–125
substance abuse and, 224, 247
television viewing and, 67,
  126–127
treatment of, 41–43, 108, 133–
  136, 267–273
Violent behavior, determinants
  of
  biological, 156–157
  psychological, 125–127, 148,
    158–159
  social, 53, 85–86, 124–125
Violent behavior, types of
  affective, 121, 155–159
  intermittent, 149
  predatory. *See* Predatory
    behavior
  sexual, 56–57, 293

Working out, 107
Working through, 107

Author Index